THE BROTHERS

ALSO BY DAVID RITZ

Biographies

Aretha: From These Roots (Aretha Franklin and David Ritz)

Blues All Around Me: The Autobiography of B. B. King
(B. B. King with David Ritz)

Rage to Survive: The Etta James Story (Etta James and David Ritz)

Rhythm and the Blues: A Life in American Music
(Jerry Wexler and David Ritz)

Smokey Robinson: Inside My Life (Smokey Robinson with David Ritz

Divided Soul: The Life of Marvin Gaye

Brother Ray: Ray Charles' Own Story (Ray Charles and David Ritz)

Novels

Take It Off, Take It All Off!

Passion Flowers

Family Blood

Barbells and Saxophones

Blues Notes Under a Green Felt Hat

Dreams

The Man Who Brought the Dodgers Back to Brooklyn

Search for Happiness

THE BROTHERS

Art, Aaron, Charles, and Cyril

NEVILLE

and David Ritz

Designed by Chris Welch

Cataloging-in-Publication data for this book is available from the Library of Congress.

First Da Capo Press edition 2001
Reprinted by arrangement with Little, Brown and Company
ISBN 0-306-81053-0

Published by Da Capo Press
A Member of the Perseus Books Group
http://www.dacapopress.com

1 2 3 4 5 6 7 8 9 10—05 04 03 02 01

Contents

Author's Introduction

BY DAVID RITZ

Over the course of the years I spent with the Nevilles — in their native New Orleans and everywhere from Vegas to Vancouver — I came to hear their storytelling voices as musical instruments. I say "musical" because they told their tales in cadences that moved in distinct grooves. I thought of melodies floating over rhythms, moons floating over lakes, clouds moving across open skies. I was exhilarated by the freedom of their speech and the urgency with which they spoke. The stories needed to be set down; the past was fully present in here-and-now accounts of what happened and why.

What happened to each brother was remarkable. Even more remarkable was the towering paradox of diversity and unity that held them together. No four brothers could be more different; no four brothers could be more fiercely connected. I felt their bond of solidarity and, at the same time, an undercurrent of tension whose source was the same: family. For the Nevilles, family is everything — joy, grief, failure, success, disappointment, hope. Family is both the private and the professional component that has come to define their essence. Without family, there is no life, no meaning, no music.

Their wildly diverse lives are connected to a self-made harmony that characterizes their artistry. The fates of the Neville brothers have been — and will always be — intricately linked. As a band, their collective identity is far greater than the sum of its parts. The same is true of their individual life stories: taken together, the result is a full-blown epic whose soundtrack reflects much of the history of American popular music in the second half of the twentieth century.

No matter how extensive their cultural and musical reach — from primitive rock 'n' roll to burning bebop, from ultrasmooth doo-wop to self-invented second-line reggae — the root remains family. If you watch them record, see them perform, go backstage after the show, or visit them in their homes, you'll feel family. Four generations of Nevilles are present at any given moment. Their children and grandchildren are welcomed, even encouraged, to come onstage to play, sing, dance, and rap. Aunts, uncles, and cousins are always in evidence; the warm affection of a family reunion is an ongoing phenomenon. You can't help but be drawn to the bosom of the family. Hang around long enough, and you yourself become an adopted Neville. With its fascinating origins and obsessive intrigues, its creative vitality and improbable balance, the family offers up generous portions of emotional nourishment. The world of the Nevilles is a world of family love.

Arguments arise. Feuds exist. The brothers, you will soon see, sometimes have conflicting agendas. I've been with them when the air was thick with tension over musical material or management. Personalities clash; old resentments smolder; verbal sparring can get serious; political differences run deep. But once they hit the stage, you witness the magic of their music melting those differences, blending the ingredients into a gumbo of such rich flavor, all you can do is praise the cooks and feed on their creation.

How do you analyze these ingredients? You don't. Little by little, you get to know each brother as an individual. You get to know his voice, his musical personality, and his own story. Finally, the stories come together as one. That's the mystery underlining the lives of the Neville brothers, and the mystery of their music as well.

Introducing the Brothers

Art

They call him Poppa Funk. Friends and family call him Artie, pronounced ArTEE. At sixty-two, Art is the firstborn. He speaks in a honey-and-molasses baritone that hangs in the air like a humid night in Uptown New Orleans. He speaks so softly, you must lean in to listen. Hours will pass when he won't speak at all. His comments, like his brilliant keyboard riffs, are subtle. He wedges his words into the small spaces of a discussion. Just as he invented his own brand of funk, he has his own brand of banter. He's a minimalist.

Like all the brothers, Artie has a strong physical presence, a broad upper body, a self-assured walk, a body language some might see as cocky. As a kid, he was quick to fight; as an adult, his don't-fuck-with-me attitude is still evident. But the attitude is only skin deep. Sweetness is his strongest characteristic. Of the four, Art may be the most protective. He is a loner, a sci-fi freak, a

Trekkie, a high-tech aficionado who, back in the fifties when rhythm and blues was birthing rock 'n' roll, emerged as a major pioneer of the new music. Like Fats Domino, his chief vocal influence, he is a singer of tremendous feeling and natural grace. Like Bill Doggett, his chief instrumental influence, he is a keyboardist with fabulous percussive flair.

As the patriarchal keeper of the flame, he still lives on the same Thirteenth Ward block of Valence Street where the boys grew up. Peering out his living room window, he says, *"I look across the street and see my mama's porch. I see that green rocking chair set out for my dad for when he was going to retire, the same chair he never got to sit in. The memories are all around me. I like living in the place where our lives began."*

Charles

A year younger than Art, he is the Horn Man. Charles is the family intellectual whose reading runs the gamut from Western literature to Eastern mysticism. He has studied with gurus, taught esoteric courses at Goddard College, and spent three and a half years in Louisiana's infamous Angola Penitentiary. He speaks about his hustling days in Harlem with unusual equanimity, even humor. His candor is startling and uncompromising. He will tell you exactly what he has been through with neither apologies nor regrets. His honesty is riveting.

Charles's passion is for the music of Charlie Parker and Thelonious Monk, the revolutionary sounds that swept over him as a child and haunt him to this day. The first brother to hit the road, he was billed as the Boy Wonder of the Sax at the Rabbit Foot Minstrel Show; he paid deep dues during decades of one-night blues-band stands in the midnight world of Jimmy Reed and B. B. King. His flawless style on sax — alto, tenor, and soprano — extends over that fertile territory where raw rhythm and blues and sophisticated jazz share common soil.

Thin, wiry, and alert, a disciplined practitioner of the focus/meditative technique chi kung, Charles has a precise mind, an easy smile, and a gentle nature. His political understanding is astute. His tie-dyed style echoes the age of flower children.

"Everything I've been through," he says, *"twenty-nine years strung out on dope, the hard time in prison, and an endless obsession with romantic entanglements — were parts of a journey that I'm just now beginning to understand."*

Aaron

He writes songs in praise of the mother of Christ. He sings with an angelic flutter that excites the heart and stirs the soul. Like big brother Art, Aaron speaks in the sweet tones of the swamp, softly slurred and sometimes hard to decipher. His eyes are also soft, in marked contrast to the dagger tattoo that adorns his cheek or the bleeding Jesus inked on his massive arm. At fifty-eight, he is a great hulk of a doo-wopper, a childlike spirit in the body of a man whose songs say what his face already reveals: he's been to hell and back.

Aaron is a devout sentimentalist. His loyalty, especially to his brothers, is ironclad. His patron saint is Jude, and he will tell you how, in his down-and-out days as a junkie, he climbed the steps of Saint Ann's Shrine on his knees, placing his hopeless cause in the hands of a higher power. When he speaks of his early successes and brutal frustrations, his sincerity is overwhelming — no irony, no bitterness. Along with Sam Cooke and Marvin Gaye, he is considered among the grand soul singers of the century.

In his home in the suburbs east of the city hard by a golf course, Aaron speaks about his turbulent life as he listens to Clyde

McPhatter and the male quartets from the golden age of gospel. At the same time, *Wrestlemania* plays on the wide-screen TV. Aaron is a hardcore wrestling fan. His clipped speech and straight-to-the-point manner is reminiscent of the cowboy stars, Gene Autry and Roy Rogers, whom he loved as a little boy.

"The little boy in me," he says, *"is always there. That's at the core of how I see the world—through the eyes of a kid."*

CYRIL

Cyril is on fire. Baby brother came up as the new generation. At fifty-one, eleven years younger than Art, he remains the most political Neville, the one who challenges and charges through the world with bristling energy and restless desire. When he speaks, sparks fly. When he sings, the sky rumbles. Cyril is a straight-up soulman, a preaching vocalist and percussionist whose polyrhythms reflect his musical cosmos — Haiti and Jamaica, New Orleans and the Native American/African American chants of the immortal Chief Jolly, his mother's brother, whose Wild Tchoupitoulas Mardi Gras Indian tribe changed the course of his life and the lives of his siblings.

Cyril's home houses an altar to Malcolm X, Sitting Bull, Crazy Horse, and Bob Marley, icons of spirituality and strength. The complexity of cultures that finds voice in Cyril's songs drives him to the edge of musical invention. He is a voracious reader and founder of the New Orleans Music and Culture Preservatory, a living museum/clubhouse where the aging deacons of the Crescent City's original music gather to tape their tales over red beans and rice. Cyril's own tale — the transformation of coarse rage into creative love — embraces many of the excesses of his older brothers.

He, too, lived the wild life before seeking salvation in the mysticism of his family's music.

"My brothers were my idols," he says, *"superheroes out of comic books. When I was just a kid, I'd crack the door open and peep inside to watch them rehearse. I felt that I'd have to turn somersaults just to get attention. First one to notice me wasn't any of my brothers, though, it was Clarence 'Juny Boy' Brown, Fats Domino's drummer. He said, 'The little cat wants to know what's happening.' When he handed me his sticks, electricity coursed through me. I came alive."*

THE BROTHERS

Valence Street

Art

The Thirteenth Ward. Uptown New Orleans. Where I started out. Where I am now.

Charles and I were born at 1016 Valence. We lived with my father and mother and my father's mother, whose name was Rowena. We called her Ma Ma. She had three sisters: Virginia — who was Auntie Cat — Aunt Espy — who was blind — and Aunt Lela. Auntie Cat, Mrs. Virginia Harris, was the power. Her husband, Peg Harris, was a master carpenter who built three houses in a row on Valence.

Let me paint you the picture, bro. Valence was a cobblestone street made up of shotgun cottages. Straight-up shotgun houses. There was an outhouse in back, and we took baths in little galvanized tubs. In those days you'd look for the iceman to come 'round with ice for your icebox. I'd scrub the splinters out of the hardwood floor with broken pieces of red brick.

The 'hood was alive with good feeling. Smells of good food and sounds of good music in the air. Good folk. Folk protecting one another. You might get three beatings a day — your mama, your daddy, and a neighbor lady who saw you do something wrong. It was all one big family. One little village. We were all in it together. I'd call it a beautiful time.

CYRIL

If you look at the way New Orleans was gerrymandered, the black neighborhoods were surrounded by the white ones. It felt like living in occupied territory. You'd have to watch where you walked. It was scary. An old white man sat on his porch on the corner of Valence. He was a grocery-store owner and a big shot at the Catholic church. As soon as he saw us coming, he'd open his gate and let out his dogs. Vicious dogs chasing us down, scaring the shit out of us.

I realize I'm remembering Valence Street ten years after my brothers do. When I was growing up, they were already gone, deep in their own worlds that had nothing to do with me. At home I mainly hung out with my older sister, Athelgra, and my baby sister, Cookie.

Charles

Valence Street was a blue-collar neighborhood on the edge of the Garden District, a major New Orleans tourist attraction made up of imposing mansions and beautiful, stately old homes. Many of the little houses on Valence were originally occupied by people who serviced those mansions. Auntie Cat was one of those people. She opened our eyes to that world — a world that was very near and very far.

Auntie Cat owned property. She was a person to be reckoned with. She worked for a white family in the Garden District on Prytania Street. She must have raised a couple of generations of kids for those white families. She cooked and cleaned and took care of business. She swept the sidewalk in front of the Trinity Methodist Church, just across the street from us on Valence, where she was a member in good standing.

Auntie Cat was light-skinned enough to pass for white, but she didn't. We had other relatives who actually did pass to get better jobs. Our parents warned us not to speak to one particular relative if we bumped into her. They'd say, *She's working at a white theater and she's passing for white.* There was a part of New Orleans — the Seventh Ward — that was *passe blanc.* It was a Creole section, and light-skinned Creoles had certain professions sewed up. The bricklayers' union, for instance, was mostly men from the Seventh Ward, while the longshoremen were darker-skinned cats from Uptown, where we lived.

The hierarchy of skin color in New Orleans has a long history. There were whites, there were slaves, and there were free people of color — Creoles. If a black mistress of a white man had a boy, he'd be schooled in France; if she had a girl, the girl would be groomed to woo another white man so her children would be even lighter. It wasn't done for shame, but for practicality; the lighter you were, the less your chance of being a victim of murderous antiblack racism.

My mother and her family — her mom, brother, and sisters — were also a big part of the village of our childhood. They had Creole roots and were Catholic — as opposed to Dad's people, who were Methodist.

Aaron

Mommee's folks spoke plenty Creole. They knew that patois, that broken French. Talkin' about Maw Maw, who was Marie, Mommee's mother. She and my other grandmother, Ma Ma, who was Rowena, would fight over me. Wouldn't let no one spank me. Put me on their laps and rocked me to the good-time gospel music — Brother Joe May, Sister Rosetta Tharpe, Mahalia Jackson, Clara Ward. That music soaked in me while I was still soaking my diaper.

CYRIL

Mommee's sisters were tremendous figures in my life. Earthy women. Big bosoms. Salt of the earth. Aunt Odile wasn't but four feet tall, but, Lord have mercy, she'd stand on a chair to punch the face of her six-foot husband. On her way to work, Auntie Deal — that's what we called her — would give you a snap of the switch, just in case you were thinking about doing wrong. We called Aunt Lena "Nanny." All strong black women who stood on their own two feet.

Charles

My mother's sisters were big in every way — bighearted ladies with big laughs who loved to dance with big movements. They cooked big meals in big pots and would feed anyone who was hungry. Their origin was more than Creole, I believe. I heard talk of Native American, French, Spanish, and even the island of Martinique.

Their maiden name was Landry. Mommee's father had disappeared. The story was that he was working on the railroad when the white brakeman got drunk and abusive. The abuse continued until my grandfather came home one night and told his wife that the brakeman had attacked him. In retaliation, Grandpa pulled the coupling pin from one of the cars and hit the motherfucker over the head, killing him instantly. "I'm leaving tonight," he told Maw Maw, "and chances are, you'll never see me again." Just like that, he slipped into the dark night, gone forever. His family didn't blame him; no one expressed anger. In the South it was understood: survival at any cost.

Auntie Cat was a great survivor, a different kind of personality. She was a pillar of the community, a representative of that generation who lived by a strict code of hard work, integrity, and self-sufficiency. She was quick to put down anyone who was not like her. And, of course, there was no one like her.

Art

We called her Auntie Cat because she had all these cats. And she'd talk to those cats all the time. She'd take us to a public swimming pool, where we'd watch the white kids swim. We weren't allowed to swim, but we got in because she looked white. White people assumed she was taking care of us. She'd take us to stores we could never have entered without her. In those days, blacks could try on clothes only in certain establishments — like D. H. Holmes. Once, we were at a food store with Auntie Cat when a woman started saying shit about "niggers." Cat grabbed a long loaf of that hard French bread and bopped the lady over the head, saying, "You're so ignorant, you don't even know when you're in the presence of a Negro. For your information, *I* am a Negro."

I also remember Auntie Cat winning the cakewalk contest at the Trinity Methodist Church. She was carrying this pretty parasol, doing her dainty steps, and, at just the right moment, dropping her hankie. Cat was something to see.

Charles

Auntie Cat would take us over to the people's big home where she worked in the Garden District. I remember playing croquet with the white kids on the lawn. It was cool, a view of another world we would never have experienced were it not for Cat.

Aaron

I was only one when we moved from Valence to the projects. Cyril wasn't even born. We'd move back to Valence in the fifties — and, of course, we'd come Uptown to visit our aunts every week. But my first real memories, especially of Daddy and Mommee, are back in those projects.

The Projects

Art

Today the word *projects* sounds scary. You picture a war zone. Today the Calliope housing projects look like a concentration camp, but back then, when the Neville family moved in, we looked at it like better living. I remember clicking on the lights and suddenly — *wow!* I mean, the shit was clean. Our apartment was on the second floor, and you had to walk up thirteen steps to get there. Three bedrooms. Me and Charles and Maw Maw in one room; Ma Ma and baby Aaron in another; and Daddy and Mommee in the third bedroom.

Calliope was way across town, or "out back of town," as folks called it. I can hear "Hey Pocky A-Way," a chant echoing through the projects. "Hey pocky a-way . . . hey pocky a-way . . . hey pocky a-way . . ." Me and Charles would bang out the beat on cigar boxes in the window. Don't ask me where the groove came from, but, bro, that groove followed me around my whole life. It's still with me.

Charles

My father really came into focus when we moved to the projects. It was the forties. The war years. You'd have to call my father a hero. He sure was a hero to his sons.

Art

They called him Big Arthur. I was Little Arthur. He was Big Artie. I was Little Artie. Auntie Cat used to say that she put the first clothes on my father when he was born, and she did the same for me. Arthur was an only child, and Ma Ma and her sisters — Cat, Lela, and Espy — adored my daddy. He was their golden boy who could do no wrong. Like Aaron, he was a big man. Six feet. Muscles rippling all over his body.

Aaron

He had strength and he had wisdom. He was a gentle man, but you didn't want to fuck with him.

Art

He had the best smile. The dude was always smiling. And he had all these different jobs. For a long while he was a Pullman porter for the L&N Railroad. From our window Mommee would point out what train he was on as we watched it pull away.

Charles

He instilled within me this sense of adventure. He ventured out into the world, and I'd think, *What's he doing? Where's he going?* Through him, I felt the excitement of the road, the lure of the unknown.

Art

He was also a merchant marine. Sometimes he and Mommee's brother, George, our Uncle Jolly, would ship out together. They'd go around the world, to countries and islands I'd never heard of.

CYRIL

For a long time I assumed Daddy and Jolly were real brothers. Just thinking about that made me feel good all over. Then I discovered that they were more than real brothers; they were soul brothers. During World War II, before I was born, they went out on merchant marine ships being torpedoed in enemy waters. They took some real chances, had some close calls, and came back with stories they'd be telling for years to come.

Aaron

Daddy was highly musical. He could whistle, but not your everyday whistle. His whistle had trails and curls. He whistled jazz. And he could sing. Sang like Nat "King" Cole and Arthur Prysock. Big, beautiful, smooth voice. Great voice.

Art

I'd hear Big Arthur singing in the bathtub — no showers in those days — and he'd sing driving around town. For many years he drove a cab.

CYRIL

Tell you what kind of man my daddy was: When I was a teenager, we were riding around in his cab listening to "Route 66" on the radio. I changed the station. James Brown came on.

"First off," Daddy said to me, "don't go changing the station without asking me. That was Nat Cole with Johnny Miller and Oscar Moore. Now, I know this new boy is popular, but I see where he puts that shit in his head." Daddy was referring to James Brown's famous process. "He don't respect himself."

Then Sam Cooke came on. "Now, that boy don't distort his looks. Let his music play." "You Send Me" never sounded so good.

Daddy was hip. He'd go down to the pool hall owned by the Soto brothers, Italian guys who were his friends. Daddy was a badass laid-back left-handed pool shark, and just before he was about to whip your ass, he'd say, "Rack man, walk slow . . ."

The other thing about Daddy is that he never lied to me. Not once. I appreciated that when I was a kid. But as an adult, I appreciate it even more.

Art

Naturally I noticed Daddy's friends. Like Smiley Lewis, the blues singer with a sound bigger than Big Joe Turner. Smiley had a deep voice like a gigantic frog, just exploding with soul. He had that coming-straight-at-you sound, pure New Orleans. Man, he was the kind of singer who didn't need no mike. He had already started recording at Cosimo Matassa's J&M Studio down on Rampart Street with Tuts Washington playing piano behind him. Smiley was one of the original cats. Later he'd have big hits like "Tee Nah Nah," "Shame, Shame, Shame," and "I Hear You Knocking." He lived right around the projects. I'd see him and my dad drive off in one of those station wagons with wood on the side. Going fishing. They'd boast about what they were gonna catch and bring these big pans to cook in. Mommee would just look at 'em and crack up laughing. Daddy and Smiley were tight. They were kindred spirits, and Daddy knew exactly what Smiley's music was all about.

Charles

When I think back, it's clear my father had exceptional musical taste. When I was still a kid, he took me to hear Charlie Parker. By then Daddy was already whistling Charlie Parker solos, note for note. That night Bird was appearing on the same bill with Stan Kenton. Turned out we couldn't get in. The thing was segregated, and all the black seats were sold out. But we stood by the doorway and got to hear. Bird was flying high, a rocket heading straight for the moon. I knew I was listening to the future. It was thunder and lightning, the truth pouring out of a golden alto sax. Daddy was standing right there next to me, digging everything

Bird was doing. Later it was Daddy who hipped me to Wes Montgomery, a master of modern jazz guitar. My father had ears.

Art

Daddy also had a feel for mechanics. That's where I got it from. I remember the Christmas when he got his first set of Craftsman tools. That same morning he started taking parts off his car and putting them back on. Naturally I imitated him. Because he was young, sometimes he felt more like a big brother than a dad. And my mom, who was a pretty lady — well, she was like an older sister. She loved to sing Ella's "A-Tisket, A-Tasket," but she also loved John Lee Hooker's boogie blues. My parents were young people with young energy.

Charles

My mother, whose maiden name was Amelia Landry, and her baby brother, George Landry — our uncle Jolly — were dance partners. They were professional, and at one point Louis Prima, who came from New Orleans and sounded like a white Louis Armstrong, wanted to take them on the road. But their mother — Maw Maw — wouldn't hear of it. I believe that broke their hearts, and they danced anyway. My mother and uncle danced for the family, danced for us kids, danced for each other, danced just because they loved to dance and had a dancing spirit that couldn't be denied. Some of my sweetest memories are of seeing Mommee and Jolly jitterbugging to Louis Jordan, the same saxophonist who made me want to play sax. Dancing the jitterbug and the lindy hop, dancing to "Choo Choo Ch'Boogie" and "Reet

Petite and Gone" and "Beans and Corn Bread." The Victrola in our house was always playing Count Basie's "One O'Clock Jump," Lionel Hampton's "Flying Home," Billy Eckstine's "Prisoner of Love." Mommee and Jolly had all the smooth moves, all that right-on-time rhythm and behind-your-back turns and flips that are back in fashion today. When they danced in front of the family, their sisters, Odile and Lena, might join in, heavy women who became lighter than air, weightless and graceful and filled with the spirit of the good-time music of the war years. "Ain't Nobody Here but Us Chickens," "Let the Good Times Roll," "Saturday Night Fish Fry" — these were the happy sounds that had our household brimming with energy.

Art

When I got to be a teenager, people thought my mother was my girlfriend. That's how young she looked. Looked like Lena Horne. She was a kind and understanding woman. Loads of energy. Like my dad, she always worked more than one job. She worked at Lane's cotton mill, and she also worked at a dry cleaners. Later she went to beautician school and did hair out of the house. She had drive and she had smarts. She went to nursing school and became a certified nurse's aid. Everyone loved Amelia Landry Neville.

She and my dad opened a little nightclub that operated on weekends called Holiday Inn. There was a jukebox and socializing, drinking, and dancing, all in this one room. The neighborhood folks would fall by. You might catch Mommee and Jolly doing their thing, her sliding under his legs or him throwing her over his shoulder. Serious dancing.

CYRIL

I rarely saw my mother put her hard-earned money in the hands of black people to buy goods or services. All the merchants around us were white. The only time our cash circulated among ourselves was when the ladies in the Thirteenth Ward gave "suppers." Up North they'd call them rent parties. Our neighbor Miss Mary might have it one week, my mom the next. They'd sell dinners and rent gambling tables from the Italian businessmen. I was acutely aware of how the system fixed it so that our money never stayed in the black community. Some kids have a high racial consciousness at an early age. I was one of those kids.

Art

We were a lively family, lots going on — people running off to work, Daddy just getting back or just heading out to sea, heading out on the train or driving his cab 'round town. No matter how busy, though, Big Arthur took time to deal with his kids. Daddy got me into boxing. He was a fight fan who idolized Joe Louis and Sugar Ray. Daddy believed in strength.

Charles

Once, my parents were out dancing when a guy stepped on Mommee's foot. The guy claimed it was Mommee who stepped on him. So he pushed her. Major mistake. Daddy grabbed him, threw him halfway across the room into a wall, and beat the dude to a pulp. Uncle Jolly said that when he and my father shipped out with the merchant marine, they called Big Arthur "Neville the Devil."

Art

Daddy would play around with me, beat me up a little. Not too bad, but just enough to wake up my fighting spirit. I started boxing in the projects, started hanging with the dudes who took it seriously — shadow boxing, running laps, building endurance. Went through the motions but didn't really know what I was doing. One Sunday all the families were on the lawn outside the projects — there was lots of clean green grass in those days — and someone gave us real boxing gloves. I didn't want to put 'em on; and I sure didn't want to take on this one particular kid, who was famous for fighting. But my dad was there, and I didn't want to let him down, so I threw myself into it. I took the kid out with one punch. Discovered I was stronger than I thought. That started me down a road. I began boxing at the Rosenwald gym and building up my chops.

I could beat up my little brothers, but if *you* touched any of them, I'd pulverize you. One brute at school splashed mud all over Charles. Threw me in such a rage, I nearly killed the guy. Each of these little gangs had their strongman, and one by one, I took all the bullies out. I was conducting my own personal crusade. I'd fight anyone — bigger the better. But I wasn't mean. This one dude stuck out his tongue when he fought. When I hit him in the mouth, he bit down and started bleeding all over me. I put him on the handlebars of my bicycle and rode him to the hospital. Wouldn't leave until I was sure he was going to be all right.

Mommee sent us to Catholic schools. I went to Saint Augustine, which one year, through the grace of God, beat Booker T. at basketball. No one ever beat Booker T. After the game I was waiting at the bus stop when some Booker T. cats started shoving me around. I punched out one, but then tripped over him. The other two dipped into their bag of pipes and sticks and chains and got me while I was down. Later I recruited some older dudes, located my assailants, and snagged one in the face with half a brick.

When I visited my auntie Cat back up on Valence, I'd go into her Trinity Methodist Church, where upstairs in the auditorium they'd show movies of Joe Louis. We'd hear the fights on the radio, but to see the man in action was inspiring. Couldn't nobody whip him. I guess I felt the same way about my father. That's what it meant to be a man. You learn to protect yourself so you can protect your family. You make it clear: *Mess with me, motherfucker, and I'll hurt you.*

Aaron

I got into fights when I was older, but as a kid I hid behind Art. I'd tell the bullies, "Fuck with me, and I'll call Artie." That's all they'd need to hear. Artie had a reputation. I loved him, not only because he was big bro but because his thing was protecting the little guy. I liked that approach and, later on, adopted it as my own.

Charles

Our father took time to teach us to box. I remember putting on those big gloves and sparring with Art and Aaron. But it was Artie who mastered it. As a boxer, he showed natural talent. He'd get into fights and level his opponents with systematic precision. Great killer instincts. He fixed it so none of us was picked on.

CYRIL

Artie was a mythical figure to me. The eleven-year age difference meant separation, emotional and otherwise. In Art's presence, I always felt a little less-than. I was in awe of him. Down at the projects I'd walk by the swimming pool next to the Rosenwald gym and hear the water splashing. I'd think, *Man, I can't wait till I'm old enough to jump in*. Then one day Artie said, "Let's go." Faced with all that water, though, I freaked. "You go ahead, Artie, I'll watch." He took me by the hand and jumped in with me. He held me up. Showed me that I wouldn't drown. He wouldn't let me drown.

Auntie Cat was always comparing us with Artie. She'd ask, "Why can't the rest of you be like Little Arthur?"

Artie also had a gift for mechanics. Everyone talked about his crystal radio sets. He could put one together in no time. Rearrange shit in the back of the television. Fix anything. I tried it myself until one day at school I saw this kid who was fooling with a repair electrocute himself. I figured I'd leave that stuff to Artie.

Art

Electronics fascinated me. I'd run Uptown to Auntie Cat's house and fix her fans, fix her radio, damn near fix anything. I'd tear an engine apart and put it back together, just for the hell of it. I'd build crystal sets and short waves from scratch, making my own antenna, copper pipe hanging out the window, wires hooked up to the screens.

I'd listen to the radio long into the night, intrigued by advertisements for a package of two hundred baby chicks. I had no idea what I'd do with them, but the idea of having two hundred baby chicks running around my room seemed absolutely wonderful. Even more wonderful were the sounds of WLAC flowing out of Nashville. Gene Nobles was the host of *Randy's Record Shop,* the show where I first heard James Brown. In those days, the airwaves were the only things they couldn't segregate.

The truth is that I was a loner. No different than I am now. I was a quiet wallflower. I stuttered severely. So I didn't say much. My sister Athelgra, who was born between Aaron and Cyril, also stuttered. Eventually my stuttering stopped as mysteriously as it had started. But it lingered a long time. No one's proud of stuttering. Stuttering will make a kid go deep inside himself.

I was also narcoleptic. Without explanation, I'd be hit by waves of sleep. My eyes would simply close, and just like that, I'd nod off. Back then, if you weren't white or rich, there were no facilities to test you. No one knew what was wrong. The teachers would yell to wake me up. Some of them assumed I was slow. Between the stuttering and the narcolepsy, I took some kidding. Maybe that's why fighting became important.

I lost myself in science fiction. Buck Rogers, Captain Video, Flash Gordon, anything spacey. I was spacey. I noticed on TV how anyone of color, like Ming, was evil. White boy Tarzan, with his high-priced haircut, was King of the Jungle.

I could do all the stuff Boy Scouts did. I could have been a Boy Scout, except I never saw a black Boy Scout. Boy Scouts were white. But I think I had that Boy Scout mentality. When Auntie Cat went to sweep the floor of the Trinity Methodist Church on Valence, I went along to help. We were cleaning the pulpit when I noticed the big pipe organ. I hit a key and — *boom!* — the sound nearly knocked me down. What I heard wasn't the voice of God, it was the voice of music — but it might as well have been the same thing. That sound turned me around. After that sound, everything changed.

I began tinkering with keyboards, just as I tinkered with radio repairs. Aunt Lela lived at 1012 Valence, and she had a piano that her son, Percy, played. Like a lot of New Orleans pianists, Percy had no single style. He could just flat-out play the thing. He was a postman and a master carpenter and was once a sharpshooter in the army. He told stories about killing people for no reason. He could still see the people he had killed. I'd watch him play the piano while he told those stories. The piano was telling stories of its own.

When I started on that same piano — I was nine or ten years old — everyone said I was playing barrelhouse. I associated barrelhouse piano with a bar in the Valence 'hood called Jack Calahan's — later it became Benny's — where they had kegs of beer. The place stank of those wooden barrels. The music seemed to carry the same smell. Never did learn to read music. But it came to me, naturally and without a struggle. Didn't think about scales or styles. My fingers worked the keys like they had a mind of their own. I didn't understand it, but I didn't fight it either.

Aaron

The music got passed down. I'd never be a singer if Artie hadn't been a singer. That's where I heard it, that's where I learned it.

Art

Singing was no different than playing. It wasn't a calculated thing. I was lucky because I was a Fats Domino freak. Fats was superhot, Fats could burn at the piano, and Fats had a vocal sound everyone loved. I ate, drank, and slept Fats. God gave me the ability to imitate Fats's sound until you'd have a hard time telling who was the real Fats and who was the Memorex me. Fats had that effortless New Orleans thing, which is sing like you speak. Just be loose and let it out.

CYRIL

When you break it down, it goes back, way before Fats Domino, all the way to Louis Armstrong. Pops was pure New Orleans. He sang the way he played, and he played the way he sang. He sang the way he was. Now historians are saying he not only invented jazz singing but invented all pop singing as well. He was the first to throw out the rules of form and follow the rules of natural expression. The result was a vocal personality that rose above the rest. When Pops sang, you could feel his life, his joy, his very being. Same with Fats. Same with Artie. They were the singers who moved me most, the ones who said, *Be yourself*.

School Days

Charles

For kindergarten and first grade I went to a school run by a black couple, the Bushes, who had a great music program. They handed out percussive instruments and put us in a little rhythm band. Our music teacher was wonderful; she played piano and had us singing the do-re-mi scale. Bush Kindergarten and Elementary School understood how beneficial the freedom and flow of music can be to kids. The teaching was so good that when I entered second grade at Saint Monica, a Catholic school, they immediately skipped me up to third.

Mommee figured religious institutions would give us the best education. In the beginning I was moved by the piety of the Mass and the somber beauty of the services. I was a dutiful kid — I loved helping my mother — and thought that I'd grow up to become a priest. What better way to please my mother and serve God? But by fourth grade I was questioning it all. If the priests and nuns were God's representatives, they represented him poorly. In our segregated all-black school, all the priests and nuns were white. A priest took us on a field trip to Werline's Music Store. Naturally we were excited. Before the streetcar arrived, the priest told us, "I'll be sitting up front. You kids will be in back. When we arrive at our stop, I won't look at you, I'll just nod my head. I'll get off and you'll follow." The fact that he wouldn't acknowledge being in the company of black children spoke volumes about his religious convictions. When one of the nuns got mad at me, she'd call me "a little nigger thing."

Not all the nuns were racists, though. One of them, Sister Damien, never showed prejudice.

Art

Sister Damien stayed in touch with us throughout the years and was always proud of our progress. She still attends our shows. Personally, I loved the nuns. I'd walk five blocks from the projects every morning to the bus stop to greet them. They'd arrive from the convent, and I'd carry their books to school.

For the very early grades, I went to Saint Monica. My classmates included Allen Toussaint and James Booker, guys who would influence my life in ways I couldn't begin to imagine. They would both grow up to be two of the baddest piano-playing dudes. Most everyone would agree that James was the badder of the two. James was a genius. We're both Sagittarians, and we were both altar boys. At High Mass, James played the pipe organ with such authority, you'd think he was born in another century. Played the shit like he was Bach's illegitimate son. Booker taught me so much stuff. Anything he heard, he could duplicate, from Frédéric Chopin to Tuts Washington, with all stops in between. James was a regular kid until he got hit by one of those *Ghostbusters* high-speed ambulances.

He was in the hospital for a couple of months, and we prayed for him. When he got out, he was playing better than ever. James never lost a lick of technique, no matter how crazy he got. As the years went by, though, his mind got messed over. After that ambulance accident, Booker's mind was never the same.

Aaron

Like Artie and Charles, I went to Saint Monica. The church of my childhood stays inside me wherever I go. I respected the white nuns. They got into trouble with the Klan for teaching black kids. They were caring women who taught me about love. The services were in Latin, and I didn't know what they were talking about, but I felt something. The "Ave Maria" stuck in my heart. Made me feel peaceful. I learned a prayer to the Madonna called "Lovely Lady Dressed in Blue." At a time in my life when I was messed-up and afraid, I remembered that prayer and turned it into a song.

I'm not saying I wasn't a wild child; I was. I called one nun Eyebrows 'cause she had the biggest, bushiest eyebrows you ever saw. She'd rap me on the knuckles, send me home with a note, and next thing I knew, Daddy was threatening to send me to boys' school if I didn't straighten up. Well, I didn't straighten up. When I got to Bush Elementary School, I got even wilder. But the lessons learned at Saint Monica stayed in my soul. I forgot those lessons for a long, long time, yet they never went away. Everywhere I went, I felt God protecting me.

CYRIL

I started out in public school, then went to Blessed Sacraments Catholic School. One of my schoolmates was Leo Nocentelli, who grew up to become a guitarist and figures in this story a little later. Blessed Sacraments is where I first learned about racism. Light-skinned children with so-called good hair were put in front, brown-skinned with medium "good hair" in the middle, the rest of us in the back. A kid named Red, who was extremely light-skinned but had kinky hair, was dumped in with us. Poor Red got hit from all sides.

The nun drew a picture of a milk bottle for each student. Every time you committed a sin — talking too much, questioning the teacher, cutting up — she'd put a black mark in your milk bottle. Well, brother, my milk stayed chocolate. Even if I could answer one of the questions, even if I jumped up and down and waved my arm around, she'd call on the light-skinned kids, completely ignoring me. If I shouted out the correct answer, she'd stick me in the corner and force me to kneel before the statue of Jesus. I felt Jesus bleeding on me, like it was my fault that my skin was dark and my hair nappy, that it was my fault he'd been crucified. The message they gave was simple — sin is black, and black is evil.

The whole scene was fucked. I'd see dark-skinned guys beating up the light skins. I'd see the priests sexually making moves on the prettiest girls and boys. After a year and a half, I was kicked out for supposedly pushing a nun down the stairs. I didn't do that, but I did give them grief, so it was the school's way of paying me back. Mommee was disappointed, but I was glad to be gone.

Art

We were all hit hard by what happened to Charles and his science project at school. We knew Charles was gifted—everyone realized that he had this incredible brain—so when it went down the way it did, it broke our hearts and pissed us off, all at the same time. You might call it an early taste, a bitter taste, of reality.

Charles

I loved math and science and took on extra-credit assignments whenever they were offered. In our grammar school we were asked to make a project relating to rockets. My project was built around experiments showing how rocket fuel propels vehicles out of the earth's gravitational field. Worked on it night and day because I was told if it was good enough, it'd be sent to the National Science Fair. If it was accepted, I'd get to go to the fair in Washington, D.C. So I built it up, got it right, and turned it in. Teacher was elated. "I have no doubt," she said, "you're going to Washington." We sent it off. Weeks passed. Then word came down. Rejected. "Why?" I asked. Teacher couldn't look me in the eye. "Because," she said, "it came from a colored school."

Looking back, I see that as a turning point in my attitude about the world. I started thinking like this: *If my intelligence isn't worth anything to them, I'll use it against them*. That was one of my rationales for becoming a criminal.

Aaron

My problems started pretty young. I was bouncing back and forth from Saint Monica to Bush, kicked out of one, then kicked out of the other. My sister Athelgra went to Bush Elementary with me. I love Athelgra. We were so close, we'd start giggling just looking at each other. That was all right until, later in life, we'd attend funerals together and have the same giggling problem.

The great buddy of my life was Melvin. We were still living in the Calliope projects. I must have been six or seven. Some Sundays I'd ride Uptown to attend Trinity Methodist with Auntie Cat. Right there on Valence Street I'd see this kid sitting on the stoop in front of his house. Melvin.

Melvin and I had a closeness that's hard to explain. I'd see him at church picnics, and when those picnics were out of town, we'd ride the bus together. Sit next to each other. Melvin was quiet, hardly said a word. Silently, we bonded. Understood each other without saying a word. Became brothers. Lifelong partners through thick and thin. Loyal to the death. They started calling us Mole Face and Melvin.

About this mole on my face: I like it. I've always liked it. I like looking in the mirror. That's me. When I was born, Mommee said I came out knees first and was ugly, wrinkled, and red. When the doctor saw the mole on my face and wanted to remove it, Mommee stopped him. "Leave it be," she said. "It's the prettiest thing on him." Thank you, Mommee. Later, when Melvin and I were getting known as fighters, a manager wanted to turn us into boxers. Took us to the gym and had us training hard. I was all set to go when a doctor looked at the mole and said it could bleed and hemorrhage and maybe kill me. My boxing days were over.

Sounds Coming 'Round

Art

Uncle Jolly played the hell out of a piano. Played like one of the professors. Like Professor Longhair, who we called Fess. Fess was a master who influenced every keyboardist — every musician — who ever heard him. Fess was a fountainhead of New Orleans music. He was a professor in the sense of learning everything there is to learn about a piano. If you wanted to play, you watched the professors and copied them. They were the cats, going all the way back to Jelly Roll Morton, who made music part of the sporting life. They made music that made people feel good. Simple as that. They took whatever was in the air in New Orleans — rhumbas and boogies, mambos and waltzes, ragtime and blues, calypso and jazz — and wove it together. It was people-pleasing music, the kind of music I grew up on, and the fact that my mother's brother played it made me love it even more. Jolly was the coolest cat in the neighborhood.

Jolly had a great attitude about the piano. It was something he just did. Didn't worry that he couldn't read or write music. Didn't worry that this dude or that dude might play better than he did. Didn't look to the piano to make him rich or famous. Piano was part of his life, part of the joy of living. When the mood struck, he'd sit down and tear it up. It wasn't a career; it was a passion. He always had odd jobs. He was the doorman at the Roosevelt, the swankiest hotel in town. But he also knew every dive and juke joint around. Jolly was the man.

CYRIL

All I wanted to do was sit and watch my uncle George. It took me a while to earn the right to call him Uncle Jolly — that came as I grew older and more experienced. When he started taking me around to his underground world of hipsters and hustlers, he'd tell his friends, "This is Cyril, my nephew, my sister's son." Seeing how everyone admired him, feeling privileged to be his blood, my chest would swell up with pride.

Charles

Jolly understood irony. He was worldly and wise in ways that made all the brothers stick close to him. We all wanted to be like Jolly.

He'd tell stories about working as a Pullman porter with my father. "Had a friend called Red," said Jolly, "with a terrible stutter. White man got on the train, looked at Red's light skin, and said, 'Damn, nigger, your daddy must have been a white man light as you.' 'N-n-n-n-no, s-s-s-s-sir,' said Red. 'Da-da-da-da-ddy was a big ol' black man and ma-ma-ma-mama was wh-wh-wh-white as snow.' White man turned red with rage while my man Red flashed his pearly whites."

Jolly and my father were close, but the differences between them were large. Jolly got high. He smoked muggles, the word for pot. Jolly sold pot. Later I saw he shot heroin. We'd get high together. But Jolly was no fall-down drunk or derelict junkie. He maintained his cool. After a night on the town, he'd come home whistling and dancing. Always sharp. Hats for days. Back then the beaver hat was the shit. Jolly had him shag beavers, bola beavers, and slick beavers. He called Barcelonas "Barcelanas" and had them in every color of the rainbow.

Aaron

I'd kill for Jolly. Jolly was raddy — that was the word for super-hip. I copied Jolly's walk. Truth is, I'm still walking Jolly's walk. I'd put on his hat, cock it to one side, and stroll up and down, imitating the slick way he'd stroll the streets.

Jolly had that touch. He'd sit down at the piano and bang out "Junkie Blues" in a way that made all the world's troubles disappear.

CYRIL

Listen here: the way I dress today — that's Jolly; the derby hats I put on my head during the shows — that's Jolly; my moves onstage — that's Jolly. Some of my sweetest memories are of Jolly coming down the street on Easter Sunday. Whatever he wore was pretty, bright colors — reds and greens, oranges and baby blues — shoes shining like glass, any excuse to dress up, look sharp, feel good.

Charles

Difference between Jolly and Daddy was that Jolly carried a gun. Jolly always had him a big, long pistol. That gave him an edge of danger. He was more like a big brother than an uncle. An exotic uncle who'd come back from Africa in a merchant marine ship with a garbage can filled with marijuana. He buried it in the backyard until Maw Maw dug it up and all hell broke loose.

CYRIL

When I was a little boy, I didn't know about Uncle Jolly and heroin, but I knew about the pot. Every time I heard he was coming to our house, I'd get excited. That would mean dancing and joking and lots of stories. When he wasn't around, I'd eavesdrop and hear his big sisters tell tales about Jolly and his women. That built up his legend even more. His arrival was an event. The crease in his pants, the way his handkerchief peaked out of his lapel and matched his tie — Jolly was clean. He'd sit in a big easy chair and hold court. When he got up to go to the bathroom, the joints he hid between his legs would fall on the floor, leaving a little trail. At that point, I'd pick up the joints and give them back to him. Few years later — at age eleven or so — I'd start smoking the joints myself.

I learned so much just by watching Jolly watch TV. Him and my father would be sitting there, for instance, watching *The Alamo*.

There's a part where a black guy throws himself over a white man to protect the white man from a volley of gunfire. Jolly would look at Daddy, Daddy would look back at Jolly, a few seconds would pass, and at the same time, they'd let loose with a long "Shit" and break out laughing. That told me all I needed to know about how Hollywood portrays race. The real side of race, the dark side, was something we'd all learn on our own. The story of Jolly being brutalized by the police was passed down over the years from one brother to another.

Art

I first heard the story from my mother. Jolly was falsely accused of accosting a white woman. The police picked him up and held him for seventy-two hours. He couldn't make a call or get a lawyer. It didn't matter that he could prove he wasn't with the woman, didn't know the woman, and had never even seen the woman. She said it was a nigger who touched her, and to her all niggers looked alike. They pressed Jolly for a confession. He wouldn't confess to something he didn't do. They pressed harder. He wouldn't give, even when they started slapping him around. Finally, they made him stand up, strip, and face a desk. Then they opened the desk drawer, placed his balls inside, and slammed the drawer shut.

CYRIL

They nearly beat him to death. They knocked him around so bad that he lost hearing in one ear. But he stood his ground. Kept his dignity under the most fuckin' undignified conditions a man could face. They finally let him go.

Art

You never saw Jolly's anger. His attitude was, *This is the world, baby, deal with it or die.* He dealt with it. His spirit never broke. He was always Jolly. He'd sit down at the piano and play like nothing had happened, like he was the luckiest man on the planet.

Cats like Uncle Jolly felt freedom in music. It was a place where they could do whatever they wanted and be whoever they were. I believe that's what drew me to music. Certain pianists had that same sense of freedom, a flow that felt right. I listened to all the piano men — Charles Brown, Amos Milburn, Lloyd Glenn, who lived Uptown — but in the fifties it was Bill Doggett's organ that wiped me out. "Honky Tonk" remains the anthem of life. When I started out, if you couldn't play "Honky Tonk," there was no reason to show up at the gig. I got to see Bill Doggett at the Municipal Auditorium. He played some other kind of shit. Doggett's keyboard attitude was too cool; he said it in a funky shorthand that made everyone wanna move. I'd never forget it, and much later in my life, that same sound would send me in a new direction and change the course of my career.

In those early days, though, the plain piano was the instrument firing me up. Except, in New Orleans, the piano was anything but plain. I'd wander through the French Quarter and see a guy called Cousin Joe playing for the tourists at the Court of the Two Sisters on Bourbon Street. History books don't pay too much attention to Cousin Joe, but I did. He played and sang and talked shit to the people. Entertained them. Can't put my finger on his style; he was all over the place. It was an old New Orleans style older than rock 'n' roll or rhythm and blues or even ragtime or jazz. Whatever it was, it was right. As a kid peeping into this place, I saw Cousin Joe killing the piano, killing the people, and making plenty money.

Another thing that boosted my education was working at

Tickles record shop, right there by the projects. It was one of those mom-and-pop places, small and cozy, where the music got all over you. When I look at the block-long superstores today, cool as they are, I wonder whether kids will ever get that homegrown feeling those early 78s gave me. I never took home a dime 'cause all my salary went straight for sides. Doo-wop wiped me out. I played the Clovers' "Hey Miss Fannie" and "Blue Velvet" until the grooves went white. I bought all the early Fats Domino records, like "Goin' Home," years before his monster hits.

We had our local heroes. Sugar Boy Crawford and the Cane Cutters cut "Jock-A-Mo," later turned into "Iko Iko" by the Dixie Cups. The Dixie Cups sang with my sister Athelgra when we moved back uptown in the fifties. "Iko Iko" is another one of those Big Easy anthems, a Mardi Gras Indian chant I can't explain, don't want to explain, but it's something I'm still singing fifty years later.

Every time I'd go to a dance, I wouldn't dance. I'd ease over to the piano players and watch. Couple of the cats hipped me to chords. Couldn't call the chords by name, but I could play them by feel. Started to feel that I could actually get up and perform myself. My first little group didn't even have a name. We worked up "Is It a Dream?" a serious doo-wop blend by the Vocaleers, and were all set to enter the talent show at Rosenwald gym, when the guys chickened out. I thought for a second — *What am I supposed to do?* Fuck it. I went out there alone. Sang the song while accompanying myself. The applause told me I wasn't crazy.

I had other jobs as a kid, but nothing as good as music. The only thing that came close was working at a TV and radio repair shop. The owner saw I had a knack for fix-it and became my mentor. That was cool until the day he took me to the Dew Drop Inn, where the baddest dudes played the baddest music. I was too young to be there, but the proprietor, Frank Painia, looked the other way. I was sitting there with my boss and his girlfriend when she got up and headed for the ladies' room. When she returned, she pulled out a gun and popped my man, right there next to me, five times through the heart. I knew he had slapped her around, I knew he had other chicks on the side, but I never guessed I'd see him murdered before my very eyes. Such things make an impression on a young boy.

Aaron

When I was a young boy, I saw something I'd never forget. I was going to the movies when I saw a grown man beat up a woman. He punched her in the face with his fist. After she fell, he kept kicking her. I wanted to run over there and protect her, but I knew he'd kill me. Just to see it, though, made me sick. I had nightmares for months. When I close my eyes, I still see the scene today. I promised myself, no matter how crazy I might get — and, bro, I've gotten plenty crazy — that I'd never hit a woman. I've kept that promise.

Charles

I was still a kid when I first hung out at the Dew Drop. Uncle Jolly took me there and introduced me around. My ears and eyes were overstimulated, my head was spinning. Music, women, drinks, drugs. The hustlers and musicians enjoyed a special rapport. The hustlers knew good music and paid good money to hear it. I was also amazed to see white women sitting at tables and standing at the bar. I saw how they were respected by the black men. In my mind, the white women who made that scene had courage. The interplay between white women and black men, which I witnessed at an early age, would fascinate me forever.

Art

Of the cats my age, James Booker played the Dew Drop before anyone. He was that good. I was so young when I played my first gigs, I had to ask Mommee's permission. I didn't know what I was doing, but I could fake it. Early in the game, I learned not to get in the way. They say silence is golden. Well, I applied that saying to music. Some musicians play a lot of notes. Maybe because I didn't know a lot of notes, I'd lay back and let the singer or guitarist or saxophonist lead. I'd never play over him. I'd play around him. A note here. A lick there. I'd come at it from an angle. Musicians talk about the "one," the primary beat. Man, I never knew where the one was. So my sense of syncopation was all screwed up. As a kid, that felt weird, but as I grew up, I came to appreciate how I kept time. It was different, and no one could say it wasn't funky.

Charles

Jazz called to me when I was a kid. I saw jazz in the form of Louis Jordan. He starred in those film clips where he played his shiny saxophone, sang his witty songs, and led his Tympany Five. The sight of his sax lit up my world. I tried different horns I borrowed from school. First there was a C melody, but that didn't do it for me. Then I played an alto, like Louis Jordan, but it sounded too feminine. I wanted a deeper sound. Before I heard Charlie Parker, I was listening to Lester Young's tenor. But more than Lester, who had a light touch, Gene "Jug" Ammons was my idol. He had the big macho tenor tone that sounded like manhood to me. I wanted Jug's sound and James Moody's technique. Moody was Dizzy's tenor player who played as fast as lightning.

My daddy said we couldn't afford a tenor sax, but Auntie Cat, bless her heart, promised to buy me one if I graduated valedictorian of my eighth-grade class. I made it and got the sax, but because I got the sax, my grades were never that good again. The horn took over.

Problem was, I didn't want to practice. I just wanted to play bebop, right then and there. Didn't want to learn scales. Didn't want to dig into chord changes. Thought I could just put the thing in my mouth, and the bebop would come flowing out. Too bad, but it doesn't work that way.

So I did the next best thing: I played the blues. The blues were simpler. Blues bands and blues singers were all around me. Rhythm-and-blues bands, doo-wop groups, early rock 'n' rollers — all this was happening when I was coming of age. Playing the blues didn't represent a step-down. It was a treat. Besides, in New Orleans there was no sharp division between bebop and blues players. The best players played both. Both were considered hot music by the hustlers and hookers of the underground world of the Dew Drop Inn.

The Turquoises was our first band, named because someone said turquoise was my birthstone. A trumpeter called J. C. Goodes and I were the nucleus. J.C. was into Miles. Later Samuel Alcorn played with us. Alcorn was into Dizzy; he loved those fast runs and high notes. When we played in the Booker T. Washington High School band, they started calling us Bird and Diz. I liked the compliment, but believe me, my bop chops were still raw.

When Art joined the Turquoises, he made it a better band, not only because he sang beautifully but because his piano was right on time for the dances and little parties we played. Another beautiful thing happened with the Turquoises: my dad became our manager. He made sure we got paid, and when we started gigging in small towns outside New Orleans, he'd drive us. That's when we got to know him better. On those two-lane blacktop highways, driving deep into Alabama and Mississippi, Daddy would open up. He'd start talking about those islands that him and Jolly visited as merchant marines. We'd hear stories about the exotic women in faraway countries who did far-out things. You can bet we listened very carefully as the pictures danced in our heads.

Art

I discovered a stash of pictures Jolly had brought back from some foreign port. We had seen sexy photos before, but nothing like this. This was a whole new world.

Charles

The world outside New Orleans was bigger and, in some ways, stranger than I had imagined. Once, playing in De Lisle, Mississippi, the cops broke in. I had no idea why. The crowd, all young black folks, were dancing to a song called "The Dog." The dance was suggestive yet, by today's standards, tame as toast. But the cops, who were white and especially fixated on the female dancers, hauled in every last patron for lewd behavior. The song was declared indecent and illegal.

Art

After the Turquoises had been together for a while, I thought we were pretty cool. Cool enough to cut a record. The coolest thing any band could do was cut a record. So we went down to Cosimo Matassa's J&M Studio on Rampart and Dumaine. That's where everyone cut everything. Whenever a record label wanted to record an r&b tune in New Orleans, they'd call Cosimo. Tommy Ridgley, Shirley and Lee, Huey "Piano" Smith and the Clowns, Earl King, Lee Allen — you'd see 'em all over at Cosimo's. You might even get a glimpse of Fats Domino. The mastermind behind Fats was Dave Bartholomew, Fats's writer and arranger. He created Fats's hit formula. Bartholomew was a bandleader before he became a studio wizard, using the best cats, like drummer Earl Palmer and sax man Red Tyler, who lived in the projects next to us. We'd hear Red's tenor coming through the walls.

Aaron

When I was seven years old, I fell in love with Red Tyler's daughter *and* his wife. That's the kind of romantic little kid I was. They were both such pretty ladies. One day Red's wife went to visit his mother and dropped dead on the stoop. When his mother came out and discovered her, the shock was too much for her; she also dropped dead. In the projects you learn about death early on.

One day I came home and went upstairs to see my grandmother, my mother's mother. She was in bed. I called her name. No response. I went over and touched her hand very lightly. This feeling came over me. Never had seen anyone so still. I knew Maw

Maw was dead. That lady who spoke Creole and gave me so much love was gone. I cried like a baby. I thought all of us would live together forever. I didn't know nothing about death.

CYRIL

I remember how she looked lying there. I freaked. I jumped down the stairs without touching the steps; I flew out of there. I was running from death, as though death would catch me and claim me just as death had claimed Maw Maw. For weeks I had nightmares about jumping down stairs and never reaching the landing. I was somehow suspended in space. I'd wake up in a sweat and remember that Maw Maw was gone. The fear was in my face.

Charles

The main fear of my childhood was white people. Back then black kids weren't running around killing other black kids. I had no fear of my own people. But the night riders and the paddy rollers were real. The paddy rollers, named in the days of slavery, were the patrollers. Patrollers and enforcers who would terrorize the neighborhoods with acts of brutality. I witnessed a black man being dragged by a car driven by whites until he bled to death. I saw the night riders, the Klan, riding on their horses and burning crosses. Scary sights for a kid. And then there were the gown men. They were said to be Tulane medical students who needed fresh cadavers. They'd ride 'round the black wards in their white vans and scoop you up, jab you with a needle — and that would be your ass. You'd never be heard from again. The cops, representing law and order, represented intimidation and fear. They'd arrest you for standing on the corner, for walking down the street, for being alive.

CYRIL

The famous quote I'd hear from my parents and aunts and uncle was "Never run from the police, even if they tell you to, or you'll wind up with two warning shots in the back of your head."

Charles

Mommee's side of the family — the Landrys — had that Creole connection with the paranormal. They were religious Catholics, but they also knew their voodoo. It was Maw Maw, for example, who told me I was born with a veil over my face. That meant I could see spirits. As a kid, I had a scientific mind; I took a scientific approach to most everything. So I didn't want to see what I saw. I didn't want to believe it was true. But I had no choice. My first experience happened when I was ten or eleven. I was visiting my aunt Lena, the one we called Nanny. She was living Uptown by the riverfront. Her front gate was on a spring that creaked when it opened. I heard the creak but didn't see anything. When I looked closer, I saw the outline of a bodiless figure entering her front gate, walking along the house, and heading toward the backyard. A buzzing feeling came over me. I was petrified. Later, still inside the house, I felt like something was holding me down. I couldn't get up, could hardly breathe. I managed to break free and run to my aunt, who calmly explained that the house was filled with spirits. Not everyone could see or feel them. It was a gift I neither wanted nor prized. That awful buzzing sensation would come back to me at critical points in my life. I didn't know why then; I don't know why now.

Aaron

I don't remember being afraid when I was a kid. What I mainly remember is music. The first music I heard is still the music I hear today, the music I love the most. Doo-wop had those harmonies that sounded like they came down from heaven. When Artie worked at the record store, he'd bring home the tunes. He brought home "Goodnite Sweetheart Goodnite" by the Spaniels, with Pookie Hudson singing lead. I loved Pookie's part, and I could sing it, but if I tried, I could sing all the parts — high tenor, middle tenor, baritone, even bass.

Artie had a little doo-wop group, the Gay Notes, with a cat called Issacher — pronounced "Isacoo" — Gordon. Issacher was bad. Sang like Sam Cooke. Sang all them pretty notes. For some reason, Issacher called me Kevin. "Kevin," he'd say, "come over here. I got a note for you." He'd show me how to build harmonies, and soon I was building my own blends. I heard everything he was hearing.

Art

Aaron would run over to me and Issacher, wanting to know what we were singing, looking to see how the notes went together. We ran him off. Didn't want to be bothered. Later I learned that Aaron had a sense of harmonics that was a whole 'nother thing.

Aaron

The harmonizing gospel groups — Soul Stirrers, Blind Boys, Pilgrim Travelers, Brooklyn All Stars singing "I Stood on the Banks of the Jordan" — these guys sang with the sweetness of the saints and the conviction of God. I also loved Clyde McPhatter. The Flamingos, Clovers, Moonglows, Orioles, Drifters, the smoothest singers singing the smoothest songs to the women they loved, songs that put women on a pedestal, like "Lovely Lady Dressed in Blue" put the Madonna on a pedestal. Songs that showed respect — "A Kiss from Your Lips," "The Ten Commandments of Love," "Crying in the Chapel."

Me and my partner Buckwheat learned all these songs and sang 'em walking down the street. We were singing fools. When we wanted to get in the movies and didn't have a dime, we'd sing "Only You" or "The Great Pretender" for the lady at the ticket counter, and sure enough, she'd smile and let us through. Same thing at basketball games. We'd sing "I'll Be Home" or "Wheel of Fortune" and walk right in. That's when I knew my voice was my ticket. Thank you, Jesus.

I have musical memories that still burn through my brain. I saw Tommy Ridgley singing on a flatback truck rolling through the neighborhood. Never heard singing so beautiful before — and done to this sweet little rhumba beat. Of all these singers, though, the one I loved best was the one I heard first, my brother. Artie had it before I did. He could sing like Fats until you couldn't tell them apart, but more than that, he could also sound like himself. He had a high natural voice that killed me. It was a beautiful voice that Artie could fix in a lot of different ways, so when the Hawketts came along, he fit right in. If you really want to know when the Neville Brothers began as a band, you gotta go back to the Hawketts.

Art

The Gay Notes faded out as the Hawketts faded in. I started out with the Hawketts about the same time we were getting ready to leave the projects. It was in 1954 when we moved back to Valence Street. I was seventeen, Charles sixteen, Aaron thirteen, Athelgra ten, Cyril six, and our baby sister, Rowena, who we called Cookie, was two. After twelve years we were back where we had started, in the heart of the family. That's when everything came together and, at the same time, when everyone started moving in different directions.

Movin' Back

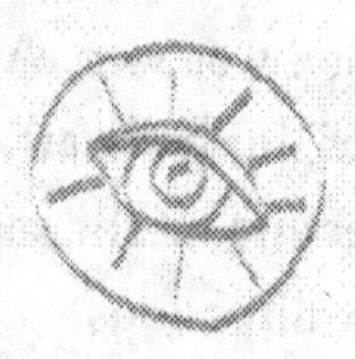

Art

Back Uptown, the big change was living in the same two-family, camelback double-shotgun house as Auntie Cat. By then our grandmother Ma Ma, who was in failing health, had already moved in with her sister Auntie Cat. Cat wanted the family closer together. We moved in to the other side of her house. She and Ma Ma were at 1104 Valence, and we were at 1106. Auntie Cat made it easier for my parents by charging very little rent, if any at all. She was a generous lady.

CYRIL

Moving back Uptown was not a pleasant experience for my mother. Auntie Cat gave her hell. Auntie Cat never wanted Mommee to marry my father. She looked down on my mother and she looked down on me. Auntie Cat never gave me respect because I was dark-skinned and nappy-haired. Wasn't her fault. That's just how she thought. She was the product of centuries of prejudice. She thought like a white person.

I'd watch out the windows when the white garbagemen would sling our cans half a block away and let the shit spill out all over the street. But when it came to Auntie Cat's cans, they'd empty them carefully and set them down perfectly in place. Auntie Cat would complain that I was playing music too loud, call up on the phone and tell Mommee the vibes were shaking her precious china closet. Even worse, Auntie Cat would tell Mommee that she was raising her kids all wrong. She gave her so much grief. One time she went too far. My mother couldn't take any more of the criticism and cursed Auntie Cat, as the old folks said, from amazing grace to a floating opportunity. When Daddy came home that night, the tension was thick. Mommee told him what had happened between her and Auntie Cat. I saw his expression turn grave, and I didn't know what he would do. I followed him through the kitchen into the living room, thinking he would call Auntie Cat. But Daddy did more than that; he walked down the steps — there was a wooden partition between her side and ours — and knocked on the door. I was standing behind him, hiding behind his legs. Auntie Cat came to the door. "Evening, Arthur," she said. I could feel him forcing himself to do something that didn't come naturally. "Look, Virginia," he said — her real name was Virginia Harris — "we appreciate how you don't charge us much rent. We appreciate living here in your house, but I don't want you getting into my wife's business. Leave Amelia alone. I respect you, but you gonna have to respect her. So that's it." I stared up to see the expression in Auntie Cat's eyes. "Didn't mean no harm, Arthur," she said, backing down. "Just make sure," he repeated, "that it don't happen again."

Man, was I a happy kid! Happy that justice was done. Happy that my father's balls were hanging right. Later I learned that part of Auntie Cat's problem was her husband, Peg Leg Harris. Some said Peg Leg would take off his peg leg and use it to beat his wife. That might account for Auntie Cat's cranky moods.

Art

I was glad when we moved back Uptown. The place next to Auntie Cat's was big — two big bedrooms upstairs, and downstairs Mommee and Daddy turned the dining room into their bedroom. I was glad to be back with all my aunts and glad to have space to rehearse. By then the Hawketts were happening. That's when the dudes started calling me Red. The Hawketts had a trombone, two trumpets, a tenor, alto, baritone, guitar, drums, and me. A small band with a big-band sound. The other hot local band was the Flamingos, led by Allen Toussaint. Allen had Snooks Eaglin on guitar, a blind man who played the best guitar of anyone in the city. We had John Boudreaux on drums and later Leo Morris, who lived around the corner from Valence and eventually went off with Sam Cooke and Jerry Butler, winding up in New York, where he became Idris Muhammad, a big-time jazz musician. In New Orleans the Hawketts were the number one band. We played everything — jazz, blues, r&b, you name it. We opened for Louis Jordan at the Booker T. Washington High School auditorium; we opened for Ray Charles when he was still singing like Charles Brown and Nat Cole. We were sharp. We had tailor-made silk shirts, khaki pants with killer creases, and old-man supercomfortable shoes.

The more I worked, the more I saw I had to be sharp. No one was sharper than Guitar Slim. Slim was from back-country Louisiana and had come to New Orleans with a guitar cord long enough to let him play out on the street and draw people in like the Pied Piper. While the opening groups were playing, Slim would be tuning up his slick guitar, drowning out everyone. When Ray Charles came through, he produced Slim for Specialty Records down at Cosimo's studio, singing "The Things I Used to Do (I Don't Do No More)," a song that caused a sensation. Slim was always causing a sensation. He was the cat who would have his valet go out and mix different dyes and paint over his white buck shoes to match the color of his suits. I tried to do the same. We were all matched to the max. Slim was just one of the gunslinger guitarists who turned up the volume on the T-Bone Walker thing. Johnny "Guitar" Watson came over from Texas — he and I became buddies — and he learned a lot from Slim. We all did.

CYRIL

I think of that line from Big Joe Turner's "Shake, Rattle and Roll": "I'm like a one-eyed cat peeping in a seafood store." Well, that was me watching the Hawketts rehearse in our living room on Valence. There was a sliding door separating my parents' bedroom from the living room, where Artie and them used to play. I'd peep through the crack in the door. At the sound of the music, especially the sound of the drums, my heartbeat quickened. I longed to be in there with them. There were times when I'd get there early and hide in the corner or behind a chair. Some of the cats might discover me and say, "Hey, little man, what's happening?" or, "Baby bro wants to play along." If I was lucky, I'd get to hit the drums. The other Hawketts paid me more mind than Artie did. Artie didn't want me in there. I guess he was busy dealing with the music. He just saw me as the pesky little brother. He didn't know it, but I was dying for his attention. I was also dying because I knew if one day

I did sing or play, I'd have to be a bad motherfucker. Listening to Artie and Aaron sing, hearing Charles play sax, I worried how I could ever measure up.

I was there the night the Hawketts won the amateur contest out at Lincoln Beach, the beach area for black folks. They won it with Little Richard's "Rip It Up." To me, Artie was the best singer around. I put him up there with Fats Domino and Chuck Berry. He knew how to cut off those notes; he had that soulful inflection and fooled with the beat until you never knew what to expect. That same night a gospel group came out with a little girl who stood on a chair and sang her lungs out. Thought to myself, *Man, I'd like to be standing on that chair, I'd like to be singing that kind of church music*.

Back on Valence we were exposed to several kinds of churches. We were supposed to be going to Blessed Sacraments. Sometimes Mommee would give me money for the charity basket and have me take my baby sister, Cookie, to the mass. Cookie was a little angel. I was a little devil. I'd give Cookie the money if she wouldn't tell on us playing hooky. I was bored silly by the Catholic service; all that business about original sin seemed to have nothing to do with me. So me and Cookie would skip out and run over to a little church around the corner from Valence called Sunlight Baptist. The tiny building would be rocking from side to side, the parking lot full of big ol' cars with country license plates and red mud splattered all over the tires. You could hear the music a mile away. Talk about making a joyful noise! We'd peep inside, me and little sis, and our eyes would pop out of our heads. There'd be these all-men quartets, cats dressed in matching kelly green suits or cherry red suits or even pink suits, their hair done up in 'dos, each group trying to outdress the others. Not just outdress but outsing, the congregation standing and shouting and carrying on like Jesus himself had returned live and in person, right there in the Sunlight Baptist Church. I didn't know anything about denominations, didn't know what to call it or even what it was. Just knew the music thrilled my soul. Compared with Auntie Cat's Methodist church, where everyone was trying to be white, everyone here was real.

Sunlight Baptist gave me the same feeling I got when, a little later, I'd follow Uncle Jolly around the corner to Jack Calahan's, the barroom on the corner. There was a section for white people up front and a side door for blacks, who had to sit in the back room. The back room was the happening room. I can still smell the beer and hear the tinkle of glasses, the raucous laughter and Ray Charles shouting "I Got a Woman" on the jukebox. The back room was jumping; folks were dancing in the back room; in the front room everyone seemed sad.

Musically, my life was set up so I always felt like I had one foot in the Sunlight Baptist and one foot in the barroom.

Aaron

By the time we moved back Uptown, I had a certain style. My walk came from Uncle Jolly, my fighting attitude came from Artie — protect the underdog — and my singing came from the cowboys. See, as a kid, I was a little cowboy myself. I loved those western movies. Had me a mop stick for a horse. I'd ride the range all over Mommee's kitchen. I'd go yodeling off into the sunset. I'd pretend to be out on the plains chasing down cattle rustlers. I was ready to rope cows. The part that got to me most, though, wasn't the riding or shooting; it was the singing. Roy Rogers and Gene Autry were my favorites. I liked how their voices were low-key and their songs simple and sincere. Real men expressing sentiments of the heart. So while I was learning Sam Cooke licks — and I could do every single last one — I was also learning "Home on the Range." I developed a yodel. Somehow I combined the yodel into the doo-wop of the day. At the same time, I was still hearing the songs sung to the Virgin Mary, the ones I learned to love at Saint Monica. The peaceful sound of praising the Blessed Lady never failed to calm my heart.

In New Orleans you learn to combine everything. My combination was the different sounds I heard and liked. So I started singing in my own way. Singing was an escape valve. I was going to sing no matter what. But I also saw that I was going to get into trouble. I was headed in that direction, and no one, not even God, could turn me around.

CYRIL

I was looking for clues about what it meant to be a man, to be a grown-up in a world where grown men would call my father and my uncle — my models for manhood — "boys." That hurt and confused me. But I was also excited by all the adults who congregated in our home on Valence. I'd hide in the kitchen closet; I'd brave the darkness and the mice just to eavesdrop on my parents and aunts and Uncle Jolly playing cards and talking shit. That's how I learned about the world. They talked about the neighbors; they talked politics; they projected a feeling of togetherness that spread warmth all over me. The rapport they shared was beautiful, the way they used humor to get by. Daddy might come in and smell something in the kitchen, saying, "Goddamnit, Lena's messing with those hog guts again." "Arthur," Lena would fire back, "I don't tell you how to drive your cab, so do *not* tell me how to cook."

Our house always smelled of delicious foods — smothered chicken, stewed hen, baked macaroni, dumplings and pies, cakes and cobblers. Every single Neville could cook, the men as well as the women; we could burn in the kitchen. Sometimes I'd be allowed to watch the big folks play cards. Daddy and Jolly would be partners, and I'd see them making signals between them. Mommee would catch them. "Look at them cheating," she'd say, "and the fools still can't win." The sound of cards slapping on the table, the beauty of their singing when the mood struck, the sense of family. Certain things left their mark on me: Me and Daddy watching cartoons, and him explaining that Bugs Bunny is black. Bugs digs a hole in the ground and comes up in Merry Ole England. An Englishman chides Bugs for knowing nothing about royalty. "Wrong," says Bugs. "I know the Duke of Ellington, the Count of Basie, and the Cab of Calloway." "See," says Daddy, "Bugs is black."

Certain sounds I still hear: the minister down the street blasting Beethoven from his phonograph while, in retaliation, our neighbor Miss Mary drowns him out with Ray Charles's "Drown in My Own Tears" or Smiley Lewis's "I Hear You Knocking (But You Can't Come In)." (A little later when pop singer Gale Storm covers the same song, I'm not sure she's keeping anyone out.)

In New Orleans there's a white Mardi Gras and a black Mardi Gras. We knew nothing about the white one. In our neighborhood everyone masked makeshift funky style. You didn't need a costume. You just went on out there with a blue or red plaid flannel shirt, a bandanna, a crazy hat. You slapped some war paint on your face and hit the streets. The party was the streets. Uptown, it started about 4 A.M. They let children in the barrooms. You could go anywhere. My daddy didn't like it. He saw it for what it was. He'd known real Africans who came to New Orleans and, seeing the Zulu parade and how it stereotyped blacks, started crying, vowing never to return here again. The Hollywood–Tarzan jungle image of our people was something my father detested.

Later I'd understand his attitude. Mardi Gras was based on European mythology in which people of color were often depicted as degenerates. Mardi Gras seemed like an excuse to glorify drunkenness, when tourists would come to town for the privilege of pissing in public on Bourbon Street. My father also explained that the private clubs who sponsored the parade and built the elaborate floats were strictly segregated. The shame of that segregation survived even during the civil rights era and lasted until only a few years ago.

From a kid's point of view, Mardi Gras was exciting, if only to shatter the routine of daily life. From the time I could stand, I never missed a single Mardi Gras. Mardi Gras also showed me how, in some sense, New Orleans is the most northern island in the Caribbean. The flavor of Carnival is an island flavor. Uptown, it was this spicy combination of island and African village. When I was a little kid, our Mardi Gras all happened, as the old folks said, "before day in the morning." If you came out of the house at 10 A.M., you might see one lone Indian heading home. Our Mardi Gras happened in the dead of night. It felt like a secret Mardi Gras, a special Mardi Gras with a mystery all its own.

Generally we were told to stay Uptown. Going from 'hood to 'hood in New Orleans was always a tricky business. White wards encircled black wards. We were fenced in. But sometimes during Mardi Gras I'd venture down to the Sixth and Seventh Wards to second-line. The great thing about second-lining is that it's spontaneous and free.

Art

Most everyone sees the original second line coming from the jazz funerals. The march to the cemetery was somber. But once the body was buried, the band broke out in a romp — and folks followed the band. Folks who didn't necessarily know the deceased — and didn't care. They just felt like dancing. Wasn't any organized dance, nothing choreographed or planned, just fall back behind the band and let loose, do a little jig, make your own moves, let the beat take you where it will. Soon this tradition started: every parade in New Orleans inspired its own second line. Everyone who felt the music became part of the music. If the music was funky, well, second line got even funkier. Looser the better.

Mardi Gras, of course, inspired the whole city to second-line. When I was a little kid, they didn't have tractors like today, only horses; and they didn't have electric lights, only dudes carrying flames. Incredible shit. From those gigantic floats they'd throw stuff — rubber cigars, whistles, brightly colored beads and necklaces — but they'd aim at the white crowds, not the blacks. I'd run behind the floats anyway and grab what I could. If you ran too far and found yourself in the wrong ward, the cops wouldn't hesitate to beat the shit out of you. Mardi Gras might look like a time when all hell breaks loose and boundaries are busted, but in the Big Easy boundaries are always there. You better watch your ass.

Charles

Growing up in New Orleans, stimulated by so much music and so many lifestyles, it was easy to get your signals crossed. This was true especially in the area of sex. When I was a kid, if a white woman said, "Hey, boy, come here," you went. Same with white men. One day walking down Napoleon Avenue, I passed a white man who stopped me to ask if I wanted to make a dollar. Sure I did. He said to follow him back into the bushes. Racial etiquette demanded I do as I was told. He gave me a blow job and then handed me the dollar. What was I supposed to think?

Black-on-black romance could be just as confusing. I had secret girlfriends who had to remain secret because their parents forbade them to go with guys as dark as me. I had sexual experiences at a young age with various girls, but the nature of the sex was perfunctory and superficial. I didn't know what I was doing — and neither did they. I also didn't know what I was doing when I got married at fifteen. Vera was a perfectly nice black girl. We liked each other; we groped; the sex act was over before it started. We thought the right thing to do was marry. That's what good Catholics did. The priest warned me. "Look," he said, "you don't have to go through with this. Y'all hardly know each other." He was so adamant, he wouldn't marry us in church. But we were even more adamant. Vera's mother had a Baptist preacher friend who did the job. When we returned to be blessed in the Catholic Church, the priest still refused. "Get it annulled," he urged. "You don't know what you're doing." He was right. All told, we would be married thirty-seven years and have six kids together. But I was never really with her, not heart and soul. My life went in a million different directions. Just months after I got married, I went on the road — and that changed everything.

A guy named Gene Franklin needed a tenor player for his House Rockers band. I couldn't wait to split, but I needed my parents' permission. I was still just fifteen. I worried that Daddy and Mommee wouldn't let me go, and wondered how I could convincingly present my case. Then I remembered my mother regretting that *her* mother had kept the dance team of Amelia and George Landry from going on the road with Louis Prima. That was a big blow to both Mommee and Uncle Jolly. "Well, this is my chance," I explained to my parents. "You wouldn't want to keep me from a career in music, would you?" They thought about it for a minute. Neither had the heart to say no. I was free.

Art

Charles was the first to hit the road, before any of us even knew what "the road" meant. That had a big impact on all the brothers. It meant Mommee and Daddy were willing to let us go if the right opportunity popped up. The door was open, the highway straight ahead.

CYRIL

Once Charles left, the comings and goings of my brothers became a fact of life. I didn't really hang with them or get to know them until I was a teen. They remained far-off figures, dudes to idolize and emulate, cats living glamorous lives.

Movin' Out

Charles

The road held a strange glamour, a self-invented glamour. Example: At the time — this is 1953 — black artists didn't have their pictures in the paper. No one knew what the stars looked like. So when we got to town, Gene Franklin, who sang like B. B. King, was billed as B. B. King. Other times Gene would bill himself as Ray Charles 'cause he could imitate Ray's voice as well. His female singer was billed as Big Mama Thornton, who had a big hit with "Hound Dog," and the crowd, who didn't know the difference, was convinced they were hearing the genuine article.

Gene was based in Tampa, and it was in Tampa — at Watt Sanderson's Blue Room on Central Avenue — that I was really introduced to the high art of making love to a woman. Before that, I didn't know what I was doing. It was on my sixteenth birthday when, I believe, I became a man. Here's how it came down:

Central Avenue was the hub for the whores and hustlers. They had money and style. The Blue Room was fabulous, but being underage, I couldn't mingle. During intermission I'd have to stay on the bandstand and watch. There was lots to see. They had tap dancers tapping to Bird's bebop licks; they had a cat called Iron Jaw stomping down on beer-bottle caps with his bare feet until the caps stuck to his soles and became taps. Then he'd tap awhile before bending down to lift up a table with his mouth. If that wasn't enough, he'd have a chick sit on the table and he'd still lift the whole fuckin' thing. He'd eat Coke bottles, bulbs, carpet tacks, thumbtacks, even double-edge razors. Then Iron Jaw would wash it all down by swallowing fire.

In the midst of all this fiery excitement, the hookers would be cruising the club for johns. The hookers were gorgeous, and most gorgeous of all was the one they called Black Beauty — Oriental eyes, large sensuous mouth, long luscious legs, sculpted booty, and big pointy breasts that sang a song all their own. All the musicians were dying for Black Beauty. So you can imagine my surprise when she approached me.

"How old are you?" she asked.

"The truth," I said, "is that in a few hours I'll be sixteen."

"Sweet sixteen!" Her shining eyes lit up. "Well, you deserve a little gift, don't you?"

"Whatever you say."

"Hey, girls," she called to her colleagues. "Baby brother is turning sixteen tonight. We need to give him a little party, don't we?"

Hours later, when the customers had gone and the club had cleared out, Black Beauty and two of her finest coworkers came to fetch me. Took me to her room. Just me and the three of them. Didn't know what to expect. They had a big cake and balloons. But they had more. The champagne went to my head. I had never tasted it before. The weed had me horny and hard. I had never smoked it before. The coke had me wired. I had never snorted before. "Ever eaten pussy?" asked Black Beauty. Not only had I never known cunnilingus, I had never heard a woman talk that way. "No, ma'am," I said, "but I sure am willing to learn."

That night in Tampa, the gods of love shone down on me. Not only were the women patient, they were specific. Black Beauty broke it down like this: "Black men always say, 'I don't eat no pussy.' They don't think it's manly. But believe me, honey, most of those men are liars. If they're getting sucked, chances are they're doing some sucking themselves. But the trouble is, they never learn to do it right. You're young and sweet, and I wanna teach you to do it right. Don't suck too hard. Lick lightly over here. Take your time. Tease. Blow softly on this spot . . . on that spot . . . put your lips here . . . put your tongue there . . . deep, deep inside . . ." No student ever paid more attention to his teacher. No lesson has ever been sweeter.

When Gene Franklin and the House Rockers weren't rocking, I'd rock out with the Rabbit Foot Minstrel Show. That was another eye-opening experience. I was privileged to catch the final go-around of a tradition in black show-business history that went back to Ma Rainey and Bessie Smith. Fact is, Ma's and Bessie's pictures adorned the big banners flanking the entrance to the tent show.

The tradition itself started three decades earlier as a black circus because blacks were barred from Ringling Brothers. The traveling show would tour the South, setting up in empty fields or deserted lots in rural areas where the African American population was denied any kind of live entertainment. No audiences were more appreciative. There were animals, fortune-tellers, a strongman, a fat lady, a girl with four legs, Siamese twins, acrobats, and, best of all, a blues tent where a big mama would tell it like it is. There were also fabulous dancers like Peg Leg Bates and Peg Leg Moffett, who worked miracles on one leg. The dancers who moved me most, though, were the gay guys, black male dancers who had the discipline and technique of classical ballet but, for reasons of racism, had been shut out of that world. They, too, were working the tents, but with such artistic sensitivity and subtle skill that, forty-five years later, I can still envision their show:

In black robes and black hoods, their faces are painted white, their hands covered by white gloves. You see nothing onstage but the lyrical movements of disembodied hands and faces choreographed to the beat of hot jazz. At some point, they throw off their robes. The fronts of their leotards are also painted white, but the backs are black. When they turn around, they disappear into the black night. Flickering lights, projected from a wheel of colored gels, as exotic as anything I'd see in the psychedelic sixties, infuse it all with a strange and sexy aura.

Even sexier is another piece danced by a company of black women set in an African village. An old man, leaning on a cane, sits on a rock. Bent over, he looks close to death. You hear the sound of jungle drums. A voluptuous woman, led on by clarinet licks, dances onstage. She circles the man, then suggestively touches him. Another female dancer appears; her dance, punctuated by a muted trumpet, is more suggestive; she, too, touches the man. After each touch, the old man straightens up — a little more, a little more — so by the time the fourth dancer sinuously winds herself around him, the cat is all the way up. Now the band is cooking. My man leaps from the rock and does a fantastic dance that has the crowd roaring; his dance of love is enough to satisfy all four women — and then some. To witness all this in a moonlit field outside a little town in backwater Alabama leaves an indelible impression. I realize I'm seeing High Art.

As a musician in the minstrel show, I was on the low end. I was billed as "the Boy Wonder of Sax." Because I looked much younger than sixteen, they featured me as a novelty. But the truth is that I still couldn't play shit. I got by on basic blues, but I was mainly growling. My dream of bebopping "Cherokee" or "Ornithology" — firing off killer riffs as fast as Bird — was far off in my future.

Art

I took whatever gigs I could find. If all the Hawketts weren't available, I'd work with a trio. One of them had Snooks Eaglin on guitar and Smokey Johnson on drums. Both those boys were bad. Still didn't consider myself a piano player, but by then I could fake it pretty good. Play some funk, sing like Fats, keep the people entertained. When Snooks and Smokey weren't available, I'd play solo gigs, anything to get over.

CYRIL

Artie was at the Araby in Saint Bernard Parish. He was playing solo that night, and for some reason, he took me along. That only happened twice in my childhood, and both times it was like dying and going to heaven. I sat by the piano, just watching his fingers fly over the keyboard. It was an all-white crowd, and Artie knew exactly how to get them dancing. In the middle of one song, two of the white boys got to fighting. I was so young and naive that I didn't think white men ever fought one another. Artie was quick to say, "Let's get out of here." The message was clear — don't fuck with white people's business; if you do, there's a good chance you'll be turned into a scapegoat.

Art

I was still a student at Walter L. Cohen High School when the Hawketts were singing on the radio for Dr. Daddy-O, the first black deejay in our area. In the fifties, r&b was played by white jocks imitating blacks. That was okay because it was the only way for the music to get over. But the irony was thick: Dr. Daddy-O trained the white jocks to talk black; meanwhile, the white jocks came in the front door of the station while he came in the back. But Dr. Daddy-O never lost his dignity. He was an educated cat; he tutored me in Spanish.

The Hawketts were hanging at the stations and studios in hopes of being heard. I'd see Fats's man, Dave Bartholomew, putting together sessions at Cosimo's. One day I got up the nerve to ask Dave to listen to the Hawketts. I thought we were ready to record. Dave disagreed. "Not yet," he said. "Go home and practice. I'll tell you when you're ready." When he finally did tell me, twenty-five years had passed.

Just by hanging around Cosimo's, I got a little taste of the action. Cosimo's is where Bumps Blackwell and Art Rupe of Specialty produced Little Richard's hit records of the mid-fifties — "Tutti Frutti," "Long Tall Sally," "Rip It Up" — all them songs. My buddy Issacher and I were there when Richard cut "The Girl Can't Help It," which wound up in the movie with Jayne Mansfield. We're the cats singing background. We each got fifteen bucks. Issacher sang so good, he got a gig going on the road with the Spiders, one of the singingest groups ever to come out of New Orleans.

The Hawketts finally did record. Deejay Ken "Jack the Cat" Elliott took us to the WWEZ studio to cut a song already done in country style called "Mardi Gras Mambo." The country version hadn't sold. He figured an r&b version might. He figured right. I sang it and didn't think that much of it. Cute song. We gave it a little mambo snap to cash in on the craze of the day and knocked it out in no time. Two mikes to pick up everything in one take. Went home and forgot about it.

But Jack the Cat didn't. He pushed it until other jocks picked it up. "Mardi Gras Mambo" became the big local hit at the Mardi Gras of 1956. Year after year it grew in popularity until it became a staple. More than forty years later I'm still singing the damn thing. Don't even ask me about royalties. All of us learned early on that, in New Orleans, control stayed in the hands of a few men. It'd be that way for decades to come. Control was tight; control was absolute. If you wanted to make a record, if you hoped to have a national hit — like Slim and Fats and Little Richard were having national hits out of New Orleans — you followed the rules. Don't ask questions. No one knew anything about lawyers; no one was offering classes in the business of music. Who knew about copyrights? Or royalties? We stayed stupid for a long, long time. All we thought about was getting on a record. Nothing else mattered.

Aaron

We called pot "muggles." I started smoking in junior high and started with heroin not long after. Uptown, copping dope was easy. Being older, Charles had started before me. Uncle Jolly sold weed, although he was the first to tell me to stay away from the shit. Charles said the same thing. But I didn't listen. Didn't listen to anyone. First time I shot smack, I was in love. Had no idea where the road would lead. Took me a lifetime to realize the real destination. In a poem — this was when I was struggling to stop — I wrote:

One day I learned to see
The ultimate high is an OD

At the same time I was using, I was always singing. A music teacher at Cohen High School, Solomon Spencer, set up a group called the Avalons. Leo Morris, the drummer, told Spencer about me, and I wound up singing with the Avalons for a couple of years. Actually, Spencer had four different groups at once — all called the Avalons — and kept them booked solid.

No money for us, but we loved what we were doing. The golden days of doo-wop were good to me. I was also the only guy who could see in an all-blind band that played the Driftwood Lounge on Bourbon Street in the Quarter. I needed Mommee and Daddy's permission to sing there. By then they were happy their sons were trying to make money making music. Daddy would take us to gigs in his cab. He even found musicians to fill in when one of the regulars fell out. My parents believed in my singing.

CYRIL

I'd always hear my mother speak of Aaron and his beautiful voice. It was clear that he had this special gift. We were in awe of it. We still are. On the entire planet, there's only one voice like his.

For a long time I was closest to Aaron because Aaron was the most accessible. He was around and willing to hang with his baby brother. I copied his walk, even before I knew that he had copped that walk from Uncle Jolly. I wanted Aaron to be proud of me. Like Art, Aaron had a reputation as a fighter. That impressed me, but it didn't necessarily mean I wanted the same reputation. Before I got to the point of throwing fists, I had to work my way through a whole battery of fears.

In 1955 my fears reached a boiling point. I was seven when I opened *Jet* magazine and saw a picture of Emmett Till, a fourteen-year-old black boy who had been tortured, shot, and drowned in a river in Mississippi. His mama had asked that the magazine publish the picture. His head was swollen and horribly disfigured. Next to the gruesome photo was an earlier picture of him. He had been a handsome boy. Emmett had gone from Chicago to visit his family in Mississippi, where, as I heard the story, he whistled at a white woman. The woman told her husband and his half brother, who came and took Emmett from his uncle's house. They said their intention was only to scare him. But he wasn't scared. He was willing to fight them, if only they'd fight fairly — one at a time. They couldn't understand him. He refused to repent. They thought, *We've never seen a nigger like this; we're able to scare all our niggers, but not this one; his attitude might rub off on the niggers down here; we've got to kill him.*

They beat him to a pulp before tying a piece of heavy machinery around his neck and dumping him in the river. The picture showed that one of his eyes was gouged out; one side of his forehead was crushed; a bullet was lodged in his skull. His brave mother insisted upon an open casket so the world could see the brutality. As a little boy, I fixated on that photo. I kept looking at it during the day; I kept seeing it in my nightmares. I still see it. For the first time in my life, I realized I belonged to more than just my family; I belonged to a people. I also realized that, in the minds of many, blacks were not human beings. We were animals without souls. The world suddenly seemed ominous to me. My mother and aunts told me stories about how black boys had disappeared right here in New Orleans, picked up off the street, never heard from again. For a while I was scared to leave the house. Inside, in the bosom of my family, I felt safe. But outside, the streets were filled with fear. It took a while, but eventually that fear turned to rage.

In a store not far from our house, I saw a white lady slam the face of a little black boy — no older than me — into a drinking fountain, smashing his nose and cutting his lip. The boy had not seen the sign that said WHITES ONLY. Seeing his blood flowing from the fountain onto the floor, I ran out. Danger lurked everywhere.

That same year — 1955 — Rosa Parks refused to give up her seat to a white person on a Montgomery bus, an act of defiance and courage that would inspire me for the rest of my life. Seeing this small woman take this enormous step stirred my soul. She was a fighter. I aspired to be such a fighter, although, on a personal level, fighting was not my thing.

My attitude about fighting was to save my energy for white boys and cops. I never wanted to hit a brother. That made no sense. So, years later when Aaron showed up at the school yard with a brother's head under his arm, telling me I had to fight him, I was reluctant. Aaron said that the guy had challenged him, but Aaron, being older and bigger, had declined. Aaron hated bullies. "So get your little bitch brother," the cat demanded, "and I'll kick his butt." I recognized the dude, who was known for throwing hands. I wanted no part of him, but if I backed off, Aaron would lose face — and I would, too. With no way out, I went to work. I got to him so quickly and effectively that in the middle of the fight I felt sorry for him. I stopped and turned away. Mistake. He snuck a punch, popping me in the eye. Now I had to finish what I started, pleasing Aaron but confusing me. "You threw down," said Aaron as I went off to throw up. Beating up a brother still didn't feel right. But the next day at school when the girls started calling me Cassius Clay, my attitude changed. My black eye became a badge of honor.

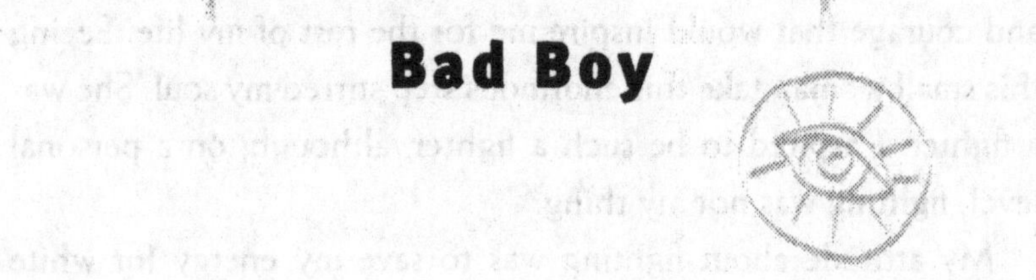

Bad Boy

Art

His name was Larry Williams. He called one of his songs "Bad Boy." And, bro, that says it all.

Charles

I met Larry Williams at the Dew Drop. He was a leader among the new rockers, the new cats. Larry was the new breed of black player, not just a hustler but the Man. His fingernails were manicured, he dressed in the finest threads, he wore those big-brimmed gangsta pimp hats, he spoke well. He had a personal valet, a flock of women surrounding him, and a pastel green Lincoln Continental Mark IV with a white convertible top, a kit in the back, and a bumper sticker that said I STOP FOR ALL BLONDES.

Art

Larry came from New Orleans, just like Lloyd Price, whose "Lawdy Miss Clawdy" was one of the biggest hits to come out of here in the early fifties. Fact is, Larry had been Lloyd's piano player. Then Larry went to California, where he had a good hit on Specialty with Lloyd's "Just Because." Larry lived in Oakland, but he was always running through New Orleans. His big smashes were songs he wrote — "Short Fat Fannie," followed by "Bony Moronie." They were novelty tunes about women with extreme anatomies and also balls-out rockers, grooves geared to attract teenagers — black and white — to the new music sweeping the country. Maybe history books pay more attention to Fats or Little Richard, but believe me, Larry Williams was their equal — and then some. The man was a trendsetter. If there's a Mount Rushmore of rock 'n' roll, you better carve Larry's face all over it. He was the architect of his own sound. As a piano man, singer, writer, and bandleader, Larry was the boss with a new style of hot sauce. He had spice to spare. For the longest, his main man and partner in musical crime was Johnny "Guitar" Watson, a clever cat who could write and play up a storm. I loved their duet record — this was years later — called *Two for the Price of One.*

Larry was the first r&b superstar to take an interest in the brothers. I believe he loved all of us — me, Charlie, and Aaron. Later he got to know Cyril. He recognized our talent and changed our lives.

Charles

When Larry recorded, he always used New Orleans cats, whether the sessions were here at Cosimo's or out in Hollywood — Red Tyler on sax, Roy Montrell on guitar, Earl Palmer or another drummer named Charles "Hungry" Williams. Hungry hooked me up with Larry when he needed another horn for his road band. That was wild. Two of the wilder times come to mind:

The Larry Williams caravan — a Lincoln Continental and a long station wagon — pulls up to a gas station somewhere in serious redneck Georgia. With his I-own-the-world attitude, Larry honks for service. The attendant looks us over and then spots the I STOP FOR ALL BLONDES bumper sticker. That's all he needs to see. He whips out his sheriff's badge. "Heard y'all were speeding," he says. "All you niggers are under arrest." Inside the station he slips on his judge's robe before banging the counter with his loaded pistol. We're each fined $150. We don't have it. He bangs the counter again. "Get your black asses in jail." There's a jail out back. We can't get sprung till Larry's agent sends money — which won't come till tomorrow. The only thing that saves us is a scrumptious southern fried chicken dinner cooked by the black lady who works for the sheriff's wife. Meanwhile, Larry never loses his composure. "Gonna be cool," he says, wolfing down some sweet potato pie. "Gonna be all right."

Wasn't all right when, at our next gig in Florida, the promoter didn't pay us and Larry promptly punched him out. Turned out the promoter had friends with weapons. The weapons had live ammunition, and we had to run for our lives, speeding down the highway, bullets bouncing off the car. Dead broke, our only recourse was to stop in some little town, break into a store, and steal some cash. In addition to being a master showman, Larry Williams was a master thief.

Art

First time I saw Larry Williams, the Hawketts were playing a club in Prairieville, Louisiana. Larry was gigging in Baton Rouge when someone mentioned us. I was singing his hits and imitating his voice. He came to check us out, and I'd never seen anyone so sharp. Larry had this aura about him. Confidence. Control. *Ain't nothing gonna get in my way*. He sat at a table in the back, sipping whiskey, not saying a word. When we were through, he came up to me and asked, "Y'all wanna go on the road?"

"What's the 'road'?" I still wasn't sure what the term meant.

"Got me gigs all over. I want y'all to be my band."

So for a while we were.

Before that, I had to get my parents' permission. "No problem," said Larry. "I'd like to meet your folks anyway." He was that kind of guy. He had a grandmother who lived at 42 Basin Street. Like Mommee's people, she was Creole. So when Larry met my mother, there was a real rapport. He could charm anyone. Daddy dug him, too. Couldn't help but be impressed. Larry had all these records out there. When he came to town, he'd get a suite at Le Pavillon, the superswanky hotel on Poydras Street.

In town he had us playing behind the Spaniels at the Autocrat Club. Out of town, Larry wasn't adverse to double-booking himself. He'd send me to one gig while he was playing another. I'd pretend I was Larry Williams, wear his clothes, play his piano licks, sing his songs. That was cool until I went to promote the show at a radio station, where the deejay took one look at me and said, "I know Larry Williams, and you ain't him." "You're right," I confessed, "but I can sound just like him."

I was just starting to have a sound of my own. Larry introduced me to Harold Battiste, who had just opened a New Orleans office for Specialty Records over on North Claiborne. Harold was incredible, a jazz musician with a feel for righteous rhythm and blues. He helped me put together some demos that he played for label owner Art Rupe and Rupe's main music man, Bumps Blackwell.

Larry Williams sang a duet with me on one of the first records, Huey Smith's "Rockin' Pneumonia and the Boogie-Woogie Flu." Given the fact that I was a nobody, Larry did it out of the goodness of his heart. He also gave me a song called "The Dummy," which took his thing about anatomical weirdness to an extreme. "The Dummy" is about a cat who falls in love with a mannequin from a department store. I wrote a couple of things of my own — "Oooh-Whee Baby" and "Zing Zing." A funky white boy who hung around Harold called Mac Rebennack — you know him as Dr. John — wrote something called "What's Going On" that I cut about the same time.

CYRIL

I was eight, maybe nine years old when I heard this song on the radio:

I drink all the tea in China
To know what's going on
I wind all the clocks in England
To know what's going on
You tell me that you love me
Then turn around and treat me wrong

When I realized it was Artie singing, my little heart nearly jumped out of my chest. Man, my brother had made a record! And "What's Going On" wasn't just good, it was great. Art was the first to record. He was destined to be a big star like Larry Williams. We all knew it.

Art

I didn't know anything. I had these older guys around me — Harold Battiste, Bumps Blackwell, Larry Williams — who encouraged everything I did. But this business about being a star . . . man, I just wanted to make records. I was meeting all these people, making all these connections. Larry also introduced me to Joe Banashak, who owned a label called Minit, where I'd work later on.

In this first phase, though, I was cutting exclusively for Specialty. One day Bumps brought a cat to Cosimo's who was also working for Rupe in L.A. Bumps said the guy was a producer, but I saw him as a promoter. Who was I to argue with Bumps? Bumps was the man behind Little Richard, and soon he'd be sending the right signals to Sam Cooke. Anyhow, the "producer" had me sing "The Whiffenpoof Song." Wanted me to do it like Fats. I did it but hated it, especially those sheepish "bah bah bah"s. The "producer" turned out to be Sonny Bono.

Mainly, though, I stuck with Harold. I remember sitting in his office over Houston's Music Store when he played me a country song called "Cha Dooky-Doo." "Think you can give it a different beat?" he asked. I didn't see why not. Started fooling with it. Took to the studio. Hungry on drums, Red Tyler on sax, Harold at the controls. Irving Charles's guitar sounded fuzzy because of a busted amp. We didn't have any choice but to leave the fuzz. Later someone wrote we had invented this hip new style called "the distorted guitar sound." It was an accident. By the time the record came out, I had given up hope that any of these early sides would sell. By then I was in navy boot camp way up in Great Lakes, Illinois. My petty officer came up to me and said, "I've been told you're the guy who sings 'Cha Dooky-Doo.'"

"How do you know about 'Cha Dooky-Doo,' sir?" I asked.

"They're playing it night and day on WGM in Chicago. Allow me to shake your hand," he said with a smile. "You're our first rock 'n' roller."

Damn, I thought to myself, *life ain't bad after all.*

Charles

In the mid-fifties, Art and I had this grand idea — join the navy. Sounded exciting. Our dad and uncle were adventurers, and hell, we'd do it, too. Besides, the navy seemed to offer all these great opportunities to guys like us who were good learners with scientific minds. Art had a keen sense of mechanics, and we both saw it as an educational opportunity. Talk about naive!

The plan was for both of us to sign up for active duty. I did, but Artie didn't; he became a reservist. Before I knew it, I was called up. My civilian life came to a grinding halt, and I found myself drowning in some of the deepest racist shit you can imagine.

Art

While Charles was in the navy, I was off with Larry Williams. I was supposed to attend reserve meetings but never made them. That didn't catch up with me till later. But something else did: a woman. I'd been loving on a sweet lady named Carolyn. When she thought she was pregnant, I did what I considered the right thing: I married her. I was all of nineteen. The marriage didn't last. How could it? Neither of us knew which end was up. Turned out she wasn't pregnant, which was a blessing, because I had no business being a daddy. I was still a kid myself, deep into teenage science-fiction fantasies. Come to think of it, I still am.

Aaron

While Charlie was in the navy and Art was running in and out of town, I started singing with the Hawketts. You might say I graduated from the Avalons and joined my brother's band, which at that time was gigging steady. I fit in. They were still doing doo-wop and hip r&b. I could sing all the styles. This is also about the time I met Larry Williams, who appreciated my brothers and, after hearing my voice, said the same about me. Naturally I was a Larry Williams fan. I loved his stuff and had heard all the crazy stories from Artie and Charlie. I was crazy about the cat.

Larry had an extra-cool process, and I had one, too. Those were the days of Tim's Barber Shop on North Claiborne. Tim did the baddest 'dos in the city. That's where all the musicians went to get their hair fried, dyed, and laid to the side. I'd watch Tim and try to do it on my pals at home, practicing on Issacher and Melvin and my friend Marvin. I might have messed up. Marvin doesn't have any hair today and says the fault is mine. He's probably right.

Larry seemed to have the right approach to stylin'. Folks said he and I favored each other. Fact is, Larry called me "baby bro." Told everyone I was his brother. "The way you sing," he said to me as he headed off to gig in some faraway place, "I'm coming back for you. One day you'll be out there with me." And one day I was.

Anchors Aweigh

Charles

I got in at sixteen and out at eighteen. In the beginning, my feeling was one of hope. The navy would give me what I never found in school — a first-rate education. After boot camp, I was stationed at Millington, outside Memphis. I took a battery of tests. By then I was well read: I was working my way through the classics — I also loved the Zane Grey westerns — and had a keen interest in history. I was a quick thinker; I made top marks. They looked at the test results and said, "We've never seen results this high."

"Great!" I exclaimed. "What does that mean I'll be doing?"

"Cleaning toilets."

I thought they were kidding. At the very least, my musical aptitude would qualify me for the navy music school. But it turned out the black quota had been filled. No more black music students would be admitted for at least two years, regardless of talent.

So there I was, me and the toilets. Sometimes strange gigs will teach you lessons you'd never otherwise learn. I'm thinking of a sailor named Johnson who was my mentor in the toilet-cleaning brigade. Johnson was a beautiful brother from South Carolina. Rather than bitch about bathroom duty, he turned it into an art form. He'd scrub commodes like they were precious jewels. He also invented a rope apparatus that he ingeniously tied to the long line of toilet lids so when the captain came in for inspection, Johnson was ready. With one quick flick of the wrist, my man snapped that rope, and like magic, every last lid would lift up at once — I mean, those suckers would pop open — as though they were smartly saluting the captain. "Yes sir, Johnson," Captain would say, "you're a credit to the U.S. Navy."

I was a debit to the U.S. Navy. I appreciated Johnson's sense of irony and ability to turn a mundane task into a vaudeville routine, but I myself couldn't take that approach. Early on I saw that rules and regulations, as ridiculous as they were, were twice as ridiculous if you happened to be black. My only escape was music. I finally found a way into the band. I played military marches by day; by night I played in a city that offered a kind of musical education the navy denied. In the mid-fifties Memphis was rocking.

I had no idea that, at this exact time, Elvis was about to break out of Memphis with "Heartbreak Hotel." I didn't know the birth of white rock 'n' roll was happening in the very city where I spent evenings avoiding the navy. The amount of black music — jazz, blues, rhythm and blues, even big-band swing — was overwhelming. Beale Street was booming. The city was a haven for great musicians in every genre; the scene was teeming with talent. I felt right at home. Beale Street reminded me of South Rampart in New Orleans, the center of black life and mecca of music.

The air in Memphis was perfumed with sweet barbecue sauce; the soundtrack of the city was live music on the streets. You'd see the old blues guys from the Delta sitting on the curb, strumming acoustic guitars, singing 'bout older days and older ways. You'd see the young dudes, their heads filled with Miles and Monk, eager to express and experiment in the most modern modes. The sounds collided but never clashed.

Sitting across from the park named for W. C. Handy, the Memphis man who wrote the book on the blues, was Mitchell's Hotel. Mitchell's reminded me of the Dew Drop Inn. Sunbeam Mitchell was patron saint to all Memphis musicians. Mitchell's was where the cats crashed, ate, and jammed. Mitchell's was also where the hustlers hustled. In my teenage way of looking at life, the universe was divided into two: the square world of the navy and the hip world of the bad folk on Beale Street. I wanted to be bad.

It was easy being bad. Weed was everywhere, and I liked how it put a warm, fuzzy focus on cold reality. The jam sessions at Mitchell's had my head spinning in two directions at once. Ferocious boppers like tenor man George Coleman, who would later play with Miles, took my breath away. George was a speed demon, a superarticulate and soulful interpreter of balls-out modern jazz. George ranks with the giants — Dexter Gordon, Sonny Rollins, John Coltrane — and I got to hear him every night in Memphis. Being a nervy kid, I joined the jams, but I was still faking it. If it were a blues-based line, I'd lope along. But on a song like "Cherokee," I'd get lost looking for the bridge. Instead of playing, I'd honk or hold a whole note.

In spite of limited chops, I found work. Old man Phineas Newborn had a band that included his sons Calvin on guitar and the piano prodigy Phineas Jr. We played some light r&b, pop, and even country. Most of those gigs were at white clubs. Saxists like Fred Ford and Evelyn Young were also tearing up the town and setting dance halls aflame. Major leaguers like Hank Crawford and Charles Lloyd were also around. Back at Mitchell's, Sunbeam let me play in the house band whenever George Coleman was out of town. And there was one time, though it's shaming to think about it, when George and I were up for the same gig.

I say "shaming" because I got the gig, despite not being in George's league. Seems like an r&b band was looking for a tenor man who knew "Honky Tonk," the Bill Doggett hit with the long sax solo. Well, I had the thing memorized — Artie played that record night and day back on Valence Street — and could do it note for note. George improvised, and that put the leader off. No matter, George remained my role model. Night and day I'd hear him practicing in his room at Mitchell's. His devotion to the horn became an inspiration, and I saw him as a hero. That became especially clear the night Little Willie John hit town about the time he was burning up the charts with "All Around the World" and "Fever." After the gig, his band came to Mitchell's to jam. About 3 A.M. his tenor man cut loose, showing the devotees that he was more than a backup for a soul singer; he was a gunslinging bebopper. When he broke out into some blistering Bird-call like "Scrapple from the Apple," I got excited. The cat was good, but I knew George could eat him alive. "Where's George?" I asked the waitress. "Upstairs asleep," she said. "Well, wake him up. Tell him we need him." Sleepy-eyed, yawning, still half dreaming, our Superman appeared a few minutes later, hooked up his tenor, and proceeded to show Little Willie's sax man that if you wanna jam at Mitchell's in Memphis, you best not fuck with Mr. George Coleman.

Back at the barracks, I thought I was settling down into the navy routine when the most unsettling phenomenon threw me out of whack. Until then, my state of mind had been good. I wasn't on dope. I spent time chilling out with June Christy's soothing recording of "Something Cool." My cool world, though, was shattered when the spirit world paid me a visit that was uninvited and unwelcome. After the childhood incident at my aunt's, I had experienced other strange stuff: I'd be sitting on my bed when I would suddenly see an indentation in the mattress; I'd feel someone sitting beside me. But this was far more dramatic: I was doing fire watch at the base, walking through the dorms and inspecting the alarms when, in one of the barracks, I felt a buzzing sensation so strong that I had to sit down. Something or someone was coming toward me. Then I saw it. As the buzzing built to an almost intolerable level inside my head, I viewed a bodiless shape covered in a hood heading down the aisle toward me. I tried not to look, but I couldn't avert my gaze. The thing was coming right at me. Unable to scream, unable to move, I was suffocated by fear. As it approached me, I saw that beneath the hood, instead of a face, was a spiral, a vertiginous cavity pulling at me, drawing me in. I fought; I desperately tried to pry myself loose and run free from this terrifying energy field, but it was no use. It was stronger than me. A second before the hooded spirit reached me, the light went on in the barracks. Someone had come in. Just like that, the spirit was gone and I was free to run. I ran like holy hell, knocking over the sailor who had saved me as I made a beeline for my supervising officer. "I'm turning in my pistol," I said, "and I'm turning in my flashlight. You can lock me up if you wanna, but I ain't going back. I'm out of here."

He heard how I was stuttering, saw that my lips were blue and my eyes the size of saucers. "Calm down," he said. "We'll go back there together." I was reluctant but followed him and his big pistol back to the barracks. We saw nothing. But because he had heard other reports of strange sightings, he believed me. Still, that wasn't enough to keep me around. I went AWOL.

I played music around Memphis until, with proper apologies and ingenious excuses, I was able to slip back into the navy's good graces. For a while. Since I couldn't break the quota and get into their music school, I joined the Ground Defense Force. That's where you learn hand-to-hand combat. Instead of just firing a .45 and M1 rifle, you were given a badass machine gun. The idea was that you'd eventually be stationed somewhere exotic, like France. France sounded fine, so I signed up for the training course. I saw it as a big adventure. Didn't take long, though, to see the real deal: our instructor said, *Forget about France*; chances are, we'd wind up in French Indochina. And with that, he snapped off the lights and ran a training film demonstrating the basic nature of the Ground Defense Force. I'll never forget what I saw: a dude with his head split open, his brain matter spilled out on the ground beside him, flies buzzing everywhere. Then they throw his ass in a body bag and zip him up like dead meat.

I didn't stay around long enough to see whether he was supposed to be the good guy or the enemy. I didn't care. I was gone.

This time, instead of hanging in Memphis, I went out with B. B. King's band. You got to love B.B. He treats his musicians right. He was riding high on his "Three O'Clock Blues," but his basic nature — humble and loving — never changed. B.B. felt like family. His wife would call my mother to assure her that I was eating right. For the month or so I got to play with him, I felt like a pro. After all, George Coleman had been in that same band. When the tour was over, I went back to the navy. Faced with my second AWOL, they gave me a choice — general court-martial or undesirable discharge. Naturally I took the discharge. I was ready to go home.

When I returned to New Orleans, I was a different person — and not only because of the powerful influence of Memphis's music scene. Something else had happened in the navy that altered my consciousness. I shot intravenous drugs. It happened when a search party was formed to find a little girl lost in the woods. Men from the base were recruited to help. I was in a detail with two white guys who had become my buddies. We were deep in the woods of Tennessee. The girl was nowhere in sight, and we stopped to rest. The guys had showed me how to drink GI gin — cough syrup with codeine — a nasty high but a powerful buzz if you chased the shit with beer. Now they were showing me something new. We'd each been given a survival kit containing morphine. Their idea was simple: we'd claim that one of the kits was lost, allowing us to shoot up that single supply of morphine. It was good. It took me out of the woods to a place of peace I had never known before. The addiction didn't kick in at once; time would pass before I shot up again. Yet looking back, that afternoon in the woods changed the course of my life. I didn't know it then, but my junkie days had begun.

Art

I escaped the drug thing early on — but it might have been luck. Just before the cats back home got heavy into heroin, I was drafted into the navy. I was pissed at the time, but now I see it might have saved me some suffering. Not that I didn't do some other kind of suffering in the navy. My narcolepsy kicked in strong. In electronics class I'd have to stand up. If I sat down, I'd drift off to sleep and be accused of inattention. Walking through the base, I'd never know when a wave of fatigue would wash over me. I'd bump into parked cars, trying to find my way back to the barracks. In spite of this mysterious disease — which I still couldn't name or understand — I was motivated to become an AT, an aviation technician. I had the right background — I'd been fooling with engines for years — and the right kind of mind. I understood mechanics. What I didn't understand, though, was that being a black AT was like being a black Boy Scout. There weren't many around, and the navy wasn't at all interested in increasing the number. So I put away that dream and did the best I could to serve out my time at the Oceania Base in Virginia Beach. The navy ordered me to shave, although there was nothing but peach fuzz on my face. It was 1958 — I was about to turn twenty-one — but in many ways I was still a kid. It was exciting to hear my "Cha Dooky-Doo" on the radio from time to time, and even more exciting when brother Charles came through Virginia Beach playing with Larry Williams. Charlie was out of the navy, I was still in, and Larry was still red hot. I couldn't wait to get out of the service and back in the mix.

Aaron

Before Artie joined the navy, I had met a girl named Joel Roux. Turned out she was my soul mate, the one and only wife of my life. More than forty years later she's still by my side, which is something of a miracle, given the changes I've gone through. Joel and I have gone through changes of our own.

We were introduced by the drummer Leo Morris, who later became Idris Muhammad. Me and Leo were bippity-bopping down the street one day when here comes this cute little Creole girl. She was on her way to pick up her prom dress being made by her aunt. I was struck by her good looks and beautiful energy. Beautiful personality, too. I acted like I already knew her and asked for her number. Not long after that I was playing piano for her singing group, the Debettes, in their church, Saint Joan of Arc. I'm not a great pianist — I play by ear — but I get by. I got by Joel's house on a regular basis. Something about her made my heart melt. She liked me, too, but her dad was a different story. He'd come home from work with a newspaper in one hand and a .45 in the other. "How are you doing, Mr. Roux?" I'd ask. He'd just look at me and snarl, convinced I was a thug. Joel's mom was cool, and her aunt Tanteen, a down-to-earth lady who owned a barroom, was extra cool. I could talk to Aunt Tanteen.

Joel understood me. She saw how much music meant to me, and she appreciated the gift God had given me. She'd come hear me sing when the Hawketts played high-school dances and union halls. Love was drawing us to each other; love was growing inside us. She was my first real sweetheart. Meanwhile, despite all my feelings of warmth and affection for Joel, other parts of me were as wild as the wind. I was a kid hanging out with other kids. And ready to rumble.

With Artie in the navy, I was the lead singer of the Hawketts. Fact is, I took over the Hawketts — or should have — until something got in the way: I went to jail. Me and my partners had been stealing cars for a while. In those days it was easy — just take the silver foil from a stick of gum, slip it behind the three screws on the ignition, shift into neutral, and *vroooom!* — the engine starts up.

We were crazy about cars. Melvin actually bought me a car — a '49 black Mercury we called the Hearse — when I was just sixteen. Melvin watched my back. We'd carry knives — small cleavers I'd take from Mommee's kitchen that I'd sharpen at the grocery store. We'd cut someone every once in a while, but only to show we didn't take no shit. Wouldn't hesitate to run up on a guy with a knife and take it from him. For a while, luck was with me and I avoided jail. There was the time, for instance, that Melvin wanted me to go stealing cars with him, but my folks insisted that I hang with Artie and the Hawketts, who were playing Lincoln Beach. That was the night Melvin and the boys got busted for auto theft. He was the only one to serve time, though; he took the rap for everyone. That's the kind of guy Melvin was.

Melvin and I did crazy stuff. With goofballs popping off inside us, we'd get in barroom brawls and start hitting everyone we didn't know, walking out of the place like James Cagney and Humphrey Bogart. Nothing scared us.

Not much later me and my buddies were thrown in a little jail in Covington, Louisiana, where we wrote on the wall, "Aaron, Marvin and Stack won't be back." Two months later we were back in the same spot, looking at those same words.

The thing that landed me in parish prison in New Orleans involved both those guys — Marvin and Stack (aka Staggerlee) — plus two other friends. Stack lived in the 'hood and was like one of the brothers; much later he'd marry my sister Athelgra, and his life and his habits got mixed up with all of us. I dug Staggerlee. But it was one of my other buddies who fucked up by telling us he was bringing his father's Chevrolet to Abita Springs for a picnic. We were already out there with a hot Ford we'd grabbed off the street. We'd been drinking wine and smoking weed when it started raining, and slipping and sliding on the muddy road, I practically totaled the Ford. We abandoned the car and switched to my buddy's daddy's Chevrolet. When the cops caught up with us, we claimed we knew nothing about no Ford. We were in the Chevrolet. Little did we know that the Chevy was as hot as the Ford. My buddy had lied to us. He'd stolen the Chevy, just like we'd stolen the Ford. The upshot was that, after slapping us around, the cops put us in a jail outside of town. While we were waiting to be transferred to New Orleans, two white dudes came by and asked for a light. They took the matches, lit them, and threw them on the floor. While they slipped out laughing, the room went up in smoke. Flames everywhere. We thought we were done for. We were never so glad to see the New Orleans police, who showed up just in time to save our asses. They hauled us off to parish prison, but anything was better than burning to death.

When I stood before the judge, I had four different charges from past convictions. Judge gave me four times the six-month sentence — but had them run concurrently. Artie was in the navy and I was in jail, so the Hawketts were put on hold. Truth is, parish prison was kind of fun. My brother Charlie had served time before me, so I had some idea what to expect. I knew most of the guys in there from the street. Half of them I had fought with. If you passed in front of the prison at Tulane and Broad, you'd hear all the different tiers — the different floors of prisoners — singing their hearts out. When you beat on the iron columns in the middle of the day room, they made a nice sound. We had a slow beat and a fast beat. Like me, there were cats in prison who could harmonize. I wasn't into writing, but I fooled with this poem called "Every Day" that I put to music. I sang it until everyone started telling me that, once I was out, I should record it. I did.

Also started giving myself a tattoo in there that was going to read BORN TO DIE. I got as far as the *B* when I changed my mind. Before that, I had a tattoo of a dagger inked across my cheek. When my daddy saw it, he hated it; he made me scrub it with a Brillo pad and industrial-strength soap. The pad and soap ripped up my skin, but the tattoo is still there today.

Those were some of the things I did as a kid. Can't tell you why I did them. I just did.

Best thing I did was marry Joel. Happened on January 10, 1959. I was underage and needed my mother to sign. Two weeks later I turned eighteen. I might have been crazy at the time, I still had no idea what the world was all about, but I felt a love for this woman, and I felt her love for me. We had to be together.

CYRIL

Joel became a member of the family. She was close to all of us — my father, my aunts, and especially my mother. She and Mommee became partners. And Joel became very important to me. She was like a sister or a second mother. I even called her Little Mommee. While no one else noticed me, she did; she saw I had talent. Thank God for Joel.

Meanwhile, my mother and aunts had jobs at Lane's cotton mill. Sometimes they'd have me stay with Mrs. Mert on Water Street during the day while they went off to work. Mrs. Mert had a bunch of kids she looked after. By then I knew how to iron my own clothes and cook some mean grits. I thought I was a little man. I was deep into reading, and Mommee, who was always talking about Job and teaching me patience, gave me little books about geography and science. I was precocious, looking to read about slavery and religion; I was curious about history's strange twists and turns. I loved studying the encyclopedia and the dictionary.

I shed my virginity at a very young age with a little girl named Crystal. I had heard about the nasty and was quite eager to get to it. It happened under our house, in that space between the floorboard and the dirt. We put up pieces of cardboard for privacy. We also lit candles under there, looking for a touch of romance. It's amazing we didn't burn down the place. I prayed not to get caught — not by my mom or any of the neighbors who were ready, willing, and able to whip your ass at a moment's notice.

Funny thing about the older women in our neighborhood. When things were calm, I'd see them as regular ladies watching over all us kids. But then when the cops would come by harassing us for no good reason, the same mild-mannered woman would transform before my very eyes into a strong black warrior queen. "Them boys ain't doing nothing wrong," she'd snap, standing her ground with a righteous indignation that could scare off an army, "so get out of our face and leave us be." That same woman wouldn't think twice about hiding the numbers man from the police. He was always the cleanest motherfucker around. I remember my mom and aunts taking him in lots of times.

I was a hyper kid — too much energy, too much curiosity, too eager to see and do everything at once. My folks encouraged my kite flying, figuring it was a healthy way to let off steam. I'd make a kite out of anything, tie up a string, run through a park, and watch the thing take off. I wanted to soar like a kite. I had ambitions early on. Naturally I wanted to be a singer and a musician, but I also wanted to be a comic like Moms Mabley and Redd Foxx, whose records made my parents howl. At Christmastime, as I watched my dad and Uncle Jolly secretly put the gifts under the tree, I thought of Redd's take on Santa: no white man dressed in no red suit with a bag full of shit would get to our house 'cause, in our neighborhood, he'd never make it that far. It was also Redd who liked to quote Confucius: Woman who cooks carrots and peas in the same pot is very unsanitary. Took me half an hour before I got that joke.

I wondered about the hair-cutting ritual for us kids. One cat in the 'hood did the cutting, and if he happened to be watching a fight or baseball game on TV, watch out. He'd cut some holes in your head that'd make you look like a martian. Best thing that could happen was to get a straight-up bowl cut. It was ugly, but at least it was even. All us kids had the bowl cut.

I was fixated on the characters who populated the world of my childhood. I remember Skin Booty. How I loved that man. A slender cat with pecan-colored skin and an easy smile, he'd been 'round the world a bunch of times and would tell me about his adventures in the merchant marine with my father. Later in life, when Skin Booty was down and out, he never lost his edge. When the big-earning longshoremen refused him thirty-five cents, he'd give 'em hell. "If you don't got no money," he'd say, "you don't need to be 'round here. You ain't shit. You ain't but one paycheck away from the poorhouse." Walking down the street, he looked like a big bird, his flailing arms, his gangly legs. Sometimes he'd be so drunk, we'd have to put him in a grocery cart and roll him home. When he was sober, he was sharp. He taught me shit I never learned in school. He was one of the funniest and most self-contained human beings I've ever known. When I got older, and the oppression of life in New Orleans got to me, he was one of the few people who could calm the rage burning in my bones. He did it with humor and by being real. No one or nothing ever got to Mr. Skin Booty.

Aaron

One night me and Joel saw Skin Booty walking around in a daze, so we took him to his mother's house. His mother was this pipe-smoking lady who did her best to care for him. But somehow Skin Booty let a cigarette drop and accidentally burned down his mama's place. Despite it all, though, Skin Booty managed to survive.

Charles

My marriage to Vera survived in name only. We had four daughters together — Charlene, Charmaine, Charlotte, and Charlestine — and two boys — Carlos and Charles. While I was in the navy, I got word that Vera had been busted for drugs. I was given an emergency leave home and, accompanied by my mother, went to juvenile court to ask for custody. My loving mother was willing to raise the girls. But the court refused and sent the girls to live with a foster family. There was nothing I could do.

From time to time I sent them money and clothes. Once, I paid them a surprise visit and discovered a daughter of the foster family wearing a dress I had sent for my kids. When my children told me stories of being mistreated and abused, I went ballistic and had to be physically removed from the premises. From then on I was barred from seeing them. Even worse, they were sent out of state, and I didn't know where they were. My daughters were lost to me.

Slippin' and Slidin'

Aaron

Little Willie John, Johnny Ace, Lloyd Price — if they didn't come from New Orleans, they came through New Orleans. I got to see them all. Larry Williams made good on his promise and came back to take me under his wing. During the time we were hanging out, he was billed with Jackie Wilson at the Municipal Auditorium. They were both hot. Jackie had his "To Be Loved" — he sure did sing that sucker — and Larry had his "Bony Moronie." As part of Larry's show, he'd jump off the stage to work up the crowd. Well, the cops didn't like that and demanded he return to the stage. "Hey, man," said Larry, "that's my act. You can't mess with my act." Jackie saw what was happening and interfered, telling the policeman it was all part of Larry's show. The cop, a black cat — I believe the only black cop in the city — told Jackie to fuck off. They got into it, and Jackie got his head bashed open with a nightstick. I'm not sure he was ever the same again. The band went to throwing instruments off the stage, and the place broke out into a riot. Right after that I went on tour with Larry. Welcome to the world of rhythm and blues.

Charles

A beautiful lady named Bobbie took me deep into the midnight world of New Orleans. It happened shortly after I came back from the navy. And like so many other things in my life and the lives of my brothers, it happened on Valence Street, where Bobbie was moving from one house to another, just down the block from us. Artie asked if I would help move her furniture. The minute I saw her, I liked her. I was barely nineteen, and she was probably twenty-nine. She had chocolate-brown skin, reddish hair, and a striking figure. She was savvy and superhip. Her new house was freshly painted, her phonograph was already set up, and Billie Holiday was singing those songs of mysterious love. Even today, the smell of fresh paint brings the blues of Billie Holiday to mind. Even today, I see Bobbie painted in hues of blue. She spoke of Miles and Bird, Coltrane, Monk, and the Modern Jazz Quartet. Bobbie knew her music and knew her drugs. The two melted together in my mind. She reminded me of the alluring women I'd met in Memphis, the people who populated the clubs, grooved on all-night jam sessions and shunned the nine-to-fives, the party people who knew the best life was the high life.

Bobbie had more than the aura of being high and hip, though. She had smarts — street smarts — combined with a physical toughness and genuinely nice nature. She had a sense of justice that impressed me along with her skills as a first-rate hustler. Most important, though, she had access to the thing I had been thinking about ever since my experience in the woods outside Memphis — drugs.

"Don't do it," she warned me. I paid no attention.

"Be careful of Bobbie," said Daddy. "She's too fast, she hangs with a dangerous crowd." I paid no attention.

At that time, Bobbie wasn't shooting drugs, but her connection was almost too good to be true. She was still close with her former boyfriend, a man named Stalebread. Stalebread had the best shit in the city. In the hierarchy of underground New Orleans, drug dealers held the highest position. Some were respected for putting money back into the community. Stalebread supported youth organizations and black charities. He was known as a bad dude who did good.

Maybe I was a good kid who wanted to do bad — I'm not sure. But when Stalebread came by the house, I was excited and eager to pay him twenty dollars for a little brown bag of heroin. I didn't realize how much was in it. The first day I started snorting it; the second day I started shooting. "You'll get sick," warned Bobbie, but I didn't — not yet. It took us three weeks to go through the bag. When the stash was exhausted, I was semi–strung out, and so was Bobbie. To keep me company, she had started using again. I moved in with her, and we began running down a road that turned out longer and more treacherous than I could have ever imagined.

The road led to South Rampart Street, where the scene was still alive. Uncle Jolly was down there, and so were Bobbie's friends Emily and Josie and a man named Good Lord the Lifter. Shoplifting was the thing. We called it boosting. At first, I just drove the car and waited while they hustled. Sometimes they'd rob stores, but never homes. Home robberies were aggravated burglaries and carried far more serious penalties.

Meanwhile, I stayed serious about staying high. Shooting dope and learning how to steal, I successfully removed myself from the workaday world of predictable routines. Bobbie's world revolved around thrills. Moving from thrill to thrill became my new way of life.

Art

Once out of the navy, I was eager to get home and back to my music. If "Cha Dooky-Doo" was making a little noise, maybe I could do something even better. Larry Williams had made it as a big star; well, I could make it, too. Fact is, I was lucky to make it back home alive. On the way to Louisiana, the bus stopped in Hattiesburg, Mississippi. It was 3 A.M. As I came out of the men's room, two rednecks calling themselves sheriffs were standing there, guns drawn. I glanced behind me and saw WHITES ONLY scrawled on the men's room door. I was in deep shit.

"What you doing coming out of there?" they wanted to know.

"Didn't see the sign," I said.

"Bullshit, nigger. You did it on purpose. Boy, what you doin' 'round here anyway?"

My uniform should have made it clear. "On leave," I said.

"On leave to where?"

"Home."

"Where's that?"

"New Orleans."

"You one of those smart-ass New Orleans niggers."

I stayed quiet.

"If you wasn't such a young nigger, we'd take your ass and put it where the navy would never find it. We ever catch you in this county again, you'll never leave it."

Scared shitless, I headed back to the bus.

Later in my life, I've heard this story turned around. Someone said I pissed on the sheriffs' shoes. Don't you believe it. If I'd pissed on those sheriffs, they would have done a lot more than kill me; they would have shot off my dick first.

Back home, I celebrated my survival with a two-day binge of red beans, something I had sorely missed in the navy. Ate myself sick. Took up with the Hawketts where I'd left off. We were playing everything from Ray Charles's "What'd I Say" to Perez Prado's "Cherry Pink and Apple Blossom White."

Charles

My first jolt in the New Orleans parish prison was in the late fifties. I got caught stealing a TV in an appliance store Uptown New Orleans. The sentence was six months with "two-for-one good time," meaning I got credit for two days for every one day I served, if I worked. I worked in the kitchen. Bobbie, older and wiser in the ways of the world, prepared me with two cardinal rules: "Don't rat on anyone, and don't let anyone fuck you in the ass." The first rule was easy, but the second required a weapon, a long safety pin presented to me by Oscar, an older junkie and buddy of Uncle Jolly. "Anyone messes with you," he warned, "take his eye out. Strike hard and strike first. Then start hollering like you're a madman." Once inside, I had some status. Dope fiends commanded respect, and Bobbie made certain her former associates knew that I was cool with her. Nonetheless, Oscar warned me: "Your manhood will be tried. You gotta fight for your manhood." I fought off the first predator who came my way. Unwanted sex wasn't the problem. The problem was withdrawing from junk. I got sick as a dog. When I finally gained back my strength, I surveyed the scene and saw some entertaining cats on the set. Dr. John —

then called Mac Rebennack — was the Zuzu man, the guy who ran around selling pencils and little candies. Only whites got that gig, but you couldn't call Mac white. His skin might be white, but his soul is black. I had known Mac as a killer pianist who'd turn up at the funkiest spots in the French Quarter. We became friends for life.

Tattoos were a big item in the parish prison. The hard-core cats all sported them, and I wanted one, too. Did it myself. Took a sharp, pointy object, some India ink, and spelled out BOBBIE. I knew she was my one and only. When I got out after serving only five or six months, she was right there. I was clean, but not for long. We decided to take a break from New Orleans and headed to Memphis. Beale Street had that great music, that fast life, and especially that cheap dope.

Aaron

When I got out of jail, I had this one song — "Every Day" — that I wanted to record. "Every day," I wrote in parish prison, "along about noon, I'm dreaming of the day that I'll be home soon / And every day, long about one, I remember how we used to have fun / And every day, long about two, I'm so lonely and so blue / And every day, long about three, well, I'm dreaming of the day that I'll be free."

Turned out Allen Toussaint was hooked up with Joe Banashak, who started Minit Records. They had hits with Jessie Hill's "Ooh Poo Pah Doo" and Ernie K. Doe's "Mother-in-Law," so I'd figured they knew what they were doing. Allen had written some songs that he thought right for me. (Don't know why, but he put down his mom's name — Naomi Neville — as the writer. She could be related to us, but I'm not sure.) At the first session I cut Allen's

"Over You" and my "Every Day." Wasn't much to it. Allen is listed as a producer, and Allen's a good musician, but as far as I can see, I just followed my instincts. If people told me what to do or how to sing — asking me to cut out my curlicues or simplify my style — I didn't pay too much attention. My style isn't anything I can change. My style is me. Whatever flourishes I bring to a melody, I bring without plan or purpose. Those are the sounds flowing from my heart. So when "producers" suggested changes in my approach, I'd listen, nod my head, and then sing the thing the only way I knew how — my way.

I cut a bunch of Allen's songs, including "How Could I Help but Love You," "Even Though," and "Over You." Artie wrote one called "Humdinger" that showed we were all listening to Ray Charles. And I wrote "Show Me the Way." Listening to the lyrics of "Show Me the Way" today, I think maybe I was talking about God without knowing it.

Banashak and Toussaint had the baddest cats at the sessions, sax men Red Tyler and Nat Perrilliat, guitarist Roy Montrell, and drummer John Boudreaux. I was honored to be in their company.

I was told the records didn't go anywhere. "Over You" was a local hit in New Orleans, but Banashak swore it never went farther than Baton Rouge. When I met the Rolling Stones a lifetime later, Keith Richards told me how he knew all these early records. "Where'd you hear them?" I asked. "When I was a teenager," he said, "they were all over England."

I was still a teenager when I made these records, and didn't know shit. I signed a contract with a company that had me running in and singing songs I learned that same day. Not that I was complaining. I wanted to sing, and I wanted records out there. The world of the New Orleans music business was — and still is — tiny. If there was any entertainment lawyer around, he worked for the record company, not the artist. Matter of fact, I'm not sure I understood what the word *artist* meant, except I was the guy who sang the song.

I was also the guy who was more interested in serious drugs. The big boys were shooting heroin, and that's the stuff that interested me. Those were the days when Charles had hooked up with Bobbie. Bobbie had the connection of connections — Stalebread. Stalebread had the goods.

Art

After my stuff on Specialty died out, I'd be a fool not to switch to a different outfit. Toussaint was over at Minit, where Aaron had recorded and where Allen was always calling for me. I went. He wrote a beautiful ballad called "All These Things." I sang it from the heart, and miracle of miracles, the thing hit big on a subsidiary label Banashak called Instant. "All These Things" became number one in New Orleans. You'd think that would mean some money for me. At least, I was thinking that way. Well, I was thinking wrong. The truth is that I didn't see a cent in royalties. I had to get a day job. While "All These Things" was being played all over town, I was running an elevator at Gaucho's, an upscale department store on Canal Street.

"All These Things" became a staple in the South, especially Louisiana, Alabama, and Mississippi. After I sang it, there were pop and country versions, but my original was the one that stuck.

Aaron

I recorded "All These Things" after Artie. I did it okay, but not like my brother. Artie *sang* that song.

Art

People were saying "All These Things" was going to be my national breakthrough, but it never got out of the South. Later I learned that the major labels were bidding for it. Mercury was hot to buy it and put it out all over the country, but Instant wanted too much money. Never happened. Meanwhile, over at Gaucho's department store, the elevator went up and the elevator went down. . . .

CYRIL

While my brothers were out there making music, I wasn't part of their world. I hung out with my little sister, Cookie, and made friends in the neighborhood — Walter "Poochie" Booth, Bobby Smith, Carol Jean Wilson, and Joseph Modeliste, known as Zig, or Zigaboo. Zig moved Uptown when I was twelve or thirteen. We became brothers, bonded in our love of the drum. We heard beats, we copied beats, we invented beats of our own. We'd listen to Leo Morris, who lived next to Buddy's Cleaners, practicing his drums. Leo had the funkiest beats. Studying his style, I'd lean my head so intensely on the screen door in front of his house that I'd have marks on my skin.

My first idol on drums, Clarence "Juny Boy" Brown, was at one time my sister Athelgra's boyfriend. It was Athelgra, by the way, who taught me a lot about vocal harmonizing; what's more, she was my favorite dance partner and taught me all the latest steps. Athelgra inspired me.

One man who should have been an inspiration turned out the opposite. He enraged my heart and confused my brain. I won't write his name, but I will say he was a preacher, respected and called a pillar of the community. He was supposed to be tutoring me in math. I went to the place he kept on the other side of the city, but instead of helping me, he started playing psychological games. He asked if I liked boys. He mentioned other boys he found attractive. He started in on the myth of black men being well hung and wanted to know how I measured up. The discussion turned me off, and I stayed silent. But that didn't appease him. He came on to me; he started getting physical. Quickly, I moved away. I wouldn't let him touch me sexually. That made him furious. He forced me to sit with my hands sticking through the back of a chair while he whupped my natural ass. It happened on my fourteenth birthday. I figured I was a man, and I vowed not to cry. That made him even angrier. "You're not going to cry, huh? Well, I'll *make* you cry." In my heart, I was crying my ass off, but I wouldn't give him the satisfaction of seeing a single tear. When I said I would tell my parents, he said no one would believe me. He hit me fourteen times, one for every year of my life. The fourteenth blow hurt so bad, I vowed that if he hit me again, I'd find the strength to kill him. When he stopped to catch his breath, I jumped out the second-story window and caught the streetcar home. When I arrived, he was already there. Having sped over in his car, he was now telling my parents some bullshit. I told them what had really happened, but they believed him, not me. That crushed me. I hated this man's fuckin' guts. For a long while, he destroyed my faith in adults. Later I understood why my folks would rather believe him than me. He was the son of a powerful man, and with my brothers in jail, my father had asked his father to use his influence to get them out. On a couple of occasions, he was able to do so. In our world we didn't know that many powerful people — and his dad was one of them. It was easier for my parents to doubt my word than his.

Later he was crippled in a car accident. Mommee and Daddy insisted I go over and help care for him. Rather than care for him, I wanted to kill him. But I loved my parents, just as I loved his mother, a sweet and loving woman. I did it for her. I went over and served him some meals. Years passed. At one point his wife and brother just up and left him. His son disappeared. Then we got the news: seated in a car, the preacher man had been doused with kerosene and set on fire. We never learned who did it or why. All we knew is that the car exploded, and trapped inside, the reverend burned to death.

All this happened after I was grown and had left home. "I feel bad," my mother said, having learned about the man's demise, "that when you came to us, we didn't believe you. We came to find out that Reverend really was funny." That was her way of apologizing. "I understand," I said. "He was a powerful man and hard to go against." "Yes," Mommee replied, "those people did help us some, but that's no excuse. If I had listened to you with my heart, I'd have heard what you were saying."

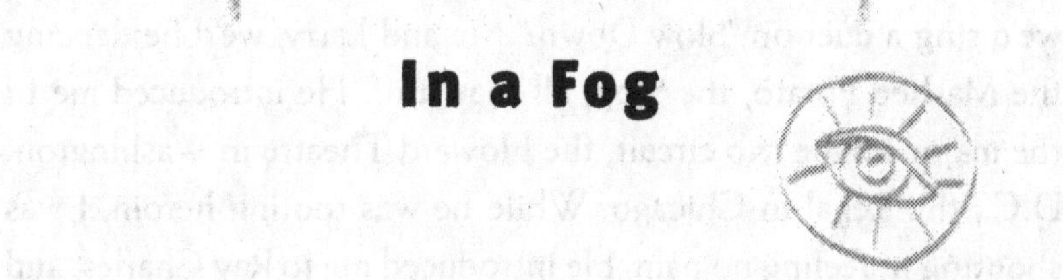

In a Fog

Aaron

I guess you could say I was in a fog, but for a long while it was a happy fog. I should have kept tabs on how and where my records were selling; I should have found a business manager or lawyer to look after my affairs. But none of that was in the cards. I was happy because Larry Williams made good on his promise to come back for me and take me on the road with him. This was the early sixties; I was just turning twenty-one and ready to roll. Being with a big-time star like Larry was a dream come true. Larry had him a bunch of big cars — a long Lincoln, a fancy Cadillac — and enough sharp clothes to last a lifetime. His clothes fit me better than they fit him. I'd fix my hair like his, I'd sing like him; everyone said I favored him. He took me to New York, where I stood in the wings of the Apollo Theatre and heard Patti LaBelle and the Blue Belles. Man, that woman kicked me to the mud; I never heard singing that like before. We played shows with the Coasters and the Drifters and the Flamingos, great singers I'd heard on the radio when I was a kid. Now they were real people with real faces telling me I was great, too. I was tripping.

I was opening the show with "Over You," which was catching on all over the country. Larry's supertight ten-piece band was rocking behind me, and I was feeling fine. Larry would come out, and we'd sing a duet on "Slow Down." Me and Larry, we'd be dancing the Mashed Potato, the Slop, all that stuff. He introduced me to the major-league r&b circuit, the Howard Theatre in Washington, D.C., the Regal in Chicago. While he was tooting heroin, I was shooting it, feeling no pain. He introduced me to Ray Charles, and one night we all got high together. That was a thrill. There he was, sitting right next to me, us getting off on the same shit, the blind genius whose music had lit up our souls. "You the cat who sings 'Over You,' ain't you?" Ray asked me. "I am," I said. "Well, you say some helluva words with that song," he said. "Some helluva words." That made me feel good all over.

For all the good times, there were scary times. Larry was more than a singer and a star; he was a straight-up gangster. He had plenty guns and plenty attitude. His guns were his guarantee the promoters would pay. His attitude kept him upbeat and sane. In Federalsburg, Maryland, when the microphone crapped out, Larry punched out the bottom of a cup and used it as a megaphone. The crowd loved it. The crowd was always with him. In that same club, Larry's man Sonny pistol-whipped a cat who was harassing the girls with our band. We thought that was the end of it. It wasn't. Cat came back with friends and pistols and chased us down the highway, bullets flying, me ducking down, glass all in my hair, Larry laughing while gunning his Lincoln and leaving the bad guys back in the smoke.

Usually Larry was joking and cracking us up. He'd do anything and say anything. But other times he'd get philosophical.

We'd be driving in the middle of the night somewhere in the middle of America. He'd always have me sitting next to him. He confided in me. It had been years since he had a hit song. Styles were changing. Fifties r&b and doo-wop were dying out. Motown was starting up. Larry was living on old glory. He saw the changes coming.

"Baby bro," he'd say, "I'm running up and down this goddamn highway like a motherfucker, and I'm tired of being pimped. That's all this business is. The record companies, the promoters, them fools do nothing but pimp your ass. Well, the pimp's the one who makes the money. Makes more sense to be the pimp than be pimped." When his music stopped selling and his fans stopped coming to his shows, that's what he became. In the slick world of slick pimps, Larry Williams was the slickest of 'em all. I know. I got to see it firsthand.

Art

Somewhere about the time when the fifties became the sixties, I married a woman named Doris. We stayed married twelve years. She's a good woman, and we had a beautiful daughter, Arthel, who became a TV personality and star in her own right. I also had a son with another woman. His name is Michael. For a long time his existence was kept from me. When I saw him as an adult, I knew he was my flesh and blood, and today we're cool. I'm not saying I was the perfect husband, boyfriend, or father. I tried to do the right thing. Sometimes I succeeded, sometimes I didn't. But I love my kids and I respect their privacy. I respect their mothers, and if I don't talk about that part of my life at great length, well, that's not my style. I've never been comfortable playing a lot of notes on the keyboard.

Charles

After I got out of parish prison, I studied six months for the general equivalency diploma. I had quit high school to go on the road but now wanted to study music theory at Southern University. I was determined to pass the test. The civil rights era had begun, yet in New Orleans civil rights always seem to lag behind. The equivalency exam was given at strictly segregated schools. I needed to take the test in summer to enter college in the fall, but the only test location was a white school. My parents knew a preacher with some influence in the community, and he was able to get them to bend the rules — or so I thought. On the morning of the exam, I showed up promptly. When I walked in the schoolroom, all the white kids looked up. By the look in their eyes, I could see them thinking, *This integration bullshit ain't about to start here, is it?* One kid made it plain. He said it out loud. "That nigger can't sit in here with us." Much to my amazement, the supervising teacher agreed with him. "All I can do for you," he said, "is have you take the test outside. I'll let you sit in my car and take it there." Writing on my lap wasn't very comfortable. Plus it was hot as hell. No electric fans, no desk, and that old feeling of being an outcast for no goddamn reason except blind prejudice. But I did what I had to do: I took it; I passed with flying colors; and come September, I became a student at SU.

Southern University was an eye-opener. Naturally I had learned from musicians on the road, but I was still keenly aware of my technical shortcomings. One night in Chicago, for example, Sonny Stitt, the great bebop saxist whose dazzling fluency echoed Bird, discussed technique with me. "Knowing your ax," he said, "means knowing scales. Everything comes out of scales. There's nothing on your horn *but* scales." Wow, what a concept! I hated hearing it, but I knew he spoke the truth. I knew I needed to buckle down and learn more music.

That wasn't true of James Booker, who enrolled in college with me. We both studied with a woman named Jo Dora Middleton. She was a first-rate blues and jazz pianist from Chicago whose class fascinated me. James and I were the only students. Unintentionally, James made a mockery of the process. He'd look over a book of Bach pieces and ask, "You want me to play it front to back or back to front?" At first she thought he was being cute. But when he flawlessly flew through the music at lightning speed, she saw it was no joke. While European theory and aesthetics might be a foreign concept to many of us, James seemed to be born with an ability to adopt any musical sensibility. No one doubted his genius.

My academic study did not exclude my study of the world of crime. To me, crime meant rebellion. My rebellion was not against my family, whom I loved with all my heart. I was rebelling against the white world. I was living according to a code I had adopted as a kid. I remember a scene from childhood that continued to resonate within me as a young adult: One day a boy from our projects showed up in a new sweater. His family, like mine, was struggling to survive. His family, like mine, could hardly afford new sweaters. My own sweater was a hand-me-down with holes at the elbows. He explained how he got it: "White people won't let my folks make enough money, so my folks can't buy it for me. I don't wanna be cold, so I'm taking it." Theft seemed justified, even noble.

"All a nigger needs," Good Lord the Lifter, a master thief, told me, "is a pencil behind his ear, a clipboard, and a dumb expression on his face. That will let you walk out of the store with just about anything." With that, we'd put on khaki pants and shirts with our names on the pocket, and head to the big appliance store on Canal Street. With pencils behind our ears and clipboards in our hands, we'd walk into the place with a hand truck, load on a refrigerator, and wheel it out. I relished the moment when Good Lord would ask the assistant manager, "Hey, boss, would you mind getting that door for me?" The guy would gladly oblige, comforted by the sight of two gainfully employed and well-mannered niggers. We'd roll that thing all the way up Magazine Street to the Thirteenth Ward, where a woman, who gave Good Lord the "order," paid us in cold cash.

Then there was my friend Slim. I met him in the early days of my criminal career. I was twenty-three, he was a little older. Slim gave the white world the impression of a black man that made the white world comfortable. He turned himself into a nonthreatening stereotype. Slim wore overalls, chewed on a piece of straw, talked real slow, walked with a lazy gait. He had a scam called the Note Game that, after buying a pack of gum, resulted in his getting twenty dollars in change for a ten-dollar bill. He did it by playing the fool and stuttering in that slower-than-molasses old-time yassuh voice. He'd roll his eyes and fumble to find the right words. Distracted by his banter, touched by his helpless ignorance, the cashier would fall for it every fuckin' time.

I liked how the best thieves made a mockery of white society. I admired their daring and skill. Good Lord the Lifter was the high priest of boosting. One day he gave me a ride home from college. He and Gilbert and Bobbie, who was still my old lady, had been out shoplifting. They had sold everything they stole except for a Polaroid camera hidden under the front seat. We were parked, hawking the camera to a fence, when a narc recognized our car and busted us. He took us back to the store, where the clerks didn't even know the camera was missing. The camera box was still in the showcase, neatly closed. Good Lord the Lifter had lifted the Polaroid without disturbing its container. That's how good he was.

Turned out my lawyer wasn't good at all. "Don't worry," he told me, "we're going to cop you out with a statement and cut you loose. No problem." But a problem did arise during the trial, when the lawyer switched my plea to guilty. Turned out he was angling to be a DA, and nailing me was part of his plan. Didn't matter that I wasn't even there when the camera was stolen. Before I knew it, I was hustled off to the parish prison for my second extended stay. I wasn't alone. Good Lord the Lifter got six months, Bobbie got three months, and I got a year.

I wouldn't call it Old Home Week, but my second stint was easier than the first. I knew the territory. I already had something of a reputation, which meant I didn't worry about being assaulted. That was doubly true because two of my partners, Fred and Red,* arrived about the same time as me. Fred and Red were knockout artists. They'd follow a guy who'd been drinking in a bar to the bathroom and, with one punch, knock him out and take his money. They were gorillas, but sweet gorillas in this sense: When we arrived at the parish prison, we saw how a clique of thugs were intimidating the weaker prisoners, the little guys serving time for lesser crimes like alimony offenses. The thugs would shake them down for money and food. They'd force one of the little guys to serve as cornerman — the cat who sits by the toilet in the shower and washes everyone's nasty underwear by hand. The thugs had such tight control and used such terrifying methods that a newspaper called the tier they ruled the House of Shock.

Fred and Red hated the House of Shock. Fred complained to the chief thug. Why did he have to fuck up the little guys? The thug responded by pulling a knife. Critical miscalculation. In nothing flat, Fred grabbed the knife, slit open the seat of the thug's pants, and stuck the knife up his ass. No more House of Shock.

*Fictitious name

Art

You might be shocked reading about some of the things my brothers did. Well, I did many of those same things. Only difference is, I didn't get caught.

Aaron

I got caught up in the idea of going to California. This was about 1962. Not much happening for me in New Orleans. I was under contract to Minit, but Minit wasn't paying any bills. That meant I worked wherever I could — painting houses, construction, odd jobs at the iron and steel plants. The docks paid the best. Valence Street is close to the river, and the river meant jobs. I liked being a longshoreman and eventually joined the union. The money was good, and the work wasn't bad. You knew what you had to do, and you did it. By then Joel and I had two sons, Ivan and Aaron Jr. I had a family to support, and if singing wouldn't support them, I sure as hell wasn't above unloading cargo. Not that singing ever left my heart. I'd be down on the docks, heaving those heavy weights, singing all the time. The guys would hear me and say, "Hey, Aaron, if Smokey Robinson is out there with that 'Shop Around,' you need to be out there shopping your own stuff around." I couldn't argue, but I also couldn't get anything out of the labels that had been recording me.

The only dude who seemed to care was Larry Williams. He was sure I could have hits. He had the experience and he had the connections. But he was living in Los Angeles. "Come on out, Aaron," he kept urging. "I want to manage you. Let me give you the break you need." I believed him, and I went. That changed my life, but in ways I could have never predicted.

Art

The Hawketts stayed alive for years. The thing about good New Orleans musicians is their ability to blend. We could keep that basic second-line-rhumba-boogie beat and still stay in tune with the current scene. And don't forget, hits were always coming out of New Orleans. In the early sixties, for instance, Bobby Marchan's "There's Something on Your Mind" was blasting all over the place, proving we didn't have to cut sides in New York or L.A. Naturally, we listened to everything out there. We heard what was coming out of Detroit; we knew exactly what James Brown was up to in Georgia; we could play pretty or we could play raggedy funk. I like funk. Ever since the big-band days of Benny Goodman and Count Basie, getting people to dance has meant happiness, not to mention monetary success. Like everyone else, I wanted both. Plus, funk comes naturally to me. With funk, it's almost more what you *don't* play than what you do play. I like those long silences between riffs; I like the empty spaces. Those empty spaces, when you stop and let the groove wash all over you, make the difference between fake funk and real funk. People as different as Frank Sinatra and Miles Davis know how to use empty spaces. Along those same sparse lines, a group called Booker T. and the MGs caught my attention. The minute their monster hit "Green Onions" came on the radio, you could smell it. Booker was like a Bill Doggett for a new generation. It was all instrumental, all low-key, but funky enough to burn down the barn. I liked the simple instrumentation. Nothing more than a rhythm section — keyboard, guitar, bass, and drums. Fact is, Booker T.'s rhythm section, in addition to having hits of its own, would be the basis of the whole Stax sound, the Memphis recording center that turned out hits by Carla Thomas and Otis Redding. For the vocal records, they naturally added horns, but the fire underneath was always Booker and his boys. I was impressed by how much four guys, cooking on all burners, could do by themselves. I wasn't ready to make such a move myself. The Hawketts were still a horn-heavy band. That's what the people wanted, and that's what the people would get. But I kept listening to what Booker was doing and wondered whether one day I could do something similar.

Bustin' Loose

CYRIL

The history of racial politics in New Orleans of the sixties is a book of its own. It's a sad and scary story about how the police went to war, sabotaging and brutalizing the black community. Change was inevitable; the civil rights movement was in full swing, but the power structure — the guys with the guns — wouldn't admit that their side was, once and forever, about to lose. In fact, the passage of progressive legislation on the national level only infuriated the hard-core haters in the city, who, rather than preserve the childhood home of Louis Armstrong, destroyed it like a piece of trash.

When I was coming up, I also saw that skin discrimination came in a variety of evil forms. Certain clubs, for instance, had a brown-paper-bag test; if your skin was darker than the bag, no admission. There were also clubs that hung fine-tooth combs over the doorway. If your kinky hair got caught in the comb, no admission.

Racism of all sorts has roots deep in the soul of New Orleans. I had seen that as a child. But as a young adult, struggling toward manhood, I felt things getting worse; respect for my own people seemed to be crumbling around me. Radicalism was the only reasonable response. Just when our country appeared to be recognizing our rights, just when Dr. King and Malcolm X were making their influence felt most positively, New Orleans reacted negatively. Self-respecting black men were viewed as targets. They came gunning for us.

It's difficult to separate personal demons from political demons. I was haunted by both. I was disillusioned with the educational system. I'd skip school and, ironically, spend time in the library. Charles and my older sister, Athelgra, were in college and I'd read their books. I went through all the work of Kyle Onstott — *Master of Falconhurst, Mandingo,* and *Black Sun.* I read everything I could about slavery and how it affected the families of my ancestors. I was fascinated by theories of human behavior and the history of ideas. When I tried to discuss what I read with my teachers at Samuel James Green Junior High, they'd say it wasn't normal for a black kid to show interest in philosophy or psychology. The teachers resented how, in spite of skipping my studies, I still managed to make good grades. They saw me as a smart-ass. When Kennedy was killed and there was a discussion afterward, I questioned what JFK had done for black people. I knew there'd been backroom deals selling out civil rights legislation, but my teacher accused me of being disrespectful. When I wouldn't back down, she got angry. That anger spilled over to the next incident, when a guy sitting in front of me claimed I was purposely bleeding on him. My hand was scabbed up from a football injury. The truth is that he leaned back, caught my hand, and opened the scab. But the teacher didn't believe me and, looking for an excuse, kicked me out of school.

My father was understanding. That doesn't mean he was

Our mother, Amelia (*All photos from private collection of the Neville Brothers unless noted otherwise*)

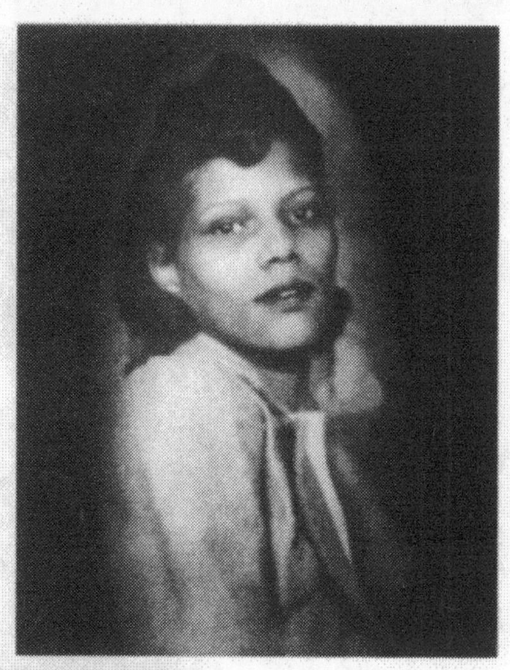

Our father, Big Arthur

Charles and baby Cyril, 1950

Art (left) and Aaron, young Hawketts

The Hawketts being cool: Samuel Alcorn (left), Aaron in dark glasses, and George French

Charles at the Dew Drop, New Orleans hot spot in the fifties

Art, age twenty-two, in a pensive mood

Aaron, budding solo artist in the late fifties

Larry Williams, the "bad boy" who took us under his wing (*Michael Ochs Archives/Venice, CA*)

Visiting Charles in Angola — a bright spot in a dark period. From left: sister Cookie, Charles, Cyril, sister Athelgra holding her infant, and Art

Our beautiful sister Cookie, just weeks before her death

Cyril (left) and the great James Booker, baddest keyboardist ever

The Soul Machine lead vocalists, Cyril (left) and Aaron

The Meters in the seventies — from left: Cyril, Leo Nocentelli, George Porter, Art, Joseph "Zig" Modeliste

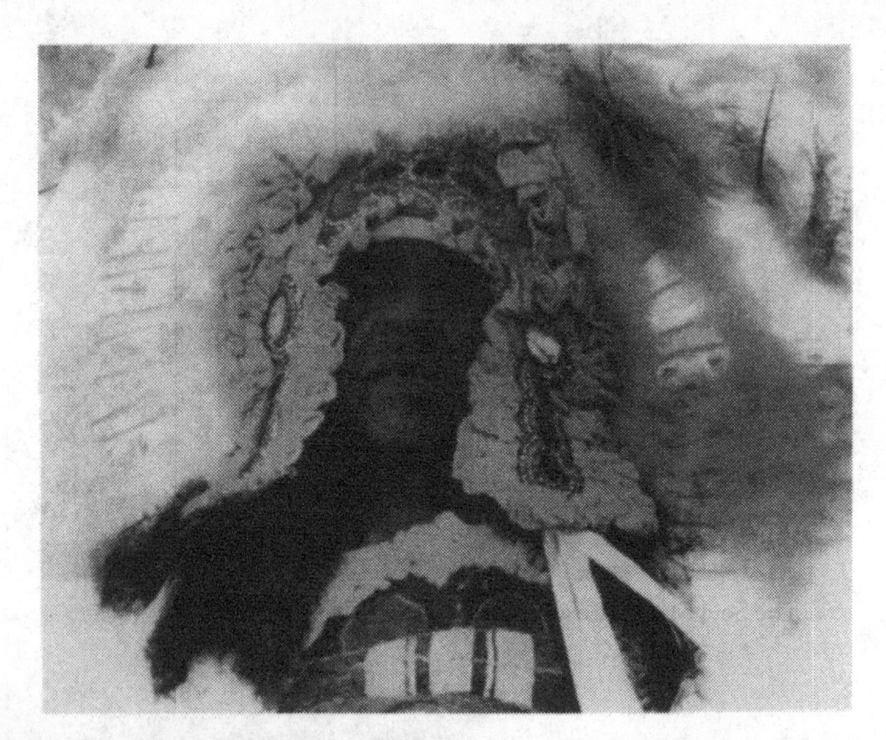

Our uncle Chief Jolly, who brought us together

In Wild Tchoupitoulas garb, the late seventies, from left: Charmaine Neville, Cyril, Charles, Tim Robinson (*Angus Wynne*)

pleased, but he showed compassion. He kept calling me a lost ball in the weeds. If I didn't straighten up, he warned, I'd never find myself. He saw a fire inside me and worried I'd burn up with rage. Then he read about the Job Corps, which reminded him of the domestic work camps during World War II. "That might be the very thing to straighten your ass out," he said. I knew he was looking at me with loving eyes, and I agreed to go. This happened when I was in the eighth grade. It was my first venture away from New Orleans. I was ready to get out of Dodge.

Aaron

I was ready to get to L.A. Larry Williams sent for me. The understanding was that he would be my manager. When he picked me up at the airport, I felt like a little boy being picked up by his father. Larry had this energy about him; he was a take-charge guy who could deal with the world, no matter how crazy the world got. I needed someone like that on my side. After all, this was my first trip to California, and Larry was acting like he was the governor of the state. Straight from the airport, he made a stop at a motel to talk to one of his women. I could see he was doing some serious pimping. For a long time, pimping had been a sideline for Larry; now it was mainline. Waiting in his tricked-out Lincoln while he discussed business inside, I was approached by a cop who knew Larry's car.

"You a pimp?" asked the policeman.

"No, a singer," I said.

"You a burglar?"

"I said I'm a singer."

"If you ain't a pimp and you ain't a burglar, what are you doing with Williams?"

"He's my manager."

The cop flashed a smug smile. "I work out of the Wilshire district," he said. "I'll be seeing you over there."

His words stuck with me.

At first there were gigs at the 5-4 Ballroom, a famous neighborhood spot where all the great r&b acts played. You'd go by and hear Ike and Tina doing "A Fool in Love" or Etta James singing "Something's Got a Hold on Me" or a young Aretha "Runnin' Out of Fools." Larry would play along with his partner, Johnny "Guitar" Watson. Two crazy characters, with me trying to keep up. Musically and otherwise, they were cats ahead of their time. They dressed far out — the original gangsta suits, the long fur coats, the broad-brimmed hats, the genuine alligator shoes. And they acted far out — they did whatever the fuck they wanted to do. They could sing and write and entertain you silly. Johnny played so much guitar that Jimi Hendrix heard what he did and, with Johnny's throwaway licks, created a whole new style. But the truth is that Larry and Johnny weren't making any real music money anymore. Their time had come and gone. Everyone wanted to twist and shout with the Isley Brothers. Rhythm and blues is a young man's music, and for all his cunning and creativity, Larry was no longer a young man. That's why he turned his attention to pimping and stealing. "Just the way the record companies stole from me," he said, "I intend to steal from the world."

Where did that leave me? I'd come to California to sing. Larry was ready to record me, but when I asked Minit Records to release me from the slave contract they had me sign, they refused.

"Fuck them," said Larry. "I still can get you all the work you can handle."

I went to live with Larry and his wife up in their big spread in Baldwin Hills, an upscale black neighborhood not far from the L.A. airport. I saw what was happening, and I wasn't happy. Larry lived like a king, but his kingdom was made up of thieves and whores. He ran a complex operation. He had a booking agency that, instead of booking musical talent, booked robberies, some in town, some in the surrounding towns. I'd sit back and watch it all happen. I felt like a hick in the big city. I'd see Larry brutalizing his women, and even more amazing, I'd see his women loving it. I hated that. I couldn't get out of my head the scene I had witnessed as a child — a big brute beating up a woman. I couldn't stand to see a woman get hit by a man. I couldn't be a pimp. Didn't have it in me. "Fine," said Larry, "not everyone's gotta pimp. We'll put you on a job."

Why did I think I could be a thief? Shooting smack didn't help my thinking any. I thought I loved the high — and I did — but my mind checked out. I just wanted to stay high. Staying high let me do things I didn't ordinarily do. Before going out on a job, I'd get high. While I was on the job, I'd get even higher. That's how I numbed out the fear. I didn't care what was happening. Then came the night Larry said we were hitting a big-time clothing store up on Sunset. "That's where the movie stars buy their suits," he said. "We can break in and wipe 'em out in a matter of minutes. Nothing to it." "Cool," I said, thinking about nothing but my next high.

CYRIL

I went into the Job Corps with high hopes. It was exciting to be away from home. We went to a little town in New Jersey to get processed, and the first thing I heard were stories from other black guys my age about racism in their cities, whether New York, Boston, or Philly. I realized if you're black and male in this society, you're going through the same shit. My worldview was expanding. From Jersey we went to Breckenridge, Kentucky, where we saw the kind of job training available to us. I went to electronics classes for a quick minute but wound up in the music and weight rooms, working out, playing drums. For a while, the novelty of the camp hid a fact that eventually became apparent: the setup was racist to the bone.

First, everything was segregated. Forget "separate but equal." It was separate all right, but unequal as a motherfucker. After a few weeks the more aware black guys got together and talked over grievances. We got different food than the white section; we got mush while they got meat. They lived in big new dorm rooms; we were holed up in dilapidated barracks. They had wider choices in courses and more lenient off-camp hours. When we were given free time, we were restricted to the black-only section of Evansville, Indiana. But in Evansville we were forbidden to hang out at the Fly, a down-home joint where the culture was the thickest. Naturally I hung at the Fly.

We took our complaints about the inferior food and lodgings to the Job Corps leaders, who promised to look into it. They never did; they didn't give a shit. Our own leader was a guy named Black Sam, a well-informed militant attuned to the times. He understood oppression and resistance. He would give us the essential texts of black liberation. He'd read from Frederick Douglass, who wrote, "Power never conceded anything without force." "Force," said Black Sam, "is our only remedy." He was the quintessential man of the sixties who helped shape my political consciousness.

Black Sam was about action. After months of nonresponse from the authorities, we were smoldering with anger. We were tired of being ignored. Sam organized a protest. I was behind him all the way. In the mess hall, rather than eat the foul food, we threw the shit on the floor. The first line of attack came from our own ranks, security guys who slept in our dorms and should have been with us but weren't. The fire trucks came; the firemen tried to hose us into submission. Some of the guys got scared, grabbed their duffel bags, and split for home. The rest of us made it to Evansville to regroup. Some of the cats' blood was up, and they went a little wild: they started breaking windows. The disturbance blew up into a full-fledged riot. They rounded us up with dogs, threw us in a paddy wagon, and took us to jail. Two of my colleagues were beaten to a pulp. It was weird and scary, raw rage electrifying the air. Next morning, at a kangaroo court, we were charged with committing a crime on a government reservation. I was thrown out of the Job Corps and sent back to New Orleans, more militant than when I had left.

Aaron

Larry Williams was on the job that night in L.A. "It's a sweet little place on Sunset," he said. "Easy score." I'd been through some easy scores since landing in L.A., so I had no reason to doubt him. We'd hit jewelry stores just off the freeway, breaking the window, scooping up gold chains and watches, and jumping back on the freeway in nothing flat. Deep inside, I was always nervous and scared, but the dope pushed down the feelings. Before taking off, I shot up. I went to that otherworld place. I acted like everything was cool. We pulled our van up to the back of the store. There were actually two stores, women's clothes next to men's. The women's store didn't have a burglar alarm, so we popped the lock. Larry and his boys busted the wall with a chisel, crowbar, and maul, making a big enough hole for us to crawl through to the men's store. I started hauling out suits and loading up the van. I was in the van, about to climb back out to get more stuff, when I heard voices coming from the women's store — voices I didn't recognize. Someone said, "Michele, people are in there. Who are they?" Larry and the crew were in the men's store grabbing more suits, unaware that the owners of the women's store — a man and woman — had shown up. "Who's in there?" the woman asked. "Come out," the man demanded. I could hear everything, and for some reason, everything sounded funny to me — probably 'cause I had smoked a joint. In my mind I saw what was happening: Larry and them had to pass through the women's store to get back to the van. The situation was serious, but the pot made it hysterical. Felt like I was watching a TV show inside my head.

Next thing I heard was the woman confronting Larry, who had crawled back through the hole. "What are you doing?" she asked. "We're the cleanup people," Larry answered. "I didn't hire anyone to clean up," she said. Now I'm laughing even harder. But the joke's over when the woman starts screaming. Later I learned that Larry hit the guy, knocked him out, and took off. Everyone took off except me. I was stuck. When I tried to slide open the van door, it wouldn't budge. I was no longer laughing. I heard Larry telling everyone to scram; I heard everyone taking off in different directions. I got the door open and went to sit on a bench. I sat there without moving because I expected to be caught. I was hoping to be caught. Went back to the van, where I wasn't waiting long before I heard the sound of sirens — first far away, then closer and closer. When I walked out of the van this time, I was surrounded by a dozen policemen and a score of spectators on Sunset Boulevard. And if that wasn't bad enough, here comes the sheriff of Hollywood.

At the moment when I should have felt the most fear, I felt something else. I felt gratitude — gratitude to God. I said, "Thank you, Jesus." Today I believe it was the Lord who kept that van door from opening; I believe it was the Lord who wanted me caught. In my heart I felt relief. I hated the life I was leading, and this was a way out. Without God's intervention I might not have been strong enough to resist Larry's influence. Larry was a sure-enough thief, but I also knew he loved and cared about me. I also loved him like a brother. But Larry had the disposition for that life. Later he told me how he ran into the Hollywood Hills, jumped over cliffs, and slid down canyons, hiding out all night and avoiding arrest. Larry was a cowboy. I wasn't. I needed to get busted.

When I finally got the door open and saw cops in every direction, I just sat down on the running board of the van and lit a cigarette.

"Hey, boy," said the sheriff of Hollywood. "What you doing?"

"Nothing much," I answered, blowing out the smoke.

"What you got in that van?"

Knowing I was caught red-handed, knowing I had no choice but to go along with the program, I didn't bother to answer.

But being passive didn't impress the police. They handcuffed me behind my back so hard that my finger is still fucked up to this day. In spite of the pain, I fell asleep in the cop car. The heroin and weed were wearing off, and I was dead tired. When I woke up in the car, it was 3 A.M., the cuffs were still on me, and all I could feel was pain.

CYRIL

Back in New Orleans I switched over to Priestly Junior High, which was in the Sixteenth Ward, where Mahalia Jackson grew up singing in the Mount Moriah Mission Baptist Church. For a while Aaron and Joel were also living over there, although Aaron was spending a lot of time in California. My brothers still weren't a part of my daily life.

I tried to relate to school. I had a hip English teacher, Miss Evelyn Gethers, who had us read "The Tell-Tale Heart" by Edgar Allan Poe. I was intrigued how the poet would start six words with the same letter, how he hooked up sounds to build up rhythms. When

I gave my book report, I did it in a style that was half Poe and half street. Teacher dug it. The class applauded. "You can be an artist like Poe," Miss Gethers said. "You understand the relationship between language and music. You can make a contribution. You can use words to rise above your condition." I was feeling good, gaining my confidence back, getting a little faith that maybe the system wasn't so bad after all. Then came the day the system caught up with me.

I was called to the principal's office. Two white guys in suits were waiting for me. Without being told, I knew what the play was. They were federal agents. "We're arresting you for committing a crime on a government property," they said, referring to the shit that happened in Breckenridge. They handcuffed me and paraded me down the hallway. Miss Gethers saw what was happening. "You don't have to handcuff him!" she shouted. "You don't have to parade him down the hallway and humiliate him!" They just looked at her and smiled. Then Miss Gethers, bless her heart, protested to the principal. "You can stop them," she said. "Don't let them make a public spectacle of Cyril." But the principal couldn't have cared less. He let the agents do what they did. By the time I was shoved into the back of their car, seemed like every student at that school was looking out the window. If I didn't feel like an outlaw before, I sure as hell felt like one now.

Charles

I was attracted to the notion of sexual outlaws. The white woman–black man connection is strong, especially in places like New Orleans, where it was so strictly forbidden. I told you about seeing white women at the Dew Drop Inn, where I not only respected their daring but was drawn to their sexuality. One of those women went with a friend of mine, Guitar Red. Her name was Sue,* a highly educated and tough lady. This was after my second stint in jail. Bobbie was still my old lady while Sue became my partner in crime.

When we first met, Sue was working as a waitress. I'd see her at the Dew Drop, where she impressed me with her ability to improvise. If the cops busted the place, for instance, looking to round up the white chicks, Sue would slap on some makeup and disguise herself as a Creole. She also proved adept at stealing.

Good boosters in New Orleans didn't bemoan racism; they took advantage of it. If a black man like me walked into any of the big department stores on Canal Street, I'd never be waited on. But I'd be watched like a hawk. As a convicted thief, my picture would be hanging in the back. And if they didn't recognize that, I'd accentuate my shadiness by not shaving for a day or two. So with half the clerks and the store dick keeping tabs on me, Sue was free to cop to her heart's content — Sue who looked like Miss White Respectability, small, dainty, and pretty as a picture. Little Sue would clean them out.

Fences were never a problem. Bondsmen were among the biggest fences. That's how they got their fancy three-piece suits for practically nothing. Lawyers and judges were also among those who bought our hot merchandise. The hustles were nonstop. The burglaries got so intense that some thieves, rather than run the risk of driving themselves, called cabs. Certain cabdrivers could be trusted to take your haul to a fence. Once, I hooked up with a couple of guys to steal some televisions. When we broke out of the store, one of the cats said, "We've called the Big One. The Big One will be here in a second." In less than a minute, the Big One pulled up. I couldn't believe my eyes, but the Big One turned out to be my

*Fictitious name

father! Daddy was driving for Ed's Cabs and was known as the Big One. I ran to hide, but he saw me.

"What are *you* doing with these motherfuckers?" he asked me.

"You know him?" the dudes asked Daddy.

"Know him? He's my son."

Everyone laughed — except me — as we loaded the TVs into the cab.

Later Daddy didn't bother to lecture me. We knew there was nothing either one of us could say.

Aaron

Larry Williams put up bail and picked me up at the L.A. County Jail, where I had spent only a day. I went back to Larry's house but didn't go back to burglarizing. I never could pimp because I never could hurt women. All I could do was concentrate on this legal problem. The cops wanted to know who I was with, so I gave them phony names, which only pissed them off. "We're sending your ass to San Quentin," they threatened. My probation officer was more understanding. He felt my spirit and didn't see me as a criminal. He said he'd help me get home to my wife and my mother and get my probation switched to New Orleans. He did all that.

Back home, my mother was praying to Saint Jude, patron saint of hopeless causes. My wife, Joel, stood by my side. Everyone wrote letters on my behalf to Judge Brand, the man who would decide my future. But when the day finally comes and we arrive at court, Judge Brand is on vacation. Another judge is up there, throwing out time like ice water. I'm scared, I'm even thinking about getting up and splitting, getting lost and never coming back. If I did that, though, I'd never get to make another record. I can't give up the idea of singing. Not even the threat of a long jail sentence can kill that dream. So I just stand there, shaking on the inside.

Judge looks down at me and says, "I'm sentencing you to the maximum." My heart sinks like a stone. This is it. My attorney has told me the maximum means one to fourteen years. "But," the judge continues — I'm holding on to the *but* like it's a piece of thread — "but I'll suspend that sentence and give you a three-year probation, providing you do the first year."

Thank you, your motherfuckin' honor, I say to myself.

"Thank you, sir," I say out loud.

A little while later I'm in a room with some other cats who received sentences. I light up a joint; I'm toking and relaxing and feeling saved. Another dude is cussing a blue streak: "Goddamn judge threw me away, gave me five to life. What did you do to him to get off so fuckin' easy?"

"Nothing," I say. But in my silent mind, I think about Joel and my mom and the prayers sent to Saint Jude. In my silent mind, I think about God's grace.

Within a month I'm flying back out to California. That's where the judge ordered me to serve my year of time. Turned out to be a whole 'nother kind of adventure — fighting forest fires.

Charles

The heat was on. The police suspected what was happening — that Sue and I had this con going, but we were careful not to get caught. I did get caught for another heist, though, and rather than go to jail, jumped my bail. When I learned that my dad had put up his car for bail, I came back, turned myself in, and did my time. Couldn't live with the idea of Daddy losing his cab.

But that was short time compared with the bust that followed. The irony was that this next arrest was a case of mistaken identity. I *was* about to commit a crime, but not the one they thought. We were fixing to stick up a doctor who had morphine. Two dudes and I were parked in front of his house, waiting for him to come out. Just down the street was a drugstore where a suspicious clerk spotted us. He thought we were after him, so he called the cops. They nailed us before the doctor ever emerged. We were accused of another crime that had happened earlier. Three black men — not us — had robbed and shot a gas attendant in the leg with a .22. Since they found a .22 under our car seat, and since we were three black men, we were put in a lineup and identified by an eyewitness. Didn't matter that I had people swearing I was with them when the man had been shot. I was charged with armed robbery and attempted murder.

My father came to my aid. My father always came to my aid. He found the eyewitness, a poor black guy who claimed to have seen the crime. Daddy, our neighborhood preacher, and my music teacher from Southern University all confronted my accuser. They told the man that I could prove I was elsewhere. How could he have possibly identified me? "The police just told me to pick someone who kinda looked like the man," he explained apologetically. "The police said they'd take care of the rest."

My attitude was, *Fuck it*. The idea of another stint in the parish prison, especially on a trumped-up charge, was too much bullshit to bear. Instead, I jumped bail, grabbed a gig with a band, and ran out of town. Motivating me even more was Bobbie. Bobbie was still my old lady, and Bobbie said she'd meet me in Florida. Man, I was gone with the wind.

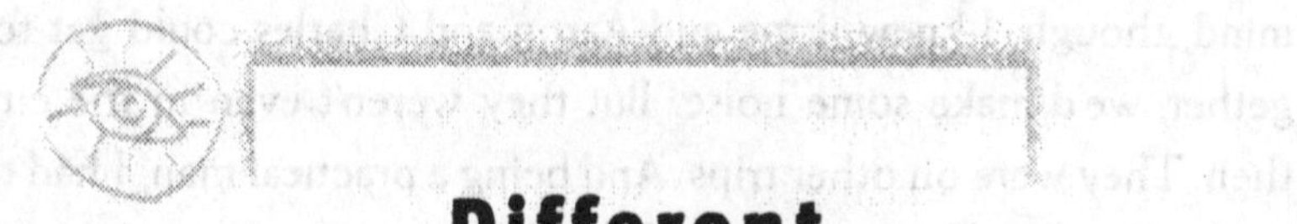

Different Directions

Art

Funny thing about me and my brothers. For a long time we weren't connected — at least not geographically. We were running in different directions. We've never been the kind of people who tell one another what to do — or warn one another. Sure, I felt protective and suffered inside when I saw them in trouble. But because I wasn't a saint myself, there wasn't shit I could say. I might have been more cautious than them; I might have been sneakier about stuff; I might have wiggled my way out of some tricky situations that kept me out of hot water. Oddly enough, my wild time would hit me when I got much older. In those early days I stayed connected to the music.

Still had my ear attuned to the funk. Funk has always been there, because funk is, after all, a form of the blues. And the blues is the basis of it all. But funk was being modernized, not only by Booker T. but by singers like Otis Redding. Modernized and accepted by a mass audience. They were calling it soul music, but I heard it as old music with a new twist — tighter horn charts, edgier grooves. I had me my little gigs with the Hawketts; I did some sessions for pocket change; I held on. In the back of my mind, though, I knew if me and Aaron and Charles could get together, we'd make some noise. But they weren't even in the city then. They were on other trips. And being a practical man, I had to deal with what was real and let that other idea simmer on the back burner.

CYRIL

I don't think Art really ever thought about me as a musician or a performer. I don't think he thought about me at all. And why should he? Most older brothers see little brothers as nuisances. My older brothers remained mysterious — faraway, mythical characters in a book that did not include me. I wanted their attention but didn't know how to go about getting it. The one who paid attention to me — at least as far as music — wasn't a brother at all; it was my sister-in-law Joel, Aaron's wife, my second mother. Joel trusted me. If she had to go out, and if Aaron wasn't there, I was the only one she trusted with her kids. I was Joel's official baby-sitter.

I remember when I started singing. Zig and I would be fooling around with Beatles songs like "I Saw Her Standing There," preparing for some talent show. Those two-family shotgun cottages had thin walls, and the music seeped through. Well, Zig and I were on one side, and Joel and my sister Athelgra were on the other. "Hey," I heard Joel saying, "that's Cyril singing. Cyril can really sing." She made it a point to come over and tell me how good I was. When I told her I was working on songs of my own, she wanted to hear them. She listened carefully and asked, "You wrote all that?" "Yup,"

I said proudly. "Well," she said, "God has given you talent." Made me feel ten feet tall. After that, I'd always let Joel hear what I was working on — no one else but Joel. At a time in my life when a single word of encouragement might have meant the difference between pressing on and giving up, Joel gave me that word.

Aaron

Went back to California, to Mount Wilson, east of Los Angeles, where I got to serve out my jail time in a forestry work camp where they taught me to fight fires. That was some tricky shit. Those Santa Ana winds will turn and twist every which way. Nearly got burned up during a bad firestorm, but luckily — I have to thank the Lord again — a Santa Ana blew the flames away at the last minute. I learned a lot that year — how to knock fire out of a tree, how to deal with the whims of Mother Nature. They told me I could have been a forest ranger, but no, thank you, I wanted to sing.

Some of the dudes up there on Mount Wilson could sing — the crooks and killers. I'd show them some stuff, and we'd wind up harmonizing for everyone. The supervising sergeant would hear me and call me over. For a while he had me clean up his office, an easy job. I'd started messing with weights and building up my body. I was completely free from drugs, and my mind was starting to clear. "Look here, Aaron," the sergeant said after hearing my story, "you shouldn't be up here. You should be down there singing." He could feel my heart. My heart was filled with songs.

My heart was also lonely. My family — my mom, dad, brothers, wife, and kids — couldn't get to California to see me. I made friends with a cat from California who let me hang with his family during visiting days. I'd sit with his mother on a bench and feel like

I was her son. I needed family around me, even if it was pretend family. By then Joel and I had a third child, a beautiful daughter named Ernestine. I wanted to go home.

Fighting forest fires was okay. Being in nature was healthy. Being off drugs helped my head. But everything I knew and loved was back in New Orleans. And on those cool California nights when the air was fresh with the smell of the wild forest, I dreamt of Valence Street and the people I loved most. I counted the days till I got home.

Charles

I was on the lam. Snuck out of New Orleans on a gig that took me as far as Mobile, where I was hired by a house band at Big Road's Tavern. Then, as luck would have it, Gene Franklin and the House Rockers, my old cronies, came through and took me to Pensacola, Florida. Gene moved on, but I stayed in Pensacola, where I found work with a black r&b band in a white club. Strange, but in those days, in the full flush of the civil rights movement, many black clubs had an attitude against rhythm and blues. They thought it represented something backward and would even ban the music in favor of something more "proper." Ironically, some white clubs appreciated it more.

Bobbie came to Pensacola and stayed with me at a whorehouse run by a dude in the hustling part of town. Everything was mellow until a white bondsman from New Orleans, on his way to Miami on vacation, stopped by the club and spotted me. Pure coincidence. Someone said I'd been recognized, so I backed off the bandstand and snuck out the bathroom window and ran back to the whorehouse.

"We gotta split," I told Bobbie. But by then the police had arrived with their bullhorn, hollering, "Come out. We know you're in there." Our only escape was under the floor; the wood floor was rotten enough for us to crawl under. The dude who ran the whorehouse was with us. He was gonna lead us to his car and over the county line. We reached the car, but once behind the wheel, the dude wasn't in much of a hurry. I knew something was wrong. Me and Bobbie kept urging him on, but by the time we passed the bus station, the dude was practically creeping. By then the police were right behind us. "Just get us to the bridge," I told him. At the bridge Bobbie and I jumped out. We were going to jump in and swim across. On the other side was the neighboring county — and freedom. But just as we were about to leap from the rail into the water, we heard the cock of a gun. A cop was standing only a few feet away. With cold-blooded dispassion, he said, "You'll be dead before you reach the water."

The dude had ratted us out. To protect his illicit activities, he'd been playing footsie with the fuzz. We waited in jail for three days until another bondsman was sent from New Orleans to take us back. The drive was bizarre and, in some ways, not unpleasant. Turned out Bobbie and I knew the bondsman. He was a dope fiend. He arrived with his girlfriend, a stripper from Bourbon Street. They were hip and, even better, holding dope. We smoked weed all the way home. At one point we hit a roadblock. The redneck highway patrol were looking for Freedom Riders. In those days state troopers and the Klan were sometimes one and the same. Seeing a car with two whites and two blacks made them suspicious.

"You ain't no goddamn Freedom Riders, are you?" they asked.

I slipped on the cuffs the bondsman had handed me.

"Hell, boss," I said, holding up my cuffed hands, "we anything *but* free."

Freedom ended back in parish prison. I was there for months, awaiting sentencing. My dad was trying everything he could to get me out, but it wasn't easy. Then one day Daddy brought a beautiful woman named Ann* to visit me. Ann changed my life. Ann's family was *passe blanc* from the Seventh Ward. Her mom and aunts owned a hip club called the Three Sisters and were friends of my family. Ann had met my other brothers but not me. When my folks said I was in jail, she asked to see my picture. Later she told me she fell in love with the picture. That's why she came to see me at parish prison.

CYRIL

Ann was a stunning Creole woman. One year Uncle Jolly, who was becoming intrigued with the Mardi Gras Indians, wanted Ann to be his Mardi Gras queen. My father took me along to pick her up and bring her to Jolly's house. When she got into the car, her dress rose up. I mean, she was total woman. Well, my man took him a good long look. "Now, now, Mr. Arthur," Ann told Daddy, tugging her dress down. She was flattered by his attention but also proper in her own way. Ann was someone who recognized my spiritual side. Later we'd have deep conversations about voodoo and its origins in the Yoruba religion.

Charles

Ann had great poise, plus a solid sense of business. She also had a window unto the world of voodoo. And strangely enough, it was voodoo that first brought us together. On that first day she came visiting, she said she could help me. We began a feverish correspondence in which she mentioned Mother Furman, her voodoo lady. Mother Furman wanted the name of the judge and samples of

*Fictitious name

his hair and handwriting. I had his name, but nothing more. I had no way of obtaining the other stuff.

A month later Ann wrote that Mother Furman's son was in parish prison for car theft. Mother Furman was able to get the kid a job in the judge's chambers, enabling him to steal the samples she needed. Meanwhile, I'd been locked up for nine months, the legal maneuvering had run its course, and I was about to be sentenced. "Don't worry," wrote Ann, "Mother Furman is on the case."

Day before sentencing, Ann gave me Mother Furman's instructions: Write the judge's name nine times. I was given a candle wrapped up with hair and handwriting and told to let it burn. With an identical candle, Mother Furman was performing that same rite.

Day of my sentencing arrives. I put on my civilian clothes and wait to be called, but the call never comes. What gives? Someone comes in with the news: last night the judge dropped dead. Unknown causes. Two days later my father arrives and lets me know I've been cut loose. I'm free.

Needless to say, once I got out, Ann and I became lovers and I broke up with Bobbie. Ann was smooth. She liked money and had her own house. She liked to gamble and worked at the racetrack, where she got and gave tips. Ann also had a job at Haskell Brothers, a big plant where they made men's suits. She got the job because she was Creole; Haskell Brothers liked hiring fair-skinned black women. Through her influence, Haskell Brothers hired me.

Haskell Brothers was a scene. Ann had a job as a cutter, and her best friend, Lily, another Creole beauty, worked as a button sewer. Lily was more happy-go-lucky than Ann. Lily loved men and loved it when men loved her. She liked turning light tricks and, together with Ann, got me started stealing from Haskell Brothers. I was a bundle boy, packing up shit, doing whatever. Mainly, though, we developed a system of carrying merchandise out of the plant into car trunks, and from there to the fences.

Art

For a time it looked like Charles and them were selling more Haskell Brothers suits than any department store in the city.

Charles

While it lasted, Ann and I had a beautiful relationship. We worked together at Haskell Brothers for a year. We made a wonderful son named Carlos, whom we both loved. But our love for each other was a crazy love because we were doing crazy things.

I continued running in and out of jail. Ann found another boyfriend — I couldn't blame her — a guy with money. Some months after I quit Haskell Brothers, I ran into Lily. When we first met, she wasn't using. Now she was. So we had that in common. We hooked up, shot up, and eventually shacked up. At one point I got busted again and needed to make bail. Because I had burned my old bondsman, I was in a bind. So I turned to a guy named Luke.

Aaron

Luke was a supersavvy drug dealer. Everyone knew Luke. He was *the* connection. When I got back home from California, Luke was one of the guys I ran into. I'm not saying he talked me into anything. No one had to. I did what I did because, well . . . I still wasn't ready to stop. Luke was one of those guys who got you what you wanted when you wanted it. And back on the scene, back on the streets, I wanted to get high.

Charles

Luke had a third-grade education, but he was brilliant. He devised brilliant ways to trick the police. You'd put in an order for a bag of heroin from Luke, and he'd tell you to go to the park, look for a beer-bottle cap in front of a bench, take ten steps behind the bench to a discarded bag of potato chips, walk toward a row of bushes, and keep walking till you hear someone say stop. That'd be Luke sitting in the car. Then you'd follow the car to an alley where, under the third garbage can to the right, the shit would be waiting for you. Luke was a master of intrigue. He never once got caught. Luke had money. He was the man to find me bail bread. When I asked him, though, he had a strange request. He didn't want collateral; he wanted Lily.

"Give me that girl you're living with," he said, "and I'll give you what you want."

Lily was a free spirit, and Lily didn't mind. She went to live with Luke, and I had my freedom back. From time to time, though, Lily and I saw each other behind Luke's back. It was a strange arrangement, but no stranger than the life led by the boosters, hustlers, and whores who made up the world I lived in.

That world was about to change. That world was about to collapse. I guess you could say that in some psychological way, I was setting myself up. But in a literal way, I was being set up by the police. My boosting partnership with Sue, Miss White Respectability, was well known among certain cops. They mistakenly presumed we were lovers. That enraged them — that and the fact that they never caught us in the act of crime. Certain cops had even told me, *We're throwing your ass in Angola*.

Aaron

My friend Melvin was fearless, but when the judge made an example of him and marked him the first dude to get life for the sale of heroin, Melvin said he felt fear all over his body. Melvin had already been to the pen six or seven times, but life in Angola was something else. Everyone was scared of Angola.

CYRIL

In the minds of black men growing up in New Orleans, the specter of Angola was always there. Angola was the threat, the nightmare, the worst-case scenario — the big, bad, dark state penitentiary stuck out there in north central Louisiana, where racism ran wild and convicts lost their minds and guards, just for the hell of it, tortured and killed.

Angola Bound

Aaron

Too many mornings gonna wake up soon and
Oh Lord, eat my breakfast by the light of the moon
Oh Lord, by the light of the moon
If you see my mama tell her this for me,
Oh, I got a mighty long time, Lord, cause I'll never go free,
Oh Lord, I'll never be free

Those are words to a song I wrote sometime in the sixties. Later, when the storms had calmed, Charlie added to it and we called it "Angola Bound."

CYRIL

The storm was still raging inside me. Daddy saw that and still thought the Job Corps would help me chill. So, in spite of the charges against me, he managed to get me into another Job Corps program in Pleasanton, California. I thought California would be cool, but the Oakland cops turned out worse than what we faced in New Orleans. There were some hip brothers there, though, who continued to school me in radicalism. One cat in particular, Akinjiju, preached how the brain is a muscle that needs to be developed. When Huey Newton came along, I was already steeped in political confrontation and knew just what he was talking about. My musical education was also deepening. In California I remember listening to Miles and *Mingus Revisited*. But it wasn't just jazz; it was also hearing Little Stevie Wonder singing "The Masquerade Is Over." More and more, I was appreciating the full spectrum of African American music as one thing — jazz and gospel, blues and rhythm and blues, the ongoing voice of a people who, despite the wounds of history, celebrated life through song. It was thrilling to think that I might be part of that tradition.

There was a weight room at Pleasanton where I started building strength. For a while I thought I was a bad boxer. Scrawny Mexican guy challenged me one day. Looked him over and said, "Man, I hate to hurt you." "That's okay," he said. Fifteen seconds later they're picking me up off the floor, and the little guy is jumping up and down. Later he showed me some of his moves. Nice cat. Taught me not to judge a book by its cover.

Also learned a lot more about weed in the Job Corps. Me and my pal Rodney planted a marijuana farm behind the dorm. We learned to cultivate the shit. And believe me, when homegrown is good, it's extra good. Roll up a fat one, take a hit, drop the needle on Coltrane's "A Love Supreme," and feel the Great Spirit close at hand.

The spirit of the times, though, was not all peace and love. The Job Corps wanted us peaceful and did, in fact, try to insulate us. They didn't want us out there marching for Martin Luther King. But the world broke through that insulation. Our country was fighting a war in Vietnam we didn't understand, a war against a people we had no interest in harming. Made no sense. And it made us angry. That anger — in many ways and on many days — nearly cost me my life.

Charles

I was hustling around New Orleans, playing with brother Art in one of his later versions of the Hawketts. White cats liked to hang around us, especially junkies, because we had the best dope. That's how I met this shy kid named Al. But Al was no junkie. He liked to smoke and nothing more. I knew he worked for the Continental Can Company and lived with his grandmother. What I didn't know, though, was that he'd been busted and threatened with a sentence in the pen. The only way to avoid that, the cops said, was to set up a big dealer. Poor Al didn't know any big dealers. He just knew me.

At the time, I was scoring from Uncle Jolly, so when Al started asking about my connections, I stayed mum. All I could do, I told him, was sell him a little pot. He bought two joints. Those two lousy joints would be my downfall. The night I sold him those joints, he picked me up for a Hawketts gig. I could see he was nervous. First he stops to buy wine. Fine. We gulp down the wine. Then he stops by his house to change clothes. Cool. When he emerges from his house, though, he's staggering; he says he's too drunk to drive. Seems like he's acting, but I take the wheel anyway. Gig's across the river, in Algiers. We drive over the bridge and are about to stop at the toll booth when he says, "Hold these joints for me, will you?" I take the joints. Seconds later two troopers jump out of the car behind us, run up, and stick pistols in our face. Plain-clothes bridge cops toting shotguns bust out of the toll booth and join them. My heart is racing like mad. "Okay, you motherfuckers," we're ordered, "put your hands on top of your head." I'm holding the joints, and as I'm raising my hands, I let them slip down the back of my shirt. The car is searched and nothing is found. We're whisked into an office for a body search. They pull my shirt out of my pants, and the two joints drop out. "Where's the heroin?" they want to know. There isn't any. Next day Al's out on bond. I'm in jail for a week. Finally Al comes and gets me out with a bondsman. Al's crying. He tells me he's the cause of the setup. I tell him he's being royally fucked, that they'll wind up sending him to the pen anyway, that he's dealing with the lowest of the low.

A long time later two homicide detectives came to see me about Al. They asked what I knew about his murder. I knew nothing. I asked *them* for the story. Al was discovered in the backseat of his car, hands tied, a bullet through his brain. He'd been shot execution-style.

When the detectives came to see me, I was in Angola. I'd been there for more than two years. The two joints — considered a class-A narcotic as illegal as heroin — got me five years.

Art

It's amazing when you think of it: five years in the fuckin' federal penitentiary for two sticks of weed. None of us could believe it, but at that point none of us — not my father, not the reverend with influence in the community — no one could do a thing about it.

CYRIL

Far as I was concerned, the incarceration of my brother Charles was another reason I viewed the system of so-called justice in America with utter contempt. I saw Charles as a political prisoner of the racist war that was quickly turning New Orleans into a combat zone.

Charles

The long and short of the story is that going to trial might have meant ten years. So I pleaded guilty and got five. Of course, there were political and racial implications to the charge. After all, this was Louisiana in 1964. I felt like a victim, but I also knew I had been toying with this kind of disaster for years. I never stopped taking drugs, never stopped stealing, never stopped leading the kind of life that could, at any moment, explode in my face.

Oddly enough, I was anxious to get to Angola. The parish prison was in the throes of a riot that I wanted no part of. I saw it as a no-win situation. The inmates were pissed about worms in their oatmeal. They complained to the warden, who said, "Tough shit. If you don't like it, we won't serve it." And the prison took it even further — they served nothing. The hungry inmates called the local reporters and began banging on the walls, hollering and screaming for hours on end. The riot squad came with their fire hoses. I stayed in my cell and watched it all happen. The hoses were turned on full blast, followed by the tear-gas grenades, which, in turn, were followed by attack dogs. Finally, the guards rounded up all prisoners — even those of us who had remained in our cells — stripped off our denim uniforms, and threw us in a big room where we were subjected to more hosing and tear gas. When the assault was over, we were told to mop up the water and tear gas. Some of the guys were seriously injured by the tear gas and the dogs. Didn't matter. Naked and shivering, we mopped until the floor was clean. When we were finally sent back to the mess hall to eat, the *plat du jour* was — you guessed it — oatmeal with worms.

The piano man's coming tonight 'cause Gus is gonna roll in the morning.

The piano man was the guy who fingerprinted you, and Gus was the truck that hauled prisoners to Angola. The expression was used by the guards to torment the young cats waiting to go to Angola. Guards can be the most sadistic motherfuckers in the world. "Once you get to Angola," they'd say, "you gonna miss this candy-ass nursery school. You gonna see a real prison."

For my part, I was ready. Parish prison was getting crazier by the day, and besides, I was going up with Snags and Pony, fellow hustlers from the street who had been cooking dope in a hallway when a lady called the cops. The bust came just as they were shooting up. Snags and Pony would be good protection for my initial entrance into Angola.

Maybe Angola was as bad as everyone said; maybe it was hell; but I'd already seen a portion of hell, and if it was my fate to descend deeper into hell's lower rungs, so be it.

CYRIL

It wasn't so pleasant in Pleasanton, California, when the Job Corps busted us. It happened on my friend Rodney's birthday, when we celebrated by bringing booze back to the dorm. That night they raided us, confiscated our liquor, and took it back to the store where we bought it. We broke into the store to get our stuff back, which is when we got caught. They threw us in the Alameda County Juvenile Home for two months. Main thing I remember is a counselor who woke us up every morning at 6:30 to the sound of Mose Allison's "Parchman Farm." That was one funky song. When I learned Mose was white, I wanted to know more about him. I knew he had a black soul and his music was as muddy as the Mississippi, and now I needed to hear all his records. With Mose waking me up every day, reminding me of the beauty and power of real roots singing, I managed to keep hope alive.

Corresponding with brother Charles also helped that hope. His letters from Angola were filled with information, his notions about race and politics and his lists of authors for me to read. If he was in jail devouring good books, I would do the same. Charles told me about *Manchild in the Promised Land,* the novels of Iceberg Slim and James Baldwin, whose *The Fire Next Time* stayed with me for the rest of my life and became the inspiration, thirty years later, for my first solo album, *The Fire This Time.*

Back in New Orleans, I was in and out of Walter L. Cohen High School. I was given five years' probation for the Breckenridge charges, which meant I had to report to federal court twice a week. The court was in the Wildlife and Fishing Building in the middle of the French Quarter. Surrounded by history, I also felt oppressed by it. I was reading Ralph Ellison's *Invisible Man* and felt invisible myself. I'd sit in Jackson Square, where my slave ancestors, their hands behind their backs, had been led from the boats to be sold like livestock. As human beings, they were invisible. I was just as invisible to the white world walking by. Walking home, so many thoughts flashed through my mind — past the mansions on St. Charles Avenue, all the way Uptown to the Thirteenth Ward. The caste system was still in place. In a strange way, the city of New

Orleans — for all its artistic grace and architectural charm — was a city of elitism and oppression. Nothing had changed.

On those same walks I sometimes dreamt of escaping the city and moving to Harlem. I was reading about the Harlem Renaissance and imagined a place where black art — not European art — dominated the scene, inspiring young artists like me. I read political and social critiques — W. E. B. Du Bois's *The Souls of Black Folk*, and *The Wretched of the Earth* by Frantz Fanon. I aspired to be a deep thinker like Richard Wright or Ralph Ellison. I also started reading about Native Americans and their own struggle with oppression. Those long walks home were deep. I thought about who I was and where I wanted to go. I'd stop to read a poem by Nikki Giovanni or an essay by Amiri Baraka. Life was uncertain; inside my heart, I felt uncertain. I was seventeen years old.

The Long and Winding Road

Art

We'd be silently riding in the car. Not much to talk about. Not much to say. We'd drive out of New Orleans a good ways. In the summertime the Louisiana air is hot and sticky. We were uncomfortable as hell. After a while the countryside would start rolling, and we'd be on this long and winding road up and down those hills. Took a couple of hours to get there. The road ended at these big iron gates. I've never seen gates so imposing. The guards would put us on a bus, and we'd ride another half hour to the visiting shed. All the time I'd be remembering the stories we'd all heard — how it's called Angola because originally slaves were brought from Angola in Africa to show the planters how to grow sugarcane, how the grounds were so enormous that they had cats who escaped, ran like the wind, and two weeks later were caught, still within the confines of Angola. Mainly, though, I would be thinking how much I loved our brother Charles. He needed to know that no matter what society said, his family valued him and recognized his worth as a human being.

Charles

When my family came to visit, I hated how they were subjected to indignities. Black visitors were treated differently than white ones. They loaded black visitors on the same smelly, nasty cattle trucks with busted wooden slats used to transport the inmates to the work fields. They didn't even provide ladders for the mothers and grandmothers, who had to be lifted on and off the truck. The trucks brought them to an outdoor shed. Black visitors were denied a decent visiting room. The whole process was geared to make you and your family feel humiliated and ashamed.

Aaron

I didn't give a shit about the visitors' conditions. I just wanted to see my brother Charlie.

CYRIL

I was amazed by the place. It was just so fuckin' vast. We'd all grown up with the specter of Angola, and here it was, staring me in the face. I thought about the police banging on our door in the middle of the night looking for Charles; I thought about my folks talking in hushed tones about how it looked like he might be headed for Angola; I thought about all the anticipation. Now it had happened. What amazed me most, though, wasn't the pen itself but the fact that my brother didn't seem scared. Charles talked about the educational opportunities inside and the musical groups he wanted to join. All his talk was positive. The joint didn't intimidate or embitter him. He was dealing with it all, doing what he had to do, being a man.

Charles

Despite the harsh conditions, visiting day warmed my heart. Daddy came once a month, and my sisters and brothers came when they could. Once, Artie brought me a joint that I was lucky enough to sneak inside and smoke. A helluva treat. Another drug treat slipped to me by a brother — cough syrup laced with codeine — turned bad. Because I hadn't been high in a while, I was sick as a dog for days. Biggest treat of all, though, was seeing my mother. Her presence calmed me; her vibe was patience and hope. The love she offered knew no limits, an extraordinary love marked by acceptance and understanding. During my years in Angola, she and I corresponded. I hid nothing from Mommee. Later she told me that my letters inspired her to go back to school and become a nurse; she wanted to learn about the root causes of drug addiction.

There was a lot to learn in and about Angola — far more than I had imagined. It was a world so isolated, so brutal, so volatile that whatever survival skills I had honed had to be rehoned and seriously sharpened. My aim was always simple — to serve my time and get the fuck out with sanity and soul intact. From the first day of orientation, staying sane was a challenge. We were told, for instance, that getting caught with a knife meant two years added to your sentence, no exceptions. Last thing in the world I wanted was more time. But as I walked from the reception area into what's called the general population, I was serenaded by the song the old prisoners sang to the newly arrived. They called it "The Walk":

You been a long time comin' but you're welcome home
Down here in Angola, Looziana, where you get your burden on
Yeah, buddy, you get your burden on . . . it's the murderers' home

An old prisoner took me aside. "Fresh meat," he called me, "take this." He slipped me a twelve-inch knife called a black diamond file. The thing was lethal, and he could see I was hesitant. "Better for them white folks to catch you with it," he said, "than these inmates to catch you without it." I took the knife.

I knew a few of the cats inside: Good Lord the Lifter had two brothers in Angola. Freddy, a friend from parish prison, was also in the general population. Daddy had a cousin, Victor, a bad motherfucker, who was about to get out. Before he did, though, he sent the word out: "Fuck with my blood, and you'll fuck with me." All that helped, but I also knew I had to prove myself. The only way was to strike first. First cat who came on to me got wasted. I attacked him viciously and screamed like a madman, "Fuck with me, and I'll tear your fuckin' eyeballs out!" After that, I was left alone.

Angola was split between the Big Stripe Side and the Trustee Side. Cats in the Big Stripe were in for more than five years; anyone under that, like me, was over on the Trustee Side, where we wore narrow stripes.

CYRIL

Don't ask me why, but I liked that small-striped uniform Charles was wearing. Maybe it represented the ultimate outlaw to me, maybe it symbolized being the baddest of the bad — I'm not sure — but I dug the way it looked.

Charles

The orientation period was rough. When I arrived, segregation was still in full force. Even the bands were strictly segregated. Wasn't until sometime in 1965 that the races could mix. My aim was to move directly into music. I saw music as my salvation and protection, but that didn't happen at first. I had to go through orientation, a process I barely survived.

The Free People were white men — sometimes in uniform, sometimes in street clothes — who we also called captains. They were the bosses over certain pieces of land and were given prisoners to work that land. Angola was spread over twenty thousand acres, so working the land was the main thing. When I arrived, I was told that the Free People could not use the bullwhip on the prisoners. "But don't you niggers forget," one of the captains was quick to say, "we can use our ax handles." Reports of inmates getting their brains bashed in were common. Truth is, I was more afraid of the Free People than of any of the crazy black prisoners. The Free People were basically the descendants of slave owners. They saw us as cattle. Maybe they treated their cattle a little better because cattle didn't threaten their manhood. When you got into the fields, they could fuck you up any way they wanted to. The guards — who are a whole 'nother story — were authorized to shoot you dead if you got within six feet of them. And, believe me, nobody had a yardstick measuring distances. You were at the mercy of merciless men.

The first day was murderously hot. They drove us out to the field on the backs of the cattle trucks and dumped us in a field of cotton. The white boss was on his white horse, right there over your ass. He had two saddlebags — one for his ax handle, the other for his rifle. We're lined up, the boss blows his whistle, and everyone takes off down the row, plucking the cotton and throwing it in the bags. Everyone's scurrying down the row except me. I've never picked cotton before; I don't know how to separate the blossom from the twigs; I don't know shit. So I'm just grabbing and dumping until . . . *WHACK!* The captain nearly cripples me with his ax handle, and I'm down on my knees. "Nigger," he said from high on his horse, "ain't you ever picked cotton?" "No, boss," I answered. "I've never seen no goddamn cotton before."

Didn't think I would make it, didn't think I could learn fast enough to keep the captain from breaking my neck. But a fellow inmate took the time to show me how to do it and, for ninety miserable days, I hung in and got by.

Still hear this work song we sang out in the fields. In Angola we called work "rollin'."

Early in the mornin' by the light of the moon
I eat my breakfast with a rusty spoon
Out to the cane field with the rising sun
Just roll on, buddy, till the day is done
Well, I don't mind rollin' but, O Lord, we gotta roll so long
Make me wish I was a baby in my mother's arms

Angola wasn't state-funded. The joint was supported by the sale of livestock and crops grown right there. The biggest crop was the sugarcane that supported the sugar mill. Cutting cane, which I did, was especially tricky because, with a machete in his hands, an angry inmate would cut you to threads. Happened all the time.

Angola didn't like executing men. Not because Angola gave two shits about your ass but because Angola wanted you out there working the land as long as your body held out. Angola's strange economic structure was also the reason there were no professional guards. They didn't want to spend the money. The guards were actually inmates who, according to prison officials, had the right qualifications. But when I learned what those qualifications were, I grew almost as afraid of the guards as of the bosses.

One morning I was with Freddy. Freddy was a bad boy who, back in parish prison, had brutally beat up these twin brothers. We didn't know the brothers were in Angola until after breakfast, as we were walking out in the yard, the brothers, hiding behind a door, jumped out and tried to knife Freddy. They missed his neck but got his arm. Enraged, Freddy broke loose, ran into the workshop, grabbed a pair of shears used for cutting leather, and pierced one of the brothers through the heart. The brother bled to death, and as Freddy was led away, we were certain he'd be tried for murder and given life.

A month later we were riding out into the fields on the cattle car when we passed by a little shed by the side of the sugar mill. Standing atop the sugar mill was Freddy, a rifle at his hip.

"What the fuck are you doing out here?" I yelled to him.

"When they found out I could murder," he said, "they made me a guard."

I was lucky to have one of my partners in that position. But other inmates weren't so lucky. If one of their murderous enemies was turned into a guard, that inmate's life wasn't worth a dime. It wasn't unusual to be riding on the cattle truck, hear the crack of a shot, and see a prisoner fall dead by your side. I never stopped worrying about the guards' aim. We were all sitting ducks.

Angola would never become a worry-free zone. Life was treacherous. I'd be sitting in the mess hall, trying to swallow the slop they served for dinner, dreaming of getting out of the cotton fields and into the band. Cat called Coca-Cola Black was sitting next to me.

I told him how I was feeling, how good it made me feel to play music, how much I missed that feeling.

"I hear you, bro," said Coca-Cola, a man the size of a refrigerator. "I get that same feeling when I stick a knife in some dude's heart and watch the life leave his eyes. Longer it takes, the more I like it."

This is my dinner companion, I thought to myself. *This is the motherfucker I'm locked up with.*

The Monkey Puzzle

Art

Ellis Marsalis is one of the great jazz pianists to come out of New Orleans. Now he's known as the father of Wynton, Branford, and his other famous sons, but in my day we knew him as a master musician. Back in the sixties, Harold Battiste produced an album on Ellis called *The Monkey Puzzle.* Marshall Smith was on bass, James Black on drums, and Nat Perrilliat on sax. Critics might have been buzzing 'bout John Coltrane up in New York, but 'Trane had come to New Orleans to hear Nat's tone. This was the same Nat who had played raw blues on so many rock 'n' roll records. Nat was another one of those local guys who could negotiate any style you name — and then go out and invent a style of his own.

CYRIL

The Monkey Puzzle was a sacred text of inspired jazz. It was modern jazz interpreted by New Orleans masters. The music was daring and brilliant and as adventuresome as anything being played anywhere. I looked up to those guys as respected elders. As a drummer, James Black was a god to me. *The Monkey Puzzle* was part of All For One, a collective of musicians-only organized by Harold Battiste who produced themselves, recorded themselves, and started their own label. It was an example of the economic self-sufficiency Malcolm X was talking about. Not only were they making beautiful cutting-edge music, they were taking care of business. Didn't matter that labels in New York or L.A. missed the importance of this music. Rather than complain, Harold and Ellis became their own means of production. Their records got out, not only inspiring up-and-coming cats like me but demonstrating that it was no longer necessary to sharecrop for the Man.

Not everyone, though, made it out of the Monkey Puzzle alive. Nat Perrilliat wound up driving a cab. He'd drive down to the levee, where I'd watch him play his sax for what he called "creation." Just wailed into the wind. He said the music biz was too vicious for him. He was another New Orleans genius who died of a broken heart.

Art

All For One was a wonderful idea. They made some pop records and had a hit — Barbara George's "I Know" — but the collective didn't last long. In New Orleans a lot of us had notions of autonomy. Seemed so simple: good cats would get together to make good music and, at the same time, figure out a way to reap the rewards. No one wanted to get screwed. So how did everyone wind up getting screwed anyway? All For One was a moment of idealism that died fast. New Orleans is strange. It's a closed town, a closed shop. It all goes back to one studio and a couple of heavyweights controlling everything. Maybe that's what the Monkey Puzzle is all about — figuring out a way to get free of that control. I know I never figured out the Monkey Puzzle, not for many, many years to come.

Aaron

I didn't stay clean long. Got busted for a little weed the first year I was back from California. That meant I couldn't leave New Orleans. I was stuck in the city that I loved but also the city where opportunity was restricted. Who was going to give me a record deal? Minit was no longer happening. Artie had kept the Hawketts alive, but it wasn't like the old days. Only a few gigs here and there. I went back to riverfronting, loading and unloading and messing up my back; no one told me about bending my knees and using my legs to lift huge weights. I was just biding my time, waiting for the right break, the right band, or the right song. Funny, but when that song came along, I didn't even know it. But Artie did.

CYRIL

Musically, I was gaining confidence. I was playing drums, writing, singing, and hanging with the musical elders. Charles was in Angola, Artie wasn't showing any interest in me, but Aaron was back. Aaron took me to his gigs and the studio whenever he got called to sing. I watched like a hawk, focusing in on Harold

Battiste and George Davis, who were savvy producers. I wanted to learn how to produce, wanted to do it all.

Aaron

I knew Cyril had a gift. He had an enthusiasm — a fiery spirit — and a voice filled with churchy soul. His voice sounds nothing like Artie's or mine. All three of us have different styles. Cyril could do more than sing; he could come up with grooves, lyrics, and melodies. Baby bro was bad.

CYRIL

No one was badder than James Brown. Anyone loving soul music in the sixties loved James Brown. This was the time of "Papa's Got a Brand New Bag" and "I Got You (I Feel Good)," when Brown's band was tighter than tight and his show righter than right. He had the funk, the moves, the pent-up energy of the real-life raw neighborhood. He didn't dodge issues and he didn't dilute jams. He was the godfather and I was a disciple.

Aaron

When I started recording again, I didn't have any model in mind. All my time in prison, all my time in California, all my time down on the docks, folks would say, "Aaron, you got the voice, you got the sound." I admired a lot of the singers out there, but I felt sure about my own thing. I just needed a chance. Music was the only thing that let my heart sing. If it wasn't for music, I don't know what would have happened.

Charles

Music protected me and saved my sanity. Without music, I'm not sure I would have gotten through Angola. Music made the difference.

When I was running the streets as a junkie and a thief, I never could concentrate on music the way I wanted. I skated by but always desired a deeper theoretical foundation. In Angola I was able to give myself that foundation and focus on learning. After the ordeal of working the fields, I was finally allowed to play in a band. That changed everything.

In 1964, when segregation was still in force, Angola had three black bands. The best was the Knicknacks, which had included my old buddy James Booker and drummer James Black — both geniuses. The Knicknacks weren't just good, they were great. They could play everything from steamy r&b to cutting-edge bop, and all stops in between. Because the Knicknacks brought diversion and pleasure, the prisoners wouldn't let anyone fuck with us. We played holiday parties for the general population as well as affairs for the administrators and Free People. Everyone wanted to book the Knicknacks. When I joined, the only tenor sax was being played by a cat named Noise, so I took up alto, which expanded my range. After months of intense work, I became a music teacher as well as director of the Knicknacks. We were cooking with gas. Given the chance, the Knicknacks could have competed with any band of that era — Cannonball Adderley, Horace Silver, Art Blakey, even Miles. We had one cat, Bug Juice, doing "Drown in My Own

Tears" sadder than Ray Charles and another singer singing "I Pity the Fool" bluer than Bobby Bland.

A white country-and-western band included a number of Ku Klux Klanners. Russell Sweets, a white bebop trumpet player, was in that band but was no redneck. He hated hillbilly music and would sneak over to jam with us. The Free People, detesting any black-white mix, threw him in the dungeon. But a week later Sweets was back, blowing "Ornithology." "It feels so good to play these Bird tunes," said Sweets, "it's worth a day in the dungeon."

When integration came in 1965, I expanded our repertoire and used a white guy, a comic-showman, to emcee, giving us a Vegas vibe that everyone dug. I also started writing charts of Broadway show tunes. To add sugar and spice, I had a real girl from the street, who sang like Billie Holiday, sing "Strange Fruit," followed by Sabu, another real girl, an exotic dancer with more moves than Gypsy Rose Lee.

Real girls were female impersonators, drag queens who had worked that way on the outside. In the bizarre homohierarchy of prison, real girls were respected. In contrast, gal boys were straight guys turned out in prison by force or trickery. They became the bitches of prisoners-predators, guys who knew they were never getting out and fixated on getting the only person-to-person sex possible.

The Knicknacks recruited a brilliant piano player, but because he was lean and muscular, we worried he'd be turned into someone's gal boy and lost to the band. This guy had no business being in Angola. He was convicted of raping a white woman, in spite of a hundred witnesses placing him at the church organ at the time of the crime. Given his good looks and innocent air, we knew he wouldn't last long. We were able to convince one especially brutal predator to leave him alone. "All right," said the aggressor, "but if another cat turns him into his bitch, I'm holding you motherfuckers responsible." Our man escaped that trap but fell into another. A more subtle predator started helping him out in the fields, treating him like a big brother until brotherly love turned sexual. Our man was seduced. I never stopped looking over my shoulder for the first predator, but fortunately he hooked up with another honey.

The erotic wars were lethal. I saw guys knock out prospective gal boys and fuck them when they were unconscious, thus staking their claim. But the violence could backfire. I also saw gal boys, desperate to get their nuts back, take those big black diamond files and stab their tormentors in the jugular.

I stayed clean during my years in Angola, not because there were rehab programs — there were absolutely none — but because I feared the drug trade. Just as I knew never to be or steal a gal boy, I also knew dealing dope was deadly. A dealer would rather plant a meat cleaver in your skull than argue over payment. Commercial transactions of any kind were fraught with peril. Gambling was another distinct danger. Coca-Cola Black won a two-cent scrip — the lowest denomination of prison money — from a man in a dice game. The man protested. Black cut his throat. "I already got three life sentences and ninety-nine years," said Coca-Cola as his adversary bled to death. "Why should I give a fuck about another life?"

I didn't argue with his logic.

Tell It Like It Is

Aaron

For years people had been saying it would happen — dudes down on the docks, cats in prison, anyone who heard me singing on the street or in the neighborhood clubs. "You gonna have a smash," they'd say. "You got the voice people love listening to." I believed them, but when it happened, I wasn't ready. Musically, I'd been preparing since I was a kid. But mentally . . . forget it. Didn't know what it meant to have a national hit. Had no earthly idea what it would do to my head.

I didn't have a record deal. I was out there working construction and digging ditches when George Davis told me he was starting a new label called Par-Lo. Red Tyler, the sax man, was part of the operation. Both Red and George were boss musicians, plus they were from the Calliope projects. I liked how we came from the same place, and I liked some of the songs George had been writing with Lee Diamond, who went all the way back to the days of Shirley and Lee and Smiley Lewis. These cats were living legends of local r&b. They had that good energy that comes when you start up a new business. They also had the backing of a businessman who seemed to know what he was doing.

Art

Aaron was pumped. He told me how George and them were cutting some tunes on him for this new label Par-Lo, and I hoped for the best. Maybe this time someone could figure out how to make hits *and* get paid. Maybe these guys could solve the Monkey Puzzle.

CYRIL

Aaron took me along, and I was thrilled. Everything was cut at Cosimo's, a place with more history than Sun Studios in Memphis. The vibe was beautiful. Willie Tee was on that session. Willie is another Calliope product, one of the funkiest keyboardists in the city, not to mention a dynamite writer and arranger. Willie, Deacon Jones, and I sang background.

This was 1966; I was seventeen and in my glory — hanging with my heroes, the main one being brother Aaron.

Aaron

The material was cool. George wrote the arrangements. Might remind some people of what Smokey Robinson was doing at Motown, but I could hear how to put in my own touch. I wrote a tune called "Jailhouse" — that's the early version of "Angola

Bound" I mentioned before — a story about someone like me or Charlie who had to face time. "Jailhouse" was twelve-bar blues with a different twist, but the rest of the stuff was highly romantic. I liked that.

Just before one of the sessions, Lee Diamond showed me this one song, "Tell It Like It Is." Went over it once or twice, then nailed it in a couple of takes. Didn't think much about it. I was actually higher on "She Took You for a Ride," a song with a grittier groove. This was the era of gritty grooves. Right there in New Orleans, Robert Parker had a coast-to-coast smash with "Barefootin'" — a straight-up dance thing — and I figured a ballad wouldn't fly. I wanted to run with "She Took You for a Ride." Thank God I listened to Artie.

Art

I heard "Tell It Like It Is" and I told Aaron, I said, "Bro, this is the shit right here. This is the serious shit."

CYRIL

The song fit the times. Sure, it was a haunting love song sung with all of Aaron's heartbreaking sincerity. But it also had this other message: "Tell It Like It Is" was an attitude. We wanted to express what was really on our minds, not just about romance but about the racial and political situation of our fucked-up country. This was the sixties.

Aaron

The song took off like a rocket. Before I knew it, it was selling forty thousand copies a week. They were playing it on the radio every five minutes. Folks were stopping me, saying, "Congratulations, Aaron, you're a rich man." Rich? I still hadn't seen a dime. Just as the song was taking off and hitting all over the country, Par-Lo was falling apart. I wasn't privy to the details, but I can tell you that no royalty checks were coming my way. Par-Lo's first shot out of the box — "Tell It Like It Is" — was a smash, but the label was in chaos.

CYRIL

It was a mess. What looked like a fantastic opportunity turned bleak and ugly. When "Tell" hit, George Davis started working on a follow-up. I had some lyrics that he encouraged me to complete. "Go on, little brother," he urged. That felt great. I was honored to be collaborating with the great George Davis. We put together three songs, Aaron sang them all, but when the album came out, they stripped off the vocals and left them as instrumentals. There went my writing credits. George and I were always cool, but George was fighting with one of Aaron's managers.

Aaron

Managers were coming at me from every direction. At least cats calling themselves managers. To me, they were wolves looking to chew off a piece of my throat. The more people tried to help, the worse it got. My mind was a traffic jam. I was still doing dope. I wasn't shooting, I was chipping, but I was flirting. And flirting with heroin is flirting with the devil. Before long, my ass would be hooked again. Meanwhile, the few dollars that Par-Lo was throwing at me wouldn't do. No one could really get any money for me until Joe Jones came along. Joe was famous in New Orleans for singing "You Talk Too Much" and managing the Dixie Cups, who had a recent hit with "Chapel of Love." Joe got me a few thousand dollars from Par-Lo that I used to buy my father a car. At the time, Daddy was also working as a counselor for a boys' home.

CYRIL

Big Arthur had a couple of strokes due to high blood pressure. That scared us, but Daddy being Daddy, he came back strong. He lost weight, his speech was a little slurred, yet he went to work anyway, moving furniture and hanging out at the stand on St. Ann's where he'd moonlight a maroon-and-white Ed's cab. He also got deeper into helping kids by volunteering at Millinger's Boys' Home, the same shelter where Louis Armstrong had been sent as a kid. The boys looked up to Big Arthur like a daddy. Watching them watching him, I remembered a big moment of my own childhood:

I had decided to skip school and go over to Soto's grocery. Got me a cookie and cold drink and was sitting on a little wooden bench in front of the store when Daddy happened to pull up in his cab. Naturally I got scared. "Get in," he said. I wondered if he was gonna whip me. After we drove around a few minutes, I was no longer nervous. Daddy was calm. Sitting shotgun next to him, I felt safe. His powerful presence always made me feel safe. "Just like my job is to drive a cab," he said, "your job is to go to school." Rather than scold, he explained.

Years later Daddy walked into the kitchen to find me sitting on the floor writing something on a beat-up four-string guitar. My lyrics were spread out on the floor. When I told him what I was doing, he looked over the stuff and started to nod his head approvingly. He asked me to play something on guitar. When I was through, he smiled. His smile said everything.

So I understood why he was so loved down at the boys' home. He had this way of talking to rabble-rousers — me included — that wasn't patronizing or haughty. He understood the restless soul. He'd calm you, not by threatening or lecturing but by listening with his heart. He taught by example, and his example was quiet strength.

Aaron

I was quietly going a little nuts, watching "Tell It Like It Is" take off all across the country while I was twiddling my thumbs in New Orleans. In the long run, the thing with Joe Jones didn't work out, but I gotta say he helped me get it together to go on tour. I needed to work, and I needed to work right away. Joe got me some clothes, a booking agent, and, best of all, Alvin "Shine" Robinson as my guitarist and bandleader. Shine was another local cat who, like James Booker, had all the chops he needed — plus a bag of chips to boot. His "Something You Got" was a big hit in 1964, and now, two years later, he was happy to back me on my tour. Me and Shine had more than music in common; we also had the get-high habit.

Before I left, I was nervous. This was my first big-time tour as a solo artist, going all over the country and into Canada as well. I wanted Artie out there with me. He agreed and came along as piano player and manager.

Art

Man, I didn't know anything about being a manager, but I did know to watch Aaron's back. That was my real job. The business side was always murky. I don't know whose fault it was, but Aaron never got paid as a solo artist for "Tell It Like It Is," only as a band member. It soon became clear that royalties were never going to be right, and the only way to cash in was to tour, long and hard, while the song was still climbing the charts.

Aaron

It was a heavy tour. Soul music was sizzling hot. I watched Otis Redding from the wings. He had his "Mr. Pitiful," his "Try a Little Tenderness," his "Satisfaction." He was a beautiful cat with a down-home delivery that gave me goose bumps. The Drifters would come out and croon "Under the Broadwalk" and "Up on the Roof" and "On Broadway." The tour was moving toward New York, heading for the Apollo. On the way we played the Regal in Chicago, where I watched Little Stevie Wonder go through his "Fingertips" and "Uptight (Everything's Alright)." He was this genius child who didn't want any help getting around. Onstage he got around those songs in a way that made me feel better than the best dope in Harlem. At the Uptown in Philly and the Howard in D.C., I shared the stage with the Manhattans. The Manhattans were my boys. They turned it out, blending up their "Baby I Need You" and "Follow Your Heart." I followed the Falcons on a couple of shows. They were singing "I Found a Love," although their former lead singer Wilson Pickett had found himself more money singing solo. The Flamingos were also somewhere in the mix. It'd been a while since "I Only Have Eyes for You" was a hit, but their version still warmed my soul.

There were big venues and little venues, three gigs in Ohio where I had to take one of those six-seater planes. Dropping through the clouds, I was scared shitless. A year later, when Otis Redding went down in a private plane in Wisconsin, I couldn't help but think how that could have been me. I still miss Otis. We were all scared of missing gigs, so we kept on keeping on, riding through snowstorms, sliding over ice, finally landing in New York City, where Shine Robinson lived. Shine knew where the good stuff was. So while the opening acts went on, Shine and I were running the streets of Harlem. By then I was second-headlining. Billy Stewart, who had that stutter style, was first, his "Summertime" all the rage. Shine and I would score, shoot, and arrive backstage just as they were saying my name. Without a second's thought, I'd slide out there and start telling it like it is. This was Christmas 1966. By March of the next year "Tell" would cross over from the black to the white charts and become the number two song in the country. Only the Monkees' "I'm a Believer" kept it from number one.

I remember one time when my set was over, a New York deejay, who'd been checking me from the wings, said, "Hey, man, I'm amazed how you sing it *exactly* like the record." Well, what did he expect? "Most of these singers," he said, "are products of the studio. When they're onstage, all they can do is fake it. You're no fake." I guess the Apollo audience, supposedly the world's toughest, felt the same way he did, 'cause after my first week I was held over for two more.

Artie and I had a few crazy adventures with a few crazy women, but that goes with the territory. The territory was expanding. We were heading up the East Coast all the way into Canada, gigging at dozens of spots along the way. Nothing was going to stop us. But something did — a lightning bolt out of the blue.

When the news came, Artie and I were in Montreal. The news stopped us cold, and suddenly nothing seemed to matter — not the big-time tour, not the hit record. Nothing.

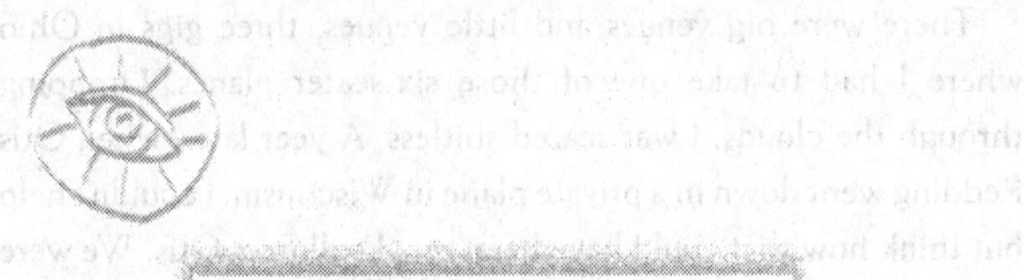

Big Arthur

CYRIL

My father and I were getting closer. This was a time when I had started dibbling and dabbling with heroin. I wasn't a full-fledged junkie but was headed in that direction. Daddy knew what was happening. He'd take me with him to shoot pool. Rather than warn me about the dangers of dope — knowing that would fall on deaf ears — he asked me about my music. Me and Zig had started a little band, and he asked us to play for his kids at Millinger's Boys' Home. I loved doing that. I loved doing anything that made him proud of me.

I was living at home, the only son still in the city. Aaron and Artie had gone off on tour, and Charles was in Angola. I was enjoying some of the attention I had long sought from my parents. I was still in school, but barely. The streets were calling me; music was calling me.

I was up in my bedroom on Valence one night at the end of

March when I heard Mommee call his name, her voice filled with alarm. *"Arthur!"* I raced down to their bedroom and saw him on the floor next to his bed. His breathing was shallow and getting shallower by the minute. He was as white as a ghost. Panicked, Mommee and I tried picking him up and putting him on the bed. At two hundred pounds, he was difficult to move. By the time we got him up there, his breathing had stopped. Mommee started crying hysterically. I was holding her, not knowing what to do or say. The ambulance arrived, the medics ran to his side. By then he was gone. Out came the body bag. I'd never seen one before. I watched them angle him into the bag. I heard the sound of the zipper when they zipped him up. It felt so cold. I felt dizzy, assaulted by thoughts of my dad: how he whistled his bebop tunes and Billy Eckstine ballads; how, when I got sick from eating our neighbor's contaminated plums, he nursed me, put his arm around me, let me sit between him and Mommee, making all my insecurities and fears go away; how he was the strongest man in the world; how he would never die.

Aaron

Artie and I flew back from Canada, not saying a word. But I was thinking, *He can't be dead; he is only fifty; he is too young, too tough to die.*

Art

His heart exploded, the heart we thought would never give out, the same heart that gave all of us so much love. I sat there on the plane with my private thoughts, remembering how he had bounced back after his stroke and his bout with a bloody colon. He wanted to be a seaman again, but he couldn't pass the physical, so he worked for the moving van company and the cab company and even drove a tow truck for Bone Ford. And then there were the kids from the boys' home.

Aaron

The funeral was at Trinity Methodist, right there on Valence. The people crying the most — even more than his aunts Cat and Espy and his brother-in-law Jolly, even more than his sons and his daughters, Athelgra and Cookie, maybe even more than Mommee herself — were those boys from Millinger's, his adopted sons. They were weeping like they'd lost their own daddy. They couldn't be consoled.

Charles

I got a leave from Angola to go to the funeral. By then I'd been in three years, so being on the outside was strange, especially in the harsh light of my father's death. I had seen him on visiting days, but it hurt that I'd been so far away during the last years of his life. It also hurt to come home in handcuffs.

Art

We were in our folks' house on Valence, with all our relatives and friends paying last respects, when Charles came in wearing cuffs. A dude was with him, a white guy from the prison. Out of respect to our father, we thought the dude should take off our brother's cuffs. The dude really pissed us off.

Aaron

Charlie did something I'll never forget: he told us to back off, explaining that the white man was only doing his duty. Mommee followed Charles's lead and offered the man something to eat. She asked him to join us. Noticing his demeanor, I saw that this was probably the first time he'd ever been in a black home. I also saw he was old enough to be someone's grandfather — and surely was. I started seeing him as a human being, not a symbol. As he warmed up to us, he took off Charlie's cuffs and even let Charlie go upstairs to be alone with his lady.

Charles

The guy was scared. He was intimidated by all these black people. The farthest he'd been from Angola was Baton Rouge, and here he was in the thick of the New Orleans ghetto. I tried to put him at ease. I said, "Look, man, I have no interest in escaping and being hunted down like an animal." He started to trust me and see what our family was really like. He let me see Lily for a little while, and that was wonderful. In the end he bonded with my family. It was something of a small miracle, a moment of warmth during a time of grief.

Art

During those days after Daddy's death, I stayed close to Uncle Jolly. He suffered the loss as much as any of us. He lost a brother. Meanwhile, me and my brothers, who had always revered our uncle, would cling to him even closer. Jolly could never take Daddy's place — no one could — but his relationship with the brothers, as our mentor and model, grew tighter.

Charles

Twisting through the hills, driving back to Angola, the dude guarding me drove in silence. The April rains had come to the Louisiana countryside. The downpour was intense, the afternoon sky a dark, angry gray. I considered my future: with time off for good behavior, I'd be getting out in a few months. I couldn't be sure, but I was hopeful that the long storm was about to pass.

"You know something," the guy finally said as rain pounded against the windshield. "You have a beautiful family back there."

"Thank you."

"And your father . . . well, he must have been a helluva guy."

"He was," I said, thinking of all the times Big Arthur came through for me, came through for all of us.

Art

The thing that hurt me most was that rocking chair. That goddamn green rocking chair. It sat out there on my parents' porch, waiting for Daddy. That was his retirement chair, where he wanted to sit and watch the world go by. By then he was the unofficial mayor of Valence, the most respected cat in the ward. I'd fantasize about the neighbors coming by and paying their respects as Daddy turned sixty, then sixty-five, then seventy, a strong and loving old man mellowing with age.

I'd see that chair during the day, and I'd see that chair in my dreams. A breeze rocked it back and forth. It was always empty. It still is.

Charles

I felt empty inside. Despite knowing I was getting out, that last stretch of time in Angola wasn't easy. I mourned for my father, mourned for the loss of my own family. I was cut off from my daughters. Ann brought our baby son, Carlos, to visit, but sometimes visits can make the pain worse. I hid from the pain in my music, teaching other inmates three nights a week. I made a diligent study of theory books, finally achieving the musical education I had long sought. I'd achieved a solid level of competence by playing on the road, but only at Angola did I find the patience to delve deeply into the complexities of chords, harmonics, and arrangements. I also started sketching seriously, moving from charcoals to pastels and oils. Painting became another outlet for exorcising my demons. I drew skulls and bones, snakes and dragons, luscious flowers and beautiful women, heroin needles, weeping moons, smiling suns. Louisiana State University set up a great book club, which was a godsend. There were only a few of us in there — a survey showed 80 percent of inmates *and* Free People during my time at Angola were illiterate — but the discussions were stimulating. I devoured dozens of books — Jane Austen, Dickens, Shakespeare,

Homer, Plato, Nietzsche, everything from Eldridge Cleaver's *Soul on Ice* to *The Life and Times of Frederick Douglass* to Aleister Crowley's *Diary of a Drug Fiend*.

The greatest characters, though, weren't in books; they were sitting across from me in the yard or mess hall. Take Kilowatt, so called because of the electric shock treatments he was forced to take. Kilowatt was a white guy bugged out on speed. Every few weeks he'd flip, so they'd haul him off to the mental hospital in Jackson, where they'd shock him up and send him back. The aftershocks were even worse, his hair frizzed out, his wild eyes bigger than saucers. I remember once he copped some fifty pills of speed. When the Free People heard about his score and were about to bust him, Kilowatt swallowed all fifty pills and, emitting an electrical charge big enough to illuminate Times Square, was bouncing off the walls for weeks.

We were all bouncing off the walls. During my time, I was hit by anxiety attacks; I suffered from claustrophobia. Watching others bang their heads on the bars, though, taught me to accept where I was. My acceptance was far from perfect, but it kept me from madness. It was enough to compare my mental state to some of the inmates. Such comparisons were sobering.

Take Joseph the Voodoo Man. The Free People didn't fuck with Joseph because Joseph would put a spell on your ass. He'd shit in bags and shake the shit bags at anyone who came near him. He was a jeffer — a con artist — but his cons were carried out with such flair that he never had to work. Same went for Bo, who displayed a different style of jeffing. Bo was a rape artist who, when murderers bragged of their great murders, bragged of his great rapes. In front of the Free People, though, his bragging turned obsequious. He became an Uncle Tom, but a Tom of such dramatic design that I considered his tomming a form of theater. Consider Bo's relationship with one old gray-haired guard who was an especially vicious son of a bitch. We called him the Ice Man because he'd pour ice on a drowning man; he'd just as soon kill you as look at you. Well, when the Ice Man approached Bo, Bo would fall to his knees and cry out, "You the boss, the only boss, the high and mighty boss, the boss we loves best, the boss who loves us, dear Jesus, thank you for giving us this boss, Lord Jesus, protect him from harm, thank you, Jesus, thank you for the boss man . . ." And on he went for half an hour, delivering his spellbinding performance with such warmth that even the murderous Ice Man started to melt.

Because Bo knew he was never getting out, he found a way to cope. I knew I was getting out, so my attitude was different. For example, when the big buck came up, I didn't participate. A buck is a strike, and in Angola strikes are futile. I heard the word come down at harvesttime, when the prison's financial solvency was on the line — "We ain't cutting no more cane. We bucking." The inmates' issues were always the same and always legitimate — the illegitimate conditions, the rancid food, the rat-infested cells, the subhuman work demands, the absence of any semblance of rehab programs. I knew this, but I also knew that I wanted out. Anything that could hurt my early exit was to be avoided.

On the morning of the big buck, I went about business as usual. I was on my way to the school building, where I intended to study.

"You ain't going nowhere," said the Free Man guarding my cell block. "There's a buck."

"But I ain't bucking."

"Don't matter. This gate's locked."

Went back to my cell and watched it all happen. Didn't take long. Here come the jeeps and the trucks, the dogs and the fuckin' state troopers. The buckers, those refusing to cut cane, were beaten to a pulp. One dude had his skull bashed in with a baseball bat, his brain matter splattered against the wall. I saw some pitiful shit. One insane inmate, excited by the buck but not understanding what was really happening, came running out of the hospital compound. This man was mentally incompetent, but the Free People saw him as a target. As he ran across the yard wearing nothing but an oversized hospital gown flapping in the wind, the machine guns took aim and fired, bullets kicking up dirt around his feet. Doing a wild ballet, he danced around the fire. The Lord had to be running with his ass, because he made it across in one piece. When he rolled himself up into a ball and started shaking uncontrollably, the guards finally realized he was a nut, not a danger. I saw how his gown was shredded by bullets, yet his body was untouched. His improbable scamper across the yard had a strangely sobering effect. Suddenly everyone was quiet — the buckers, the riot police, even the barking dogs. The first phase was over, but the buckers still refused to cut cane.

The second phase was marked by the inmates' demand to speak to the governor. Demand denied. "The governor ain't coming," said the Free People. "The governor don't give a fuck, and neither does the warden. Matter of fact, since you're bucking, we Free People intend to kick up a little buck of our own. We don't wanna work, so we're locking you up in your cell blocks. We ain't opening the fuckin' gates to the yard for anyone. And the mess hall is closed 'cause the mess hall workers are saying, 'Since everyone's bucking, we're bucking, too.' " I looked in my locker and saw a little bread, some Spam, peanut butter, and Kool-Aid. Day one was rough; day two rougher; by the third day, we were starving, and making matters worse, the Free People turned up the heat by turning off the water. Couldn't flush the toilets, couldn't wash, couldn't take a shower. On the fourth day, the buckers caved. "Okay, boss," they said, "we ready to go back to work."

Aaron

I wasn't ready to go back on the road after my dad's death, but I did. "Tell It Like It Is" was still happening. Man, that song had a long life. Today, more than thirty years later, folks who come to our shows still get mad if I don't sing it. So I sang it and sang it and sang it some more. I'd send money back to Joel in New Orleans. I called when I could. But I could feel myself wandering off into another fog. Artie sensed that as well, so he went home. I couldn't blame him. I was just out there, looking to get high.

Art

I liked helping out Aaron, but I've always had my own musical ideas. After the "Tell" tour fizzled out, I felt it was time to put those ideas into action. I wanted to take charge of my own life and make the kind of music I wanted to make. And I wanted to make it funky.

Art Neville and the Neville Sounds

CYRIL

As a performer, I really knew only one song — James Brown's "Please, Please, Please." Once, while still in high school, I played in a band with Snooks Eaglin, the blind guitarist who was as good as any who's ever lived. Snooks could sing and play all the way from deep-bayou blues to cutting-edge street soul. Just to fuck with him, cats would untune his guitar minutes before he went onstage. But before five bars had passed, Snooks had his guitar back in tune and was rocking harder than the whole band put together. I didn't know anything about keys, so when it was time for me to sing "Please, Please, Please," I'd go over to Snooks and sing the first note in his ear. That's all he had to hear. He made the rest right for me. After months of singing that song, people started comparing me with the Godfather himself, heady stuff for a teenager on the verge of quitting high school and following my brothers into a life of music.

Aaron

At the tail end of the "Tell" tour, my life got strange. Well into 1967 the song was still superpopular, especially down South. So without Artie, I traveled down through the Carolinas, working clubs all the way to Florida. Turned out I was in big demand in Tampa, Clearwater, and Miami. I was deep into my drugs when I hooked up with a white act called Johnny and Joe Ford and the Better Ideas. (Back then the ad slogan was "Ford has a better idea.") The Fords were hip. They sang Otis Redding and let me stay at their house. Florida turned into a long, heavy hang. Latimore, the smooth soul singer, was down there, and Jimi Hendrix came through and sat in with me and the Fords. Hendrix was stretching out from straight r&b into his psychedelic shit. I stayed for another month and moved into a motel filled with vaudeville troupers, elderly black entertainers looking to chill out. The vibe was kicked-back and cool. Every day I'd sit by the pool and bullshit with a retired army officer and his wife, nice proper people. I had a cat in Harlem copping me smack and mailing it to Miami, so I was okay — until the packages stopped arriving. Suddenly life became hell. I didn't know where to score and, going through my jones, grew desperately sick. I went through the sweats, tearing off sheets and ripping up the mattress. The old motel janitor saw that I was hurting. I saw pity in his eyes and said, "Hey, man, do you have any fucking idea who's holding around here?"

"You been looking at him every day," he explained.

"Who you talking about?" I had to know.

"The soldier. The dude you been talking to. He's the man."

What? He seemed so square. I looked out the window and saw him sitting by the pool. I went out there and asked him straight-up.

"Sure, I got what you need," he said.

"Why didn't you tell me before?"

"You never asked."

"Well, now I'm asking like a motherfucker."

For the rest of my time in Miami, I was cool.

Charles

The day of my release, I thought I was cool. Thought I had learned my lesson, thought I had it all under control. Three and a half years in the joint — including a good spell of hard labor — and I was still in one piece. My mind was clearer than ever, my body fit, my heart filled with gratitude to my family. I was especially grateful to Artie and Aaron for hooking me up with Joe Jones, who signed papers saying I would road-manage the Dixie Cups. That allowed me to be paroled in New York City. Before I was due there, though, I had ten days to see everyone in New Orleans. The first place I hit was Valence Street. I wanted to see my mother.

I was standing on the porch, carrying my sax and a box of letters and drawings, about to knock on the door. My heart was filled with excitement and love. Then, out of the corner of my eye, I spotted our old friend Stagger "Stack" Lee. Just a few doors away, I saw Stack reach under the steps of his house and pull out a package. My body suddenly convulsed with withdrawal symptoms. Hadn't been high in nearly four years, so I knew the symptoms were psychological. But the mind controls the body, and my body was screaming. I turned around and, before going inside to see my mother, went down the street and shot up with Stack. A week later I was headed for New York, dreaming of that potent heroin they sell in Harlem.

Art

By the time Aaron got back from Florida, I had the makings of a new band. "Tell It Like It Is" had run its course, and with the label gone belly-up, there was no real follow-through. I could see that for all his incredible talent, Aaron needed some direction. I figured I needed to take responsibility and put something together. The old Hawketts, born in the fifties, were played out. New energy was needed — and a new name. I called the band Art Neville and the Neville Sounds because I wanted my brothers up there with me. Charles would play with us whenever he was around, but after Angola he anchored himself in New York. That left Aaron and Cyril.

CYRIL

Art Neville and the Neville Sounds was the first time my brothers — especially Artie — took full notice of me as a performer. My James Brown thing was supertight. I was in shape and I was motivated like crazy. I'd been waiting my whole life for a chance to stand onstage and sing with my siblings — and I wasn't about to blow it.

I didn't. I did splits, I did slides, I rolled over backward, I dove off the goddamn stage, I went nuts.

Aaron

Cyril showed us parts of himself we'd never seen before. We always knew he was good, but up there with Art Neville and the Neville Sounds, he wasn't just good, he was fuckin' great. He turned into Mr. Soul.

Art

Cyril surprised us. He was more than a voice or a drummer. He was a serious front man, the kind of performer who can ignite an audience.

CYRIL

Nineteen sixty-seven was a hell of a year for soul music. Aretha busted out with "Respect"; Stevie was screaming "I Was Made to Love Her"; Wilson Pickett was tearing up "Funky Broadway"; Jackie Wilson had "Higher and Higher"; Sam and Dave did "Soul Man"; and James Brown worked up a "Cold Sweat." Combine that with the political fever of the day, and brother, the thermometer down in New Orleans couldn't climb no higher.

The big bread for bands was in the French Quarter, where tourists spread the money around. But black patrons still weren't allowed in those clubs, and black bands, aside from traditional jazz, were seldom booked. Our territory remained Uptown. Art Neville and the Neville Sounds worked in a club close to the Thirteenth Ward, the Nite Cap on the corner of Louisiana and Carondelet, where the clientele was strictly sisters and brothers. The club was only about twenty blocks from Valence, and sometimes Aaron and I would walk to work.

From the jump, the band was smoking. This was the first year of the New Orleans Saints, and the players came out to party, building up our buzz. Within a month or two, word got out — Art Neville and the Neville Sounds were the shit.

Art

Gary Brown was our saxman. Gary was a bad boy. I mean, he'd walk the bar blowing "Soul Serenade," giving anyone — King Curtis, Junior Walker, you name 'em — a run for his money. By the end of the night, his sax would be stuffed with bills.

CYRIL

Got to the point where I was picking up a hundred dollars a night off the floor from folks throwing money at me. By then I'd quit high school and was making more money off tips than my brothers. I started sporting custom-made pants and shirts and hats with superbad brims like Jolly wore. I went to the same Jewish merchants on Magazine Street where my uncle and father had shopped. Those were the guys who'd give you a break on the price and understood our style. I had to be sharp.

Musically, I'd come alive. All the cats were saying, "Watch out, Artie, don't let him learn piano, or he'll be taking your gig." But the great thing was that although Art was the leader, the gig belonged to all of us. When Aaron sang "Tell It Like It Is," the place exploded. We were the most explosive thing happening in the city.

Art

In the beginning, the personnel shifted. At one point Smokey Johnson, another New Orleans monster musician, sat in on drums. But after a few months, the lineup stabilized. The front line was me and my brothers plus Gary Brown. Then the rhythm section caught fire. Besides myself, I had three cats I knew from around town, all a generation younger than me. Drummer Joseph Modeliste — called Zig, or Zigaboo — was Cyril's buddy from the 'hood who'd hung around the Hawketts, learning whatever he could. He learned lots. George Porter Jr., Zig's cousin, was originally playing guitar when I suggested he switch to bass. His funk feel came out better on bass. Leo Nocentelli came from downtown, and of all the wicked young guitarists around town, he was wickedest. Meanwhile, I'd convinced the Nite Cap owner to pop for a Hammond B3 organ, meaning I could dip deep into my Bill Doggett and Booker T. bag. With George, Zig, and Leo prodding me on, with Gary blowing hard, with Cyril's congas and bongos, and with Aaron's sweet harmonies, the Neville Sounds were soaring. Night after night, month after month, the crowds got bigger as the grooves got grittier. The walls of the joint were wet with sweat. My dream band was taking off.

Rip Van Winkle

Charles

Imagine this: Three and a half years in Angola, where the operating mode is mistrust and murder, where fear runs rampant and hatred among men — not to mention hatred between the races — is so commonplace that you forget the world runs on anything but smoldering resentment and vicious anger. Then one day I leave that world and suddenly find myself in Central Park in New York City on a summer day with clear blue skies and puffy white clouds and frolicking white girls in granny dresses and braless halters offering me free weed and free love. I'm in the midst of a goddamn love-in.

Was I dreaming?

No, I'd just been locked away in one world and, when I woke up and was let out, entered another. Moving from the world of pain to the world of pleasure shocked my system. I was a dude who originally got five years hard labor for two joints. Now two hippies —

his hair longer than hers — were passing me a joint and saying, "Take as much as you like, man. We love you." After a toke or two, I loved them, too. Fact is, I loved all hippies. What wasn't to love? They loved black music, they loved black people, and they loved good dope. Like me, they were rebelling against a system they found intolerable; like me, they were searching for a spiritual connection to the universe. If such a connection was aided by drugs — as the accepted advanced wisdom of the day was saying — so much the better. Besides, the hippies were gentle, a quality I had sorely missed behind the bars of cold-blooded Angola. In Angola friction led to killing. In Central Park the hippies were killing me with kindness. Instead of bland prison uniforms of oppression and shame, I now saw a universe of vibrant color, a psychedelic rainbow of free expression.

For a week or so, I helped out the Dixie Cups. But that was just a temporary job set up by Joe Jones to legitimize my parole. I moved into the Bryant Hotel at Fifty-fourth and Broadway, by the Ed Sullivan Theater, wondering where I was going to find work. I had money for one week's rent, and no more. Enter Honey Boy.

Charles "Honey Boy" Otis was a drummer and patron saint of New Orleans musicians. He'd been with everyone from Fats to Fess and always kept track of his homeboys. Now Honey was playing with John Hammond Jr., the guitarist-singer who'd begun his career by celebrating authentic Delta blues. John had fallen in love with the rural roots music of the South and played with authentic attitude that brought Robert Johnson to mind. He was white, but you'd never know it by his sound and style. He hired me on the spot.

The gig was at the Gaslight Café down on MacDougal Street in the Village, where the burgeoning hippie culture and old folk music scene met. The mostly white crowds were young and appreciative. That knocked me out — the notion that white kids were loving the blues. A blues renaissance, supported chiefly by whites, was under way. Even my old boss, B. B. King, was crossing over to an audience of hippies and college kids who, following the lead of their heroes like John Lennon and Eric Clapton, were discovering the original sources of rock 'n' roll.

Fueling the musical fires, Jimi Hendrix was also playing on MacDougal, right across the street. I'd known Hendrix from his Little Richard days. Seemed like a thousand years ago that he was strumming while Richard was shouting "Tutti Frutti." This, though, was the new Jimi, the Jimi of "Hey Joe" and "Are You Experienced?" The new Jimi reminded me of Coltrane, busting boundaries and breaking through to higher levels of technical and emotional expression. I loved it when he came over and sat in with us. To hear Jimi jamming with John, you understood that, for all his pyrotechnical genius, Hendrix's rock-solid foundation was blues-based.

The Hammond gig died out after a month or two, bringing me back to ground zero. Prospects were dim. My days consisted of walking around Central Park; nights were spent practicing in my little room. This went on for weeks, and just as I was down to my last buck, fate knocked on the door. When I opened it, a pretty white woman was standing there.

"Heard you playing," she said. "You sound good. You looking for work?"

"Always."

"Well, my brother's a drummer in a band looking for an alto player."

"Whose band?"

"Tony Ferrar. Ever hear of the Band of Gold?"

"Afraid not."

"They're white guys playing soul music. Are you interested?"

"Very. Just show me the way."

The way led to the Village, back to MacDougal, to a club called the Eighth Wonder, where my life in New York City would take another couple of unexpected turns.

CYRIL

The thing that happened to Art Neville and the Neville Sounds was very unexpected and, to my mind, very unfortunate. It hurt me then, and it still hurts now.

AARON

Art had to do what he had to do. It was a business decision. I understood completely. No hard feelings. If anything, what happened probably brought me and Cyril closer together.

ART

Wasn't anything I planned out. The truth is that it came out of the music — naturally. It was spontaneous combustion, this thing between me, Leo, Zig, and George. There was so much funky feeling in that rhythm section, so many free-flowing ideas, that the hookup was inevitable. The catalyst was an offer I couldn't refuse. The Ivanhoe, a Bourbon Street club in the Quarter, needed a small combo to perform on a small bandstand, and the owner made it clear — there wasn't room for more than four musicians. Used to be called the Ivanhoe Piano Bar when it was all choked up with the suit-and-tie set. The musical requirement was something sophisticated but something different. With all that in mind, my move was clear. I'd go over to the Ivanhoe with my rhythm section. By then the unit was tight. The Neville Sounds lost two Nevilles but gained new momentum. Even though the contributions of Aaron and Cyril and Gary Brown were tremendous, losing their powerful voices meant all focus on the funk. Rhythm became everything. Because I'm a percussive keyboardist, and because Zig and Leo and George are so inventive rhythmically, the groove became king. As opposed to playing songs, we were flat-out grooving, vamping on beats that could go on for an hour. Left to their own devices, the boys might go into Miles Davis or Wes Montgomery. But I had to have it simpler than that. My job was to get down and stay down. Ain't nothing like low-down grooves to get folks dancing. So we stayed low-down, and the Ivanhoe stayed packed.

Aaron

We had a captive audience at the Nite Cap that we wanted to keep. Me and Cyril also wanted to keep Gary Brown, who was the blowingest motherfucker around. So with Sam Henry on piano, Bull Dog Bonnie on drums, and Richard Amos on bass, we started the Soul Machine. Maybe 'cause we had something to prove, or maybe 'cause the chemistry was so strong — whatever the reason, the Soul Machine was a monster. We kicked ass and took numbers. We were probably the best cover band in the world; we wore out those soul hits — "Mustang Sally," "I Heard It Through the Grapevine," "Gypsy Woman," "I Want to Take You Higher." We were looking to get high between sets and might be gone an hour and a half hunting down drugs. But the crowds loved us, and they'd wait till we got back, and believe me, bro, we made it worth their wait.

CYRIL

It took a while, but I got over being excluded from Artie's new band. The Soul Machine helped divert my anger. The Soul Machine cranked on for years. It was a serious band with a serious snap. And more than soul, we did shit by Chicago and Three Dog Night, we busted up the Beatles, and broke down the Doors. When we switched from the Nite Cap to the Desert Sand, on Clairborne and Esplanade in the Seventh Ward, we started singing "Light My Fire" so strong the owner made us stop 'cause folks were waving lit matches until it looked like the joint would go up in flames. The joint wasn't really made for live music. There wasn't even a bandstand. We just stood in the corner and wailed.

The political times were heavy on our heads. On April 4, 1968, we were in the middle of a set when we heard Martin Luther King had been murdered in Memphis. The news shook me to my core; I felt frozen; I felt ice water washing over my heart, ice water coursing through my veins. My body parts went numb. Nothing made sense except to sing the songs — James Brown and Marvin Gaye songs — with such furious intensity that I somehow made it through the night. In the morning, though, my grief turned to rage.

How could I feel otherwise? Dr. King was about nonviolence, and it was violence that brought him down, a violence that triggered my own violence. By then New Orleans had become a city of infamous racial violence. I responded by becoming more radical. My texts were *Down These Mean Streets* and Huey Newton's *Revolutionary Suicide*. I knew I was living in a war zone. Many of the local cops had come back from 'Nam. You'd hear them say, "You fuckin' niggers are no different than the gooks." They were out for blood.

This was when I met Alfred Rudolph, called Jake, or Jake the

Snake. Before Jake, I traveled alone, without a partner or crew. When he first moved Uptown from the Sixth Ward, I'd see him sitting in front of his house. I'd throw him the power sign and keep on stepping. Then one day we started rapping. Man, it was like finding a long-lost brother. We saw the world the same. We knew we were living through a moment of history that was turning black men into an endangered species. Together, we threw away our combs and grew wild and woolly Afros. I got Jake to stop buying his clothes on Canal Street, where he was putting money in the Establishment's hands, and shop on Magazine Street, where our street uniform became bell-bottom jeans and formfitting jeans jackets. I also hooked him up with my gurus, Akinjiju Ola and Babtunji Ahmed, who hipped us to what J. Edgar Hoover was doing to our cause. We took on African names: I was Umbuku, Jake became Kumbuka. We were affiliated with the Panthers and other groups willing to put their lives on the line. Because of those affiliations, Jake and I became marked men. Certain cops swore they'd get us. Their attitude only reinforced our radicalism. That's one of the reasons drugs became important, as both an escape and an expression of our alienation from a culture intent on killing us.

The killing was real. There were search-and-destroy teams. There were famous cases, even mass murders. I knew one girl, sympathetic to our case, who was murdered in her bathtub. The lady next door to her house heard her pleading for her life. But the cops shot her eyes out and killed her boyfriend and two other people before throwing her son out on the street. The cops were killing with the vengeance of the American army raiding a Vietnamese village. My friend's son described his mother's murder; the presence of a small boy in no way stopped the cops. Another woman, also close to the movement, got over there before the ambulance came, and took pictures. We saw the gruesome photos. I still see them. My insides still jump when I think about it. I wonder where her son is today. Some wounds — call them soul wounds — never heal.

I have a wound on my neck, the result of a throat-slashing from this same crazy period in my life. I see the scar as a symbol not of political struggle but of a struggle so deeply personal it nearly cost me my life. My love life, along with everything else about me, was in turmoil.

Charles

My love life came alive when Sue, my former partner in crime, arrived in New York. With the money I'd been making with Tony Ferrar and the Band of Gold, I was able to buy her a plane ticket and help her out of a jam. She was just getting out of jail in New Orleans and, according to a mutual friend, could not risk staying in the city, not even for a night. Certain police officers had threatened her life. So she went directly from prison to the airport. Before then Sue and I had been just friends and working associates. I admired her mind and her style. She looked soft but was tough as nails. She was also attractive. The two of us, alone in my hotel room in midtown Manhattan, became lovers. She was the first white woman with whom I had sex. In New York the sexual restraint between the races, so oppressive in New Orleans, was lifted. My affair with Sue couldn't be characterized as wildly passionate. It was more a matter of convenience and gratitude; we were friends first, willing to help each other through tricky situations. If we could also satisfy each other sexually, so much the better. Beyond that, I was still feeling the liberation of a man no longer living in the South.

As a kid I'd learned that to merely look at a white woman was a crime punishable by death. The white woman was forbidden fruit.

To finally taste that fruit was a thrill that carried an addiction all its own. My sense of the heat behind interracial sexuality was confirmed when I read Lillian Smith's *Killers of the Dream,* a brilliant analysis written by a white southern woman in the late forties. Smith showed how white women, as much as black men, were imprisoned by sexual stereotyping. White men looked to illicit encounters with black women for uninhibited gratification, while white women were seen as models of nonsexual propriety. The result was a confusion and misunderstanding that injured everyone's essential humanity.

New York opened me to these new ideas. It was there, for example, that I met a prostitute, a white woman, who had sex with white men for money but with black men for pleasure. Her preacher father had warned her that black men were wildly oversexed and to be avoided at any cost. "The first time a black man inadvertently brushed his arm against me," she said, "I came."

Reading theories of social psychology, I remembered my own childhood and the way black women protected black men. It was easier for a black woman to get a decent-paying job in the white world. For many such women, it became a point of pride to protect their men from the South's bitter prejudice. *"My man don't gotta kiss no white man's ass to make a dollar if I can help it."* I heard that statement, in one form or another, from dozens of ladies. For all its understandably good intentions, it's an attitude that contributed to the black man's sense of himself as a gigolo whose roguish ways were unwittingly underwritten by the women who loved him most.

Sue loved to live fast and dangerously, and New York didn't scare her in the least. Neither did Harlem. She had connections up there and got a job at the Club Ho Tai, where a big statue of Buddha with his arms raised to the sky greeted the patrons. We moved into a dingy apartment at 117th and Morningside; Sue adopted three cats and a giant German shepherd to protect her when she took walks. The dog looked like a wolf but was a real pussy. That winter when I took him out so he could shit in the snow, he never would. The second we got home, though, he'd take a huge dump in the middle of the living room. Finally I took him to Central Park and left his ass there.

My next gig in the city, the Band of Gold, was cool while it lasted. Tony Ferrar, like most of his sidemen, was Italian. The baritone saxist was Jewish, and I was the only black. The vibe was straight-up soul, Tony singing in the raspy-voiced style of James Brown and Otis Redding. The cats wore mohair-and-silk burgundy suits with an astounding variety of silk linings. I fit in fine. Even wrote a number of arrangements. Happy to be working. After the last set, I was also happy to be in the basement of the Eighth Wonder when they started passing around sugar cubes. I'd never seen LSD. My experience with drugs had been smack, weed, and coke; I welcomed anything new. Turned into a hip trip. We wound up at some club where the Day-Glo-painted walls and ultraviolet lights started moving and melting before my eyes. Learning this was my maiden voyage, beautiful hippie chicks began hugging and kissing me and laying me out on pillows spread over the floor. No wonder I became a tripper.

Acid didn't keep me from junk. Harlem was a junkie's paradise or, as I'd soon see, a junkie's hell. Either way, I'd never seen so much heroin. When I first arrived in New York, I was hesitant about scoring. I was used to New Orleans, where you'd never score from an unknown source. Through a junkie who worked with Sue at the Club Ho Tai, I learned that Harlem was a free zone where you could score from anyone anywhere.

Before Harlem I'd never seen a shooting gallery. My first encounter was in the basement of a tenement at 118th Street and Eighth Avenue. The gallery was enormous, a labyrinth of coal shoots, piles of coal, hot-water tanks, exposed plumbing, and leaky pipes. Filthy mattresses stinking of urine, their springs exposed, were scattered on the concrete floor. No sounds except hacking coughs and a hissing furnace. Junkies everywhere, ghostlike figures, who actually lived there. One dude behind a desk ran things, bartering dope for hot merchandise brought in by hustlers. Mostly people scored their shit elsewhere and came here to shoot. In New Orleans it was against the law just to possess the paraphernalia; not so in New York, where the gallery rented works for twenty-five cents. No matter how depraved, no matter how dismal, it also seemed safe. In contrast to New Orleans, where fear was my constant companion, Harlem accommodated my lifestyle; Harlem understood my obsession; Harlem eased me into a get-high, stay-high state of mind where the supply was endless and the real world far away.

Meters and Machines

Art

It happened faster than I thought it would. Happened so fast, in fact, we probably made some bad business decisions. But if extra-thick funk was a hallmark of this new group, so were bad business decisions.

The beautiful part was the music. The beautiful part still is the music. We found a niche and made it our own. In the late sixties soul was in flux. Sly Stone was coming on strong. His "Dance to the Music" and "Everyday People" had a sophisticated syncopation — a newfangled funk — that had everyone taking note. Sly even made Miles change his tune. Over at Motown, Norman Whitfield took a similar approach with the Temptations on "Cloud Nine" and "Runaway Child, Running Wild." James Brown was hitting his stride with "Mother Popcorn" and "Ain't It Funky Now." Well, it *was* funky, and the funk was coming out of virtuoso bass players like Larry Graham and Bootsy Collins, cats who gave the music a pop it never had before.

It was clear to me that our bass player, George Porter, could pop it as hard as anyone. Leo Nocentelli had a flow and feel on guitar that went with Zigaboo's incredible beats like ham and eggs. These young boys were bad, and I, the old man of the group at thirty-one, found a way to punctuate their sentences, punching my organ in the margins of the music. As a result of all this synchronicity, the four of us came up with a Sound — tight, sparse, and funky as the fuckin' devil.

During our run at the Ivanhoe, we were almost too successful. I remember finding, together with five-dollar bills, bullets buried in our kitty jar. Some of those bullets had our names written on them. Some of the customers were jealous that we were making more money than them. Fortunately the jealousy never passed the point of a threat.

The vast majority of the customers left in a state of bliss. Night after night, the sold-out dates were making one fact increasingly clear — Art Neville and the Neville Sounds had reached a new plateau. Now we needed to make records. At that time, Allen Toussaint had broken off from Joe Banashak and hooked up with another businessman, Marshall Sehorn. They had some big hits on Lee Dorsey — "Ride Your Pony," "Get Out of My Life, Woman," and "Working in the Coal Mine." Hearing there was a buzz on my new band, Allen and Sehorn checked us out at the Ivanhoe. They liked what they heard and started using us at Cosimo's new eight-track studio. Working behind Lee Dorsey and Betty Harris, we began a career as the city's most prominent rhythm section. Eventually, we'd record with everyone from Paul Simon and Paul McCartney to Joe Cocker and Patti LaBelle.

We also started recording on our own. The first sides, "Bo Diddley, Parts 1 and 2" and "I'm Gonna Put Some Hurt on You," were issued under my name. Nothing much happened. But then came the bomb: we pretended the studio was the Ivanhoe and started riffin' like we did at the gig. Strictly head charts. We wrote collectively, or better yet, we improvised; we made up shit on the spot. If there were ever four genuine co-collaborators, that was us. Leo wrote lots of the early stuff on his own, but our genius was in the jam, the spontaneity, the surprise of not knowing where we were going but getting there anyway. One of the jams was simply called "Art's Thing." Allen and Sehorn thought it needed a more commercial title and, borrowing from Rufus Thomas, called it "Sophisticated Cissy." The name has no particular meaning — I didn't see it as a reference to homosexuals, as some claim — but a simple signal of a groovy attitude. Two other tunes from that session, "Cissy Strut" and "Here Comes the Meter Man," would, along with "Sophisticated Cissy," help put us on the map.

These were all vocal-less instrumentals, with a clear debt to my heroes, Booker T. and Bill Doggett. I wasn't all that confident about the commercial potential of these songs. Instrumental hits were still rare. Toussaint and Sehorn tried to get us a deal, but the majors all passed. Finally Jubilee, a small outfit in New York, agreed to release the stuff on the Josie label. The suits felt we needed a more commercial handle than Art Neville and the Neville Sounds, especially since I was the only Neville. I agreed; our name should more aptly reflect our music. Our music was about syncopation; we had this strange measured approach to funk. Someone suggested the Metrics. Not bad. Then someone said the Meters. Better. The Meters were born.

The Meters hit the soul charts in 1969. "Sophisticated Cissy" went to number seven and "Cissy Strut" strutted up to number four. We were on our way. The problem was not the music; the problem would never be the music. The problem, like most problems in life, concerned control: Who was in control of our careers? Who controlled our songs, our copyrights, our direction? These were the issues that plagued us. I can't think of a group who needed less production help than the Meters. Put us in the studio, turn on the lights, and let us do the rest. You might see other people's names as producers on our records, but just for the record, let me assure you — we were our own built-in writers-producers. What we lacked, though, was management — we lacked the ability to manage ourselves and, even worse, the resolve to hire a righteous manager. The result was rip-roaring success accompanied by years of emotional and financial chaos.

Aaron

Maybe if the personal shit hadn't been so chaotic, the Soul Machine would have recorded. We never did. Aside from some private tapes floating around, there's nothing to document all that sweet soul music. That's a shame, because that was a time when me and Cyril were really in sync. We weren't writing that much, but we were flat-out singing. The Meters were going great guns, and I was glad for them; after all, that was my brother Artie who started the thing. When Allen Toussaint and Marshall Sehorn got their Sansu enterprise together, they also asked me to do some solo stuff. I saw it as a continuation of the old New Orleans story: these dudes were about the only game in town, so I agreed, singing stuff like "Where Is My Baby?" a beautiful ballad written by Allen. Nothing much happened. My solo career stayed quiet, but the Soul Machine was cranking hard and keeping me high.

CYRIL

I was dealing with so many emotions — frustration, anger, political rage, personal confusion — I couldn't sort out my feelings. Getting deeper into dope only muddled my mind. But you couldn't tell me that. You couldn't tell me shit. I didn't even see the wild danger in front of me. Once in a great while, a ray of calm hope would break through the dark night. I saw Floyd Gibson, the cat we called Mojo, as one such ray of hope.

Mojo was beautiful. He was an A student at Xavier Prep and poised to go to college. Everyone loved him. He'd play hooky to hang with me and Jake — calling us Umbuku and Kumbuka — and he'd come by every weekend to hear the Soul Machine. He was a clean-cut little guy with a razor-sharp intellect, a neatly combed Afro, a heart of gold, and a cool way of expressing himself.

Mojo hipped me to the etiquette of taking a chick to a prom, something I'd never done before. In fact, we double-dated. He went with Jake's cousin, and I took a date and, square as it sounds, even bought a corsage. Mojo was with me every step of the way. Didn't matter that my date turned into a self-centered pain in the ass; I had a ball anyway. Mojo was more than my little brother; he was the hope of the future. He could hang with the nerds, he could hang with the hipsters, he could face down the cops when it came to his rights. The boy could excel at anything. His political militancy wasn't based on knee-jerk emotions; he had read and absorbed the lessons of the great revolutionaries. Mojo knew what time it was. He was a beautiful little warrior.

Then one night when the Soul Machine was playing at the Desert Sand, the barmaid came up to me during the midnight break. "Call Jake," she said. Something had to be wrong. Our routine was to play from ten to midnight, then take a two-hour break to score Uptown, then play till six or seven A.M. Why should Jake be calling when he knew I was on my way Uptown to see him? I went to the phone booth at the corner, my stomach churning.

"Umbuku," he called me. "You ain't gonna believe this."

"What?"

"Mojo's dead. They stole Mojo from us."

The phone slipped out of my hand, but I could hear Jake crying.

Later I learned the story:

Walking to our Uptown homes, we had to pass by a park close to a number of cops' homes. The cops' kids played in this park, kids who, adopting their dads' attitudes, loved to throw shit at us and scream, "Niggers!" Mojo and his date were walking past that park when the white boys started fucking with him. At first, he didn't respond to the taunts, but as they worsened, he moved his girlfriend out of the way, sensing things would get worse. Before he could respond, they shot him in the chest. If he hadn't gotten her out of the way, she would have been murdered, too. After the killers had fled, the uncle of Mojo's date happened to walk by. He ran over. Half-conscious, Mojo asked, "Is this a brother? 'Cause I don't want no honky touching me." Minutes later Mojo died in his girlfriend's arms.

Mojo's death was another soul wound that would not heal. At that point in my life, I had been shot at, I had OD'd, I had been in vicious fights, but I was still alive. Mojo had one single incident and was dead. Why him and not me? The shock was as deep as any I'd ever felt. The shock left me bitter. What's the use of living if this is how a good man dies?

Jake and I swore not to let it die. We went to the police station and demanded an investigation. Good luck. We went to the NAACP but discovered, at least at that moment in time, that the organization, as Malcolm said, was really the National Association for the Advancement of Certain People. We — and Mojo — were not those certain people. We went door-to-door asking sisters and brothers to ask their church members to join in protest; we organized a march to demand an inquiry. But all that happened during the march was more harassment; the police jumped out of their cars and, without provocation, shoved us to the ground. We would have fought, but we would have died. Something in my head said Mojo wouldn't have wanted us to go down the way he did.

In my history book, Mojo goes down as one of the martyrs of the civil rights movement. I put him up there with Fred Hampton and Jonathan Jackson [George's brother], brave leaders, beautiful human beings who were silenced by a system fueled by hatred and fear.

Charles

Our place in Harlem became oppressive. We shared a bathroom and kitchen with four other apartments and were jonesing for more space. That's when Sue learned that Lucky and Lola,* hip white girls from back home, had moved to the city, where they turned tricks for a big-time madam. The madam set them up in a plush penthouse with a terrace that ran all around the building on Fifty-fifth Street near Third Avenue. They invited us to move in, and just like that, a new adventure began.

I dug all three women. Lucky and Lola had taken on the New Orleans cops, no mean feat. After Frank Painia, owner of the Dew Drop, won his case that allowed whites in the club, the cops stepped up their harassment. They especially liked fucking with white chicks, charging them with tricking even when they weren't. Sue wasn't hassled, because she'd darken up and look Creole. But

*Fictitious name

Lola and Lucky, who loved the Dew Drop, were too white to camouflage and, even worse, wouldn't take no lip. One night a policeman asked Lucky why she couldn't find a white boy to date. "If I had to choose between you and the lowliest nigger," Lucky said, "I'd choose the nigger." With that, the cop beat the shit out of her, just for the hell of it. That's when she and Lola decided to get out of Dodge.

Lucky was a big woman, soft and round and inclined toward laughter. She had a kind disposition and easygoing way of looking at life. Lola was a professional dancer, peppy and slender with gorgeous blond hair, hard blue eyes, and a severe face. She was street, sexy, and given to changing moods. I was definitely attracted to Lola.

Soon as we moved in, Sue started scrutinizing the relationship between Lucky and Lola and their madam. She saw how Lola would gig for twelve straight hours and come back with modest money, while the madam made ten times as much. Sue, who was turning an occasional trick herself, decided to start her own operation, assuring Lola and Lucky the lion's share of their earnings. With a loan from a mobster friend, Sue took over the operation. I wondered whether there would be recriminations from the replaced madam, but there weren't, and the reason might have to do with Sue's new boyfriend. He was a black narcotics officer in Harlem who'd threaten drug dealers with his gun and badge, saying, "Give me the dope, or go to jail." In other words, he was a stickup man and a dope dealer himself. Fact is, some of the best dope I ever got in New York came from Sue's new man — which is partly why I didn't mind being replaced by him as Sue's lover.

The other part had to do with Lola. She became my new girlfriend. The result was supersteamy sex. Lola was an incredibly sensuous woman; as a dancer, Lola had wonderful moves. She was into her body and the pleasure it gave men.

For a while, Sue recruited me into the prostitution business as Lucky and Lola's would-be pimp. When they hung out in the Times Square area and wanted everyone to know they had protection, I came along. They bought me pimp clothes — the silk red-flamed shirt, the tight white bell-bottom double-knit pants, the shiny alligator shoes, the broad-brimmed hat. Though it was a ruse, I liked playing the part. I also liked watching the tricks who came to the penthouse. The girls would put me out on the terrace and leave the blinds open so I could see what was happening. If the guys got rough, I'd run in with a pistol and warn them to back off; if that didn't work, I'd hit 'em over the head. I was shocked by some of the stuff I saw. The cats who killed me were the straight-looking business types who'd come in with wet towels and demand that Lola whip their asses. There was also a dentist, looking squarer than Lawrence Welk, who turned up with the most potent pharmaceutical liquid coke known to mankind. I shot the shit up and soared to the moon.

My parole officer would show up from time to time. Once he came when I wasn't there. Lola gingerly explained she was a friend who appreciated my musicianship and had merely given me a place to rest my weary head. On one level, Lola was telling the truth. These relationships — me and Sue, Sue and her cop, me and Lola — were based more on survival than love. Love existed, but it was the love of kicks and exotic head trips.

Sue married the narcotics officer, Lucky went out on her own, and Lola asked me to move in with her to an apartment on Seventy-ninth and York. That threw us into the hip Upper East Side hustle scene. At trendy clubs like Catch a Rising Star, pimps and mobsters were in VIP rooms snorting big piles of coke with hundred-dollar bills. The sixties were giving way to the seventies.

180 Stitches

CYRIL

The mixture of booze and drugs and women was lethal. I was cruising for a bruising — and caught one that came within a fraction of an inch of killing me.

At the apex of my craziness, I was with two women who became mothers of my children. I could go on and on about those women, but I won't. My own responsibility in those intense affairs is clear. It takes two to tango, and I sure as hell wanted to tango. One night at the Desert Sand, one of my girlfriends, wanting to be a player, was playing with a dude at the bar. Whether it was something she said or did, I'm not sure. All I know is that she came into the dressing room and told me the brother had smacked her in the face. The macho in me — or the madness in me — blew up. I was also flying high on heroin. I rushed out into the club, and on my way to find the dude, a barmaid warned me. "Cool it, Cyril," she said. "Find out what really happened before you do anything." But

I was beyond reason and restraint; I was looking for the cat who'd hit my woman.

I didn't like that it was a brother who'd done the damage. I didn't like fighting brothers. We were outside when I told the dude I just wanted to talk about it and see what had really happened. But he had an attitude. Maybe he was just being defensive because Aaron and I had reputations as two Uptown dudes you wouldn't want to fuck with. Whatever the reason, he played me off like I was a little bitch. That enraged me. Just then, just as my woman came out to see the fireworks for herself, someone pushed me into her assailant — and the rumble was on. I knew he was carrying something, so I quickly got in a couple of fierce licks. Next thing I know, his buddy is holding me down and my man is slicing me with a razor, across my neck and over my shoulder. But I'm too high to feel the pain and too enraged to do anything but break loose and fight back like a rabid dog. By now Aaron is out there, trying to separate me and the cat with the razor, when I see blood and wipe it away, only to stick my finger inside my neck and feel it slip all the way to my nerve. Now I'm bleeding like a hog and Aaron is yelling, "You killed him, you killed my brother," and I'm thinking, *Fuck that, I ain't dead yet,* and the two cats are running across the street, up underneath the overpass, and we're chasing after them, and we catch them, we're kicking their asses, and one of them says to Aaron, "Hey, man, don't do this to me, we worked together on the riverfront," and Aaron says, "Well, work with me now, motherfucker," and Aaron kicks his ass even harder when Sam Henry comes over and says, "Cyril, we gotta get you to the hospital," which is where they needed 180 stitches to sew my neck together and where my pal Poochie got me some Demerol to get me even higher and let me go back to the gig — that same night — where I carried on, singing "Cold Sweat" and "Heard It Through the Grapevine" as though the shit had never happened.

Aaron

Man, the atmosphere was poison. The police were getting so crazy, they'd bust you for just being alive. Called it vagrancy, but what it really meant was that you couldn't even stand on the sidewalk. They even arrested my wife, Joel, a peace-loving woman, because she got sassy with the police when they arrested me for doing nothing. They didn't book her, but they did haul her down to the station.

The world seemed unreal. I was looking down on the world from cloud nine. There were lots of nutty ladies around, but I think I scared them off. They saw me as a thug; they also saw that my real love affair was with Lady Heroin. Maybe I wasn't aware of how frustrated I was after the success of "Tell It Like It Is," seeing my solo career trail off like a cloud of smoke. If you asked me, I'd say I was fine. I'd say everything was cool 'cause the Soul Machine was gigging steady, and me and Cyril were up there every night singing our hearts out.

One night I was Uptown with Cyril, standing on the sidewalk between two barrooms, Zalias and Club Sorrento. The cops cruised by and started demanding that we get off the street. "Fuck that noise," said Cyril. "I'm tired of feeling like a roach running for a crack every time someone turns on the lights. I'm tired of worrying about someone stomping me like a worthless piece of shit."

"Whatever," I said, used to baby bro's radical rap. "Just cool it till the cops go away." The cops had a history of manhandling Cyril, but they had never put their hands on me. Well, just then Jake pulled up, got out of his car, and joined us on the street.

"We better get inside," I said, " 'cause these cops are out for blood."

"It's as much my goddamn sidewalk as theirs," said Jake. "Fuck them."

The police — there were two of them, two guys who hated Cyril and Jake — circled back, parked down the street, and came at us. We backed into an alley that sat between the two barrooms. By now Cyril and Jake are going off on them, declaring their rights and calling them every name in the book. The first cop loses it; he grabs Cyril, sprays him with Mace, and whacks him over the head with a flashlight. That's when I lose it. That's when I see God or the devil; that's when I see my brother being violated. So I grab the cop's wrist and squeeze it so hard I leave my fingerprints deep in his skin. The second cop, standing a few feet up the alley, draws his gun and takes aim. I see his eyes are scared; I hear him saying, "Don't do it, Aaron." I say, "If anyone hits my brother again, we're all gonna die in this fuckin' alley." The first cop — his left hand squeezed by me until the circulation has stopped, his right hand holding a flashlight that could beat my brother's brains out — begins trembling. He knows that with my free hand I can grab his gun and blow *his* brains out. His partner knows that as well. "We all gonna die in this alley," I repeat, "if you motherfuckers don't back off."

They back off.

"Okay," I say, "take us to the station and book us with your bullshit." We get in their car — me, Cyril, and Jake — but instead of taking us straight to the jail, like they should have, they drive to the corner of Napoleon and Prytania, where six other patrol cars are waiting. They drag us out and start calling us dirty niggers, provoking us and hoping we'll go after them so they can mow us down for assault. Jake and Cyril are ready to die right there and then. I'm not. I think about my singing. No matter how fucked I am, I know I'm a singer. I don't want to die; I want to sing.

"Look," I tell the police, who are lined up like a firing squad, "at least thirty people back there saw what happened in the alley. They saw you take us away. If you don't take us to central lockup now, those thirty witnesses are gonna know you fucked with us. So just take us in and stop the bullshit."

Somehow that stopped Cyril and Jake from saying another word. The cops stayed silent for a few seconds. Those seconds lasted a lifetime. I didn't know what to expect. Then, with no explanation, they let us back in the car and drove us to the station, where they booked us for vagrancy. Those same two cops would harass Cyril for years to come, but that night we got away with our lives.

CYRIL

I'll never forget the incident in the alley. I was hotheaded enough to do us all in. And angry enough not to care. But Aaron had presence of mind. He knew what to say and do. The police respected Aaron; they sensed his strength. I could say a lot about that night, but the most important thing is this: brother Aaron saved my life.

Art

Maybe it's the mixture of frustration and funk that gave the Meters such a distinctive groove. I'm not sure. And I don't want to point fingers, don't want to play the blame game. But the fact of the matter is that we had hit records and couldn't cash in. We were on the chitlin circuit, playing dives and roadhouses, and never hit the big time. The record label didn't know how to put us over, and because the band itself couldn't agree on management, we lingered in the boondocks, even as our national reputation grew.

Our reputation grew on grooves like "Look-Ka Py Py," based on a beat that I'd been hearing my whole life. We shouted out some stuff — couldn't even call 'em lyrics — that you'd hear on the streets of New Orleans. God knows what the lyrics meant. We were just meaning to keep the music low-down and true to the kind of chants we heard growing up, those second-line grunts and groans.

If you look at an early picture of the Meters, you'll see four guys decked out in skinny-lapel suits with skinny ties and Afros cut all neat and trim. Later that changed to beaded bell-bottoms and tricked-out jeans jackets, but our first flush of success had us looking almost square. Before our egos blew up, we were four guys playing with the head and heart of one soul, four dudes just having fun. You could feel the fun in the music. My hope was that the music would keep catching on. And it did. Charles would tell me that up in New York even the far-out jazz fans were digging on us. We had a buzz going, and I was praying, given the talent in the group, it wouldn't be long before we'd blow up big.

Charles

Every time I went home, I sat in with the Meters, just as I'd jammed with Art Neville and the Neville Sounds. Artie was always looking for ways to refine essential funk, and this time he did it. The Meters had an edge that even the most sophisticated musicians appreciated. The Meters also developed a cult following among young people; they became an underground phenomenon that slowly spread out over the country. If you dug the Meters, you really knew what was happening in music.

My own musical journey took me to Minton's, fabled bebop hangout in Harlem. I went there with George Coleman, my friend from Memphis who wound up playing tenor with Miles, and walked in the night they were having a birthday party for Monk. To hear George blow a bop riff on "Happy Birthday" while Thelonius sported his self-styled dance was the treat of treats. For all its glory, though, bebop has always been a brutal way to make a living. For a sideman, there was more money in soul, which is how I wound up with Joe Tex.

Joe was known for "Skinny Legs and All." With her gorgeous legs, Lola would come to the show and take over the dance floor, her spectacular moves turning men to toast. Joe's band was smoking and included the one and only James Booker, who, like me, came to New York in search of better dope. One stormy night at a black club on Long Island, the Joe Tex Show hit a high point. This was when big-wig hats were all the rage, and always the clown, Joe had a habit of snatching them off the heads of ladies dancing around the bandstand. The usual reaction was a roar of approval. Not this night. When he snatched a wig hat off one particular woman, who was the size of a small refrigerator, she screamed in horror; underneath her hair was a scramble of short tufts held together by blue rubber bands. Infuriated, Miss Thing started throwing salt shakers, then silverware, then bottles. We ducked. But when we saw her extract a long-ass pistol from her purse, take aim, and start shooting, we ran like hell. Joe Tex survived, but I never did see him snatch another wig hat again.

Aaron

For years I was a wanderer. I stayed married to Joel, stayed devoted to my kids, but I wandered. The average person seeing me on the street wouldn't want to approach me. I'd be silent; I'd be sulking; my eyes would be glazed over; and if I wasn't high, I wanted to be. If you saw into my mind, though, and looked into my heart, you'd see someone who just wanted to sing. Sing with the Madonna. Sing with the angels. Sing the dreamy doo-wop, sing like Gene Autry out on the range, sing the old love songs, sing my prayer to God to find a way to get off the dope that was turning my mind to black night.

I'd find a moment of determination. I'd go to Greyhound and, without telling anyone, buy a ticket to New York. I'd pack a few shirts, an extra pair of jeans, some underwear, and a toothbrush. No drugs. Just climb on that sucker and find a seat in the back and sit and sweat it out. Sit and suffer. Sit as we drove up Arkansas and Missouri. Curl up in a fetal position, all fevered, throwing up in the bathroom, sweating and suffering through Indiana and Illinois, up all night, up all day, not eating, not drinking, just sweating out the dope, cold turkey through Ohio, cold turkey through Pennsylvania, cold turkey into New York, where I found my brother Charlie.

I stayed with Charlie and Lola. Charlie was playing different r&b bands around town, and I stumbled upon a gig or two. But the main thing I stumbled on were those shooting galleries in Harlem. I got to the city clean, but the clean didn't last. Those shooting galleries matched my mood — dark and lonely. No one could find you there. I'd never seen anything like it. I remember women with forearms as big as Popeye's, looking for a clean vein to hit where there were no clean veins to be found. I saw women stick needles in parts of their body you don't want to know about. I didn't want to know about anything except floating away from a world filled with pain.

I stayed in New York for a while, but because nothing much was happening, I floated back to New Orleans.

Charles

Whenever my brothers turned up in New York, I took them in. I only wish, though, I had more to offer them in the way of exemplary behavior. The truth is that we were all still scuffling. From the gut-bucket r&b of Joe Tex, I slipped back into hippieland. I'd call Sunshine Conspiracy a hippie band — and also the beginning of the end of my relationship with Lola. Sunshine Conspiracy was about to do a tour of navy bases in Puerto Rico and Newfoundland. Joe Tex had moved on without me, so, with the approval of my parole officer, I auditioned and got the gig. It was a whole revue, including songs like "Age of Aquarius," comedy skits, and a sensational singer-dancer named Chris, a white girl who, during rehearsal, recruited me to dance with her during "Mustang Sally." Chris did the dance in a way that had us rubbing bellies. That was fine with me, if only Lola hadn't been there watching. "You're fucking that girl, aren't you?" I wasn't, but I certainly wanted to and suspected I would as soon as we hit the road. "You're not going on the road," Lola announced.

A blizzard hit New York the day of departure. Snow blowing hard. "You're not going," Lola reiterated. "I need the work, I need the money, I gotta go," I said, grabbing my sax case and suitcase and heading downstairs. When I reached the street, people were pointing up at our apartment. I looked up and saw all my clothes — socks, underwear, ties, jackets — floating down onto York Avenue. Lola was dumping out all my belongings. No time to argue. The subway was down, the cabs were full. Finally I just jumped into a cab that already had a passenger. Coerced the driver to take me to Kennedy, where I grabbed the last plane out before the storm closed down the airport. When I left, it was seven below; when I arrived in Puerto Rico it was seventy-two, the sun shining, a tropical breeze kissing my face.

My Latino buddies in New York hipped me to enough Spanish so I could score in San Juan, where you got three times more and better smack for your money. We were staying at a marines base, where I wound up shooting up on the floor of the guard booth. Turned out the guards were part of a heroin ring. After I left, they were busted and discovered to be supplying most of the base. My name came up, but I was never charged. By then — a month after we'd landed in Puerto Rico — Sunshine Conspiracy had moved to Newfoundland, where we played another couple of weeks.

Lola had called me in Puerto Rico, but I never called her back. Her prediction had come true — Chris and I became lovers. Justifiably angry, Lola went to my parole officer and offered up the following information: Charles Neville is still using drugs, and — in violation of a restriction that parolees have sex only with their spouses — Charles Neville has not only been fucking me, Lola, but another chick named Chris. Soon as I returned to New York, the officer was in my face. He looked at my arm with a magnifying glass and saw the telltale tracks. I thought of the Smokey Robinson song "The Tracks of My Tears."

"I'm sending you to the Tombs," he said, referring to the Manhattan Detention Complex. "I'll give you thirty days to dry out. And it'll give me thirty days to think about what I want to do with your junkie ass."

The Crown of Life

CYRIL

I got shot in the hip; I got crapped on by the police so many times, it became routine; I ran so much shit up my veins, it's a miracle my body didn't implode. Yet my time with the Soul Machine was precious because it represented the first time I felt on equal footing with one of my brothers. I'm not saying I'm the singer Aaron is; we sing so differently, and besides, no one on earth sings with Aaron's unearthly beauty. But Aaron did nothing but encourage me. He treated me like a full-grown brother.

Aaron

The day came when Cyril had to report to the draft board. I took him down there 'cause he was real nervous. His friend Poochie had gone off to Vietnam, and Cyril was worried they'd ship him out in a hot minute. He didn't have to worry. When we showed up, I was practically carrying him in my arms. He had a scar in his neck from that night at the Desert Sand; he had a bullet in his hip from some romantic fuck-up; he had one of his elbows in a cast and, just to make the point, was walking on crutches. "Man, what was Vietnam like?" one of the draftees asked him. "I don't know," Cyril said, "this shit is just from the 'hood." When it came time to sign the forms, I had to sign for him 'cause both his arms were in casts, his hands all bandaged over. He never had to serve. We walked out of the draft board and walked back into our own war, the one being fought on the streets of New Orleans.

Art

I always had my eye on Cyril and figured at some point he'd come in the Meters. We needed a lead singer, and his voice fit our funk. I encouraged Marshall Sehorn and Allen Toussaint to look at him as a solo artist, and they did.

CYRIL

Marshall Sehorn drove me to Macon, Georgia, where he was cutting sides on the Meters. He wanted to cut a few things on me, hoping I'd sign a contract, which I never did. He was looking to get on my good side. It was a strange ride. We didn't say much, we didn't trust each other, and the silence was deafening. At one point we passed a chain gang of black men repairing the highway. To see the cats chained together, heaving those hammers and chisels on the boiling blacktop in 100-degree heat — man, it was a scene out of slavery days. Sehorn saw how it affected me and stopped the car. A little stand had been set up where the overseer was selling wallets made by the chain gang. Sehorn bought four. It was his way of saying, *Hey, I'm not a bad guy after all*. I didn't say anything.

I had books filled with songs of my own, but the ones we recorded in Macon were written by Leo Nocentelli. There was lots of dissent over business dealings, and Sehorn was trying to placate the Meters by using their tunes. Anyway, "Gossip" was a funky thing with a theme I could relate to — a woman who couldn't be trusted. Another Leo song, "Tell Me What's on Your Mind," also pushed my right vocal buttons and made me feel that I was up to the Meters' standards.

Art

Cyril fit the Meters' vibe like a glove. He sang the shit out of Leo's stuff. He was the obvious and logical fifth Meter, the same generation as Leo, George, and Zig. He was their soul mate, he was right for us, and it should have worked out.

CYRIL

The Macon trip was eye-opening. After recording, I walked out of the studio and heard blues in the air. There was an outdoor festival around the corner. The blues was of the filthy low-down variety, and I couldn't wait to see the brothers who were turning it out. When I took the turn and looked up at the bandstand, I was shocked: the brothers were white. Someone said they were the Allman Brothers, and I thought to myself, *Man, look at what they got going on in Macon — white boys playing blacker than black*. I loved it.

Duane was smoking the guitar and Gregg destroying the keys. They had two drummers, and one of them, a brother called Jai Johanson, had him a wooden earring. I thought that was the shit, and soon as I got home, I tore up my earlobe with a safety pin to make a hole big enough to hold wood. Later that same day I watched Arthur Conley, Otis Redding's protégé, who sang "Sweet Soul Music," receive the keys to the city. Macon was all right with me.

Art

Macon should have been the turning point. One of the reasons we went there was to meet Phil Walden, the manager responsible for Otis Redding's career. Walden dug the Meters. By then another one of our jams, "Chicken Strut," had caught on; we were on fire. Walden saw our potential. He talked to us straight-up: "If you don't put your trust in a manager with a bigger vision, you guys are going to be playing dives forever." I was ready to sign, but the Meters weren't. I thought of a song we'd recorded, "Rigor Mortis," which said it all for me. I put up a big enough stink so that the others, convinced I was holding them back, decided I was no longer needed. Didn't matter that I had begun the group. They threw my ass out.

Charles

I wasn't surprised that Lola threw me out and turned me in. I stayed in the Tombs for thirty days, where I was given a choice between going into the general population or in the ward with the cats who were kicking. "I got a habit," I admitted, preferring the section where they'd give me drugs when I got sick. But the druggie/

alcoholic section was filled, so they moved me in with the mentally disturbed. My cellmate was a cat who couldn't stop talking. That wasn't so bad, except he was convinced he was talking to Eleanor Roosevelt. I got tired of being called Eleanor. I also got pissed when, after thirty days, I couldn't get out. My parole officer, the only one authorized to release me, was on vacation and wouldn't be back for another month. At last they found a place for me in the druggie ward, where there was a good band. Playing music did me good, and when I left, I was clean.

"You got a choice," the parole officer told me after I'd served my time. "You can go back to Angola or go on methadone." I went on methadone. I also went to live with Chris, who had a tiny apartment in the Village on Eleventh Street between Fifth and Sixth. Chris was the one woman who was moving my life in one direction, even as methadone was moving me in another.

Chris was different than any girlfriend I had ever known. Her central concern was spiritual evolvement. She had a guru from India named Kirpal Singh and gave me his book, *The Crown of Life: A Study in Yoga*. Chris was interested in purification; she ate no meat, drank no liquor, and asked that I not smoke in her apartment. Not smoke? I'm an addict trying to stay off smack. Who gives a shit about a little tobacco?

The better part of me, though, followed Chris's lead. By living with her, I avoided the wild life I'd been leading with Lola, Sue, and Lucky. Besides, as a kid I had been attracted to prayer. If it hadn't been for the racist hypocrisy of the nuns and priests, I might have found solace in the Catholic Church. My heart hungered for spiritual nourishment, and having it offered by Chris in the form of Eastern mysticism, I found myself eager to learn.

Methadone was another matter. As the sixties turned into the seventies, many medical experts saw methadone as a source of hope for heroin addicts. In some ways it was; in others it wasn't.

For me, it ultimately represented another form of mental and physical imprisonment. When I began the treatment, though, I hardly had clarity of thought. I followed the program and, for the most part, I suffered.

Methadone blocks out the euphoria of heroin. While you're on methadone, you can't get high on smack. And because methadone is dispensed by regulatory agencies, you're allowed to live a normal, productive life. You no longer have to run the streets looking to score. When I started, the program was still experimental. Every month I got $800 through the welfare office as disability compensation. I saw the money as the government's way of saying, *We ain't sure what this shit will do, so we'll pay you to take it.* The legal dose was 100 milligrams a day, but in some cases, that brought on methadone poisoning, resulting in several deaths. James Booker started meth the same time as I did, but James, being a mad genius, concocted a scheme where he had three addresses in metropolitan New York and consequently received three $800 checks. For a while, I ran the same scam.

Something about meth encouraged scamming — maybe because it continued my lifelong habit of drug dependency. One of the ways it stops heroin craving is through a high all its own, at least for the first three weeks. When you become accustomed to meth, though, the high dissipates and you take it just to keep from getting sick. Well, the psychological mind-set of addicts isn't merely to maintain normalcy. Addicts want to feel something; addicts want to get off. Which is why I ultimately started selling and trading my meth for other kinds of dope. Meth, for instance, doesn't block a cocaine buzz. So snorting and shooting cocaine ultimately became another obsession of mine.

The methadone program had other problems. If you couldn't get to the clinic, if you were out of town or the buses weren't running or a storm closed down operations, you were fucked. Withdrawing from meth is worse than withdrawing from street drugs. The suffering is unimaginable. The result was that, legal or not, you were still a slave to a chemical substance.

Reading *The Crown of Life,* I saw that true freedom was not a substance but a spirit. Kirpal Singh also said that "the spiritual path is essentially a practical path." And the practicality of the matter meant I had to assume responsibility for my own actions and condition. This was a new attitude not easily adopted. I had assumed that I was a victim of an oppressive system — that's how I started stealing, that's how I started drugging, that's how I wound up in Angola. This country's socioeconomic system had set me up and turned me out. But Eastern thought was taking me deeper. The guru was saying that I had autonomy to change not only my behavior but my mental condition. Rather than see myself as a helpless victim, rather than use that as a rationale for escaping reality, I was given tools — meditation, prayer, spiritual readings — that let me leave the sordid life I'd been living.

It all sounded great, and I would continue on the path, but it wasn't easy. I'd backslide, again and again and again. I'd fall to temptation, I'd get back up, I'd fall back down. I'd surrender and fight and resurrender to the methadone program for decades to come. I made a mess and, in the process, came close to blowing my brains out.

Art

When I was out of the Meters, I did what I had done before — found any kind of goddamn work to keep myself going. There were occasional music gigs, but mostly I was working at Lane's cotton mill, hauling shit in lumberyards, helping bricklayers, and driving delivery trucks. I was back where I started, scuffling to make ends meet. There were some other bands — Deacon Jones started up Duck Butter and Electric Soul Train — but they never took off.

CYRIL

I played in Electric Soul Train and Duck Butter with Artie. Even though we've never been emotionally close, musically we're closer than close. Maybe 'cause he's the oldest; maybe 'cause he was the first to be in a band and the first to record; maybe 'cause he really is Poppa Funk and by then my real poppa was dead — whatever the reasons, I've always sought his approval and, at the same time, never felt it. Anyway, Artie couldn't provide a steady gig for me. If I had any security at all, it came from my place in the Soul Machine, where I stood shoulder to shoulder with Aaron.

Aaron

I saw Artie going through some tough changes. You might think that maybe me and my brothers would now finally get together and form a band. But the time still wasn't right. The Soul Machine had built up a local reputation, and it was mainly me and Cyril, along with Gary Brown's sax, that were bringing in the crowds. Charlie was off in his own world, and there was no talk of his coming back. So we all just kept on keeping on.

Charles

I never lost touch with New Orleans, which is how I wound up playing Las Vegas with Fats Domino. I was tight with the cats in his band, and whenever they came to New York, we hung. I never knew Fats to indulge, but the band itself was divided into two factions, the older guys who loved to drink and the younger guys like me who loved to drug. I joined up, buying a bunch of Harlem heroin and heading out with them to New Orleans, where we replenished our drug supply before moving on to Vegas. We shot up the last of our stuff at Hoover Dam, so by the time we hit the Strip — at 4 A.M. — we pawned our instruments for dope money. The city was blazing with good entertainment — Elvis was singing "In the Ghetto," Nancy Wilson had her "Guess Who I Saw Today," Ella Fitzgerald was playing showrooms, Lou Rawls was playing lounges, and Redd Foxx was funnier than ever.

Wasn't funny, though, when Fats wouldn't loan us the bread to get our instruments back. Our gig was at the Flamingo, where, disgusted that I couldn't get my sax out of hock, I saw a sign posted by the hotel kitchen: HELP WANTED. Why not? I took a job washing dishes, lying that I had no jail record with the knowledge it would take them a month to find me out. By then I'd be gone. I lifted my arms out of a sink of soapy water and heard someone ask me, "Hey, man, you fuck around?" A white boy had noticed my tracks. I wanted to know why he wanted to know. He knew these rich white boys looking to score but lacking a connection. The white boys, in their early twenties, were brothers who lived in their parents' mansion. They were also musicians. Before long, I was in the seedy section of Vegas buying in bulk; I bought enough heroin to supply not only these white guys but Fats's cats as well. The white boys took a liking to me and had me over to the folks' estate tucked away behind a gated community. The folks were in Europe. It was an elaborate compound — a main house, a servants' quarters, a freestanding recreation center stocked with booze and pool tables and a wide assortment of guns. The guys themselves thought nothing of spending two or three hundred dollars a night on dope. They gave me enough business that within three weeks I quit my dishwashing job. I wasn't sure where my life was going, but at least for now, I'd found a scene that suited my style and kept me high. I suspect I would have stayed longer were it not for something that made me — and my brothers — stop dead in our tracks:

On March 6, 1970, we lost Cookie, our baby sister.

Her Prom Dress

CYRIL

I was twenty-two when it happened. I wasn't expecting it, though I probably should have been. I was probably in denial. Cookie was so sweet, so loved by everyone who knew her, I never wanted to recognize how sick she was. It began when she was ten. She started growing at an accelerated rate, her heart became enlarged, and she was suddenly double-jointed, able to put her arms behind her back and kiss her elbows. For years she took calcium pills that I mashed up because they were too big to go down her small throat. Only once I remember discord: My older sister, Athelgra, and I were bitterly arguing with Cookie when Mommee stepped in. She asked Cookie to leave the room before telling us, "I'm not sure whether I'm gonna get a chance to raise this girl, so I'm giving her as much love while I have the chance — and I expect you both to do the same." I'd never seen my mother look so serious; I wanted to know what she meant. "I don't want to go into explanations," she said. "Just trust me and love her good."

It was easy to love her good. Not only did Cookie give love to every member of our family, she extended her love to all the homeless winos in the 'hood. She was always giving them money and food. Our yard was filled with the stray cats and dogs she insisted on feeding. As the years went on, her own health deteriorated in ways that frightened me. I heard talk of a toxic thyroid gland, a heart murmur, a hole in her heart. All the talk was hush-hush. And then came her seizures. I was scared by their violence but somehow found the presence of mind to hold her until the convulsions stopped. She also suffered bone spasms that had her writhing in pain. She lived with enormous pain.

High-school graduation is a time of hope. Cookie was an A student looking forward to a bright future. Her heart was set on the prom. Mommee and Athelgra helped her select a beautiful white lacy prom dress. A few days before the prom, she and some of her girlfriends were at Artie's. He was living across the street from my mother on Valence and had just bought a movie camera. He was showing Cookie home movies he had shot of her — the happy graduation girl. She was laughing and feeling good and eating some heavy foods, hot dogs and burgers, that were not on her highly restricted diet. Suddenly she began regurgitating; she breathed in her bile; her lungs filled with toxins. I was across the street when it happened, getting dressed for a Soul Machine gig. Auntie Deal came running in, saying that Cookie was desperately sick. I ran over to Artie's and saw her stretched out on the bed, white as a ghost. I knew mouth-to-mouth resuscitation — I had applied it when friends had OD'd — and desperately tried to revive her. I picked her up, still blowing air into her mouth, and carried her to Miss Mary's, our neighbor. Maybe Miss Mary could help. She called the doctor. "It's no use," Artie said, "she's gone." "Bullshit!" I cried. "She can't be." I kept breathing into her mouth, I never stopped, I was going to save her, I had to save her, someone had to save her. I went a little crazy, wouldn't let anyone touch her till the doctor arrived. He examined her and said, "I'm sorry. There's nothing I can do." But her hand was still warm. "What do you mean?" I screamed. "You got to do something, you gotta save her!" I got rough with the doctor, and Artie had to pin me to the wall. "Cyril," he said, "no one can do anything." I pushed him away and was on the verge of doing major damage when my mother came up to me and, rather than speak, put her arms around me. She held me like I was a baby who needed comforting. I was. I was questioning everything and everyone, including God. Why create a beautiful human being only to destroy her at the brink of womanhood? The world seemed so ugly to me, so fucking senseless. When the ambulance took away her body, I couldn't stay in the house. That night we had a gig. We went and played. Mommee said, "Cookie would have wanted it that way."

Aaron

When I saw her in the casket, she looked like an angel. She was wearing her prom dress, all white and frilly. In between their tears, my mother and aunts took pictures of her. I was sobbing. I couldn't handle it.

Art

I'm not sure my dad could have handled it. Somewhere in my mind I was thinking, *Maybe it's better that Daddy went before Cookie.* Daddy loved her so much — we all did — that the sight of her in that prom dress might surely have killed him. She was eighteen years old.

Charles

When Cookie died so young, I believe something died within all of us. At that point all the brothers were dealing with frustrations, personal and professional. We all had our demons and our confusions. Seeing what happened to Cookie — there was no rational explanation, no sense of divine justice — threw us deeper into a despair that no one wanted to name. We buried her; we wept; we went on with our lives.

Back in New York the readings of Kirpal Singh continued to touch me. I even went as far as to write the guru himself in India, asking advice about my seemingly hopeless addiction. He wrote back reminding me that this was a common problem. I had to pay off my debt in this lifetime, but that didn't mean my early death. I had to change my behavior completely; I had to accept responsibility for my actions. Stopping drugs required a strong resolve and a decision to turn my trust and spirit over to God. I must live according to the laws of the universe; I must get in tune with God's energy; I must let love lead me to a place of silent surrender where grace was possible and healing imminent. All this was within my power to achieve.

I went to meetings; I heard the guru speak and began to feel the possibility of such power. When Chris connected me with a friend of hers who was a hippie and high-ranking administrator at Goddard College in Vermont, and when that friend actually offered me a teaching job, I saw the possibility of profound change in my life.

Those were the halcyon days when little liberal-arts colleges were a hotbed for alternative lifestyles. Goddard had a Third World studies program that hired paraprofessionals, not based upon their degrees but upon their life experience. I already had enough life experience to equal several Ph.D.'s and was assigned courses in the history of black music and jazz theory. Other than the joy of teaching something I loved, I had another motive to move to pastoral Vermont — I wanted out of hopped-up New York and into an environment where I'd have a chance to get clean.

For the first two weeks, kicking meth and smack, I was sick as a dog. When you withdraw, your sense of smell intensifies. The campus was next to an apple orchard, and the scent of apples was so strong I nearly lost my mind. Now I can never smell an apple without thinking of kicking dope in Vermont. There were some compensations. Arriving in September, I went straight to my dorm room. When a naked white girl walked out of the shower and simply said, "Hi, I'm your roommate," my belief in God — and the beauty of hippie women — was reinforced. Turned out she had a boyfriend, though, with whom I gallantly but reluctantly switched rooms. My new roommate was a character I called Mr. Big Fro. He was a brother from California, a rich kid dying to be down and militant. He wore combat boots and Black Panther black power T-shirts; he read Stokely and Malcolm; he talked about Fidel and Che and Chairman Mao; but the truth is that this was his first time out of the suburbs, and he didn't have a clue.

There were real radicals at Goddard. These were the years when the Weathermen were actually blowing up banks and white kids were dodging the draft. The black dorm housed militants on the run as well as regular students looking for an education. I dug the whole scene. There was the woods, the big pond, and acres of lawns and shady trees where I'd hold classes and talk about Muddy Waters and John Coltrane. A student might come by my room early in the morning with his guitar and ask me to explain some chord structures. "I got some acid," he'd say. "Wanna drop some?" So we'd sit and discuss chord construction while the LSD deconstructed our brains.

There were some early signs that my former way of life wasn't entirely behind me. I rationalized dropping acid; after all, I wasn't sticking a needle in my arm. But that same rationalization led me to buy cough syrup laced with codeine and morphine. I happened to spot the bottle in a drugstore in Plainfield; the same brand that was outlawed almost everywhere else was on sale for $1.50 in this most all-American setting. Seemed so innocent, seemed so easy. Since I was clean, it took only an ounce to get me off. Two days later I'd buy another bottle, and then another. Soon I was feeling withdrawn and thinking about the heroin up in Harlem. Meanwhile, the college was cool — the avant-garde jazz pianist Cecil Taylor was passing through, the students were digging my courses — and I was thinking I could do this forever.

I couldn't. New York was heavy on my mind. By the time fall turned to winter, I was ready to roll into the city. I found out there was money to buy a flute for the program, and borrowing the college station wagon, I drove down to New York, where I headed straight for Manny's Music Store in midtown. Mr. Big Fro kept me company. I asked Mr. Big Fro to watch the car while I went into the store. But he wanted to check out the instruments himself, and when we emerged from Manny's with the new flute, the station wagon had been towed from the no-parking zone. I didn't have the sixty dollars to claim it. Thinking fast, I called Stickup Sam,* a fellow hustler and get-high partner from New Orleans, who understood such predicaments. He suggested we stick up a parking-lot attendant. Curious about the underworld, Mr. Big Fro came along to watch. The stickup worked, we got the car out of the pound, but it wouldn't run. The repair shop on 110th Street said it would take a day to fix, so we stayed uptown at the basement crash pad of other New Orleans friends who were big-time dope dealers.

We got there — me and Mr. Big Fro — just as they were bagging up a fresh shipment of smack. They were selling the shit out

*Fictitious name

of the basement window, where cats slipped their five-dollar bills through the bars. Watching all this, I was naturally going to get a taste for myself. I was back in my element when, half an hour later, the cops were at the door. There was barely time to hide the dope under newspapers covered by a big chessboard. By then the police had busted down the door with guns drawn, and Mr. Big Fro, in total shock, was trembling. Mr. Big Fro shit his pants. This was more underworld than he'd bargained for. "What's wrong with that nigger?" the police wanted to know. "He's a college kid from the 'burbs," I explained. One of the cops spotted the chessboard and asked if anyone played. I did. We sat down, and for the sake of goodwill, I let him win. They had no search warrant, no dope was visible, and flushed with victory, the chess-playing cop left us alone.

Next day I went to get the car, only to find someone had stolen the tires and wheels. That meant I needed more money. By then I was shooting up like crazy and helping my friends sell smack through the window. I made enough to send Mr. Big Fro back to Goddard on the bus. A week later an arm reached out to grab me through the basement window. It was the chess-playing cop, demanding that I go around and open the door for him. Fortunately, we were clean out of drugs, so there was nothing he could do except demand another chess game. This time I kicked his ass.

It took a month, but I finally got the car together and drove it back to Goddard. Of course I got canned. "If you had just called," my supervisor said, "we would have sent you money." My mind wasn't working that way. I could only apologize. He also said Mr. Big Fro had been telling stories about stickup men, cop busts, and shooting galleries in Harlem, but no one believed him. I smiled, thanked the man for the positive experience, and hitchhiked back to the city.

Struttin' Down Cabbage Alley

Art

Struttin' was the third and last album the Meters did for Josie. In the early seventies the label went belly-up. By then I didn't care, since the cats had kicked me out of the group. I thought of one of our tunes — "Sehorn's Farm" — that had a meaning that took me years to appreciate: we were all slaving away on a work farm without shit to show for it. But just when it seemed that me and the Meters would never see eye-to-eye, fate took a left turn and threw us back together. Warner Brothers wanted to sign the Meters, but only if Art Neville was on keys. The boys asked me to rejoin. I figured a deal with an international record company was a good incentive for us to bury the hatchet. Besides, I missed the Meters' music. The Meters had a kind of organized freedom I'd never before felt in a band. I liked how we never rehearsed and never practiced. It was good to get back to all that spontaneous combustion. Warner put us on its Reprise label and left us alone to do what we did best — jam. I don't think Warner knew much about our kind of music. Of course, it was Sehorn who cut the deal and Sehorn who was still pulling the strings, but at least for a while, that was okay; my attitude was that Sehorn was better than nothing.

Aaron

At one point the Soul Machine started to break down in New Orleans and found a gig in Nashville at a club called the New Era. It *was* a new era — folks around Nashville said we were the best r&b band they had ever heard and kept us there for months at a time — but it was also an old era. The old problem of getting a deal as a solo artist was staring me in the face. I was singing cover songs — Bobby Womack, Bill Withers, you name it — and making just enough to get by, still wandering, still wondering.

CYRIL

I've heard cats say they got into music to get girls. Not me. I got into music because music was in my soul. I've never been a womanizer. In my whole life, I've had serious relationships with only three women; I've claimed the children born out of those relationships and put them in my will.

It began in the seventies. That's when I had five different children with two different women, all born close together. Daughters Talitha and Imami and sons Louis, Cyril Jr., and Kenric are all dear to my heart. I tried best as I could to help them. But because I wasn't in my right mind, because I was drugging and drinking and filled with righteous rage, I had one of the most fucked-up family situations you can imagine — different kids with different ladies being born at the same time. It was crazy. The kids didn't ask to come along; the kids wanted nothing but the love of Mommy and Daddy. I wish I could have given them more. I'm still trying. But I was as wild a man as AmeriKKKa could produce.

Living between two women, between two families, I was living nowhere at all. I was playing these women just like they were playing me. But the play was turning into a tragedy, and I didn't see any way out. People with low self-esteem, people like me, look for love in all the wrong places. An elderly friend of my mother's called my relationships "graveyard love." Confusion was my constant companion. The park was my church; I slept under the trees.

My mother saw the chaos surrounding me; she saw the danger; she said, "I spoke to Charles, and he's expecting you in New York." New York? Could I see myself in New York? My mother gave me no choice. More than anyone, she saw that it was a matter of life and death. I had to get out of New Orleans.

Art

Cabbage Alley symbolized the funkiest side of New Orleans. Daddy and Uncle Jolly would talk about going down to Cabbage Alley, this slither of a street where anything could happen, but I never figured out where it was. I saw it as a state of mind. My mind was hopeful when the Meters cut our first Warner album and called it *Cabbage Alley*. Cyril came in to the studio and helped us out with vocals and percussion; you can hear him on several of the tracks.

CYRIL

You can hear me if you get a hearing aid 'cause I'm buried so far back in the mix, I'm barely audible.

Art

Cabbage Alley," the title song that re-riffed Professor Longhair, was more than a bad groove; it's where we came from. Songs like "Soul Island" pointed to where we were going — the Caribbean. "Soul Island" showed an influence that's always been felt in the Crescent City but, starting in the seventies, got even stronger. We were expanding our repertoire — and our touring. We went to Trinidad and played with the great Mighty Sparrow. The island sounds were all around me, the old sounds of my childhood, the new sounds of reggae, the time-honored funk taking nasty new turns. For the first time in a long time, I felt good about music again. Fresh spirits were pouring in.

CYRIL

They say New Orleans is the most northern port of the Caribbean, and a sense of island life — island dreams, island songs, island rhythms — is definitely part of our heritage. The slave trade with Africa, souls being shipped and abandoned, cultures confused and commingled, the sense of oppression, the sense of relaxation, humid heat hanging over your head like a hammer, carnivals and rituals and a beat that goes from morning till night, drums that talk like singers and singers who sing like drums — the Caribbean really started calling to me in the seventies when Artie returned from the islands. He played there with the Meters and came back with some records. He wouldn't stop talking about Jimmy Cliff and the new reggae music that he swore had the heart of our r&b but was spinning it in a new direction. "Cyril," he said, "this is some serious shit that's gonna wipe you out." He was right. Not since I was a kid and heard Ray Charles, B. B. King, Etta James, and James Brown had music hit me this hard.

Meanwhile, I was running to New York to keep from getting killed by the New Orleans cops, but I was also going to a city that was filled with the sounds of island people — Jamaicans, Haitians, Puerto Ricans — whose music, no matter how fucked-up my mind, filled my heart with joy.

Charles

I was glad to see Cyril in New York. I missed my baby brother and wanted to reconnect. Seeing as we shared the same lethal habit, I hipped him to the methadone program. Wasn't perfect, but it was the only thing I knew that could keep anyone off heroin — at least for a while.

By then Chris and I were through. She had written Kirpal Singh about us. The guru replied that our relationship seemed obsessively carnal and that, for the sake of her spiritual growth, she should break it off. I couldn't argue. Chris had helped me in so many ways that I'd do anything to help her, including getting out of her way.

Off and on, I had been working with Joey Dee and the Starliters, whose big hit, "Peppermint Twist," dated back to the early sixties. Lots of great musicians had jammed with Joey, even Hendrix. Beyond "The Twist," we also did jazz stuff like "Watermelon Man" and "Sidewinder"; sometimes I'd blow sax and sometimes I beat the cowbells in the rhythm section, happy to lose myself in Joey Dee's good grooves.

Through the cats in Joey's band, I met a group of white musicians living on Ocean Parkway in Flatbush who were into weed, 'ludes, barbiturates, and acid. They were also dabbling in smack but didn't have a solid connection. I started supplying them with Harlem heroin. They lived in a commune setting, which is where I met Heather,* the next great love of my life. It was a balls-out seventies scene, complete with wild swinging and wife-swapping. I remember one of the cats having fits convincing his wife that it was okay to change partners. When he finally prevailed, she got into it so passionately he got jealous and demanded she stop. But it was too late. "Now that I know I can get laid easier than you," she said, "I'm just getting warmed up."

Among the craziness, Heather stood out as a square. She was a beautiful woman of Irish heritage whom I saw as an innocent, a soft and gentle soul who had a baby boy and was always volunteering to baby-sit everyone else's children. Her husband was a short-tempered bully who didn't hesitate to slap her around. She and I started talking music, and I brought her several 45s. She had a good collection of her own, and from the very start, I felt how she longed for the company of someone who understood her sensitivity. We became friends. But when her husband discovered we were talking, he berated her, forbid it, and beat her up. One night I was gigging at a private party and asked her to come along. She had never heard me play before. I drove to Brooklyn with my homey Stickup Sam. Just when Sam, Heather, and I were about to leave, her old man comes running down and whacks her before she can get in the car. I whack him back, and he's about to retaliate when Stickup Sam pulls out his pistol and aims it at hubby's head. "Do

*Fictitious name

not shoot him," I tell Sam, who's crazy enough to shoot anyone. Hubby retreats to the house and starts throwing all her shit out the window. Heather runs inside and picks up her son, being cared for by another lady, gathers her clothes off the ground, and, infant in arms, drives off with me and Stickup Sam.

Heather and I stayed together for six years. We wrote poems and beautiful love songs together. Eventually we had a child together, a girl named Rowena, after my sister. We never married, but we were soul mates. I adored Heather. She's a fine writer and a wonderful woman. In the beginning we lived in the homes of different friends all over the city. But we finally settled in a place back in Brooklyn, two floors of a hip brownstone in Park Slope that cost $400 a month. That's where Cyril found me when our mother sent him to New York.

CYRIL

I arrived by bus, and the first thing I wanted to see was Harlem. I wanted to see the Apollo, the palace of legendary black entertainment. I pictured it a block long. I had dreams in my head of James Brown's *Live at the Apollo,* the greatest live album ever made. Charles told me how to take the subway from Brooklyn, and I could hardly sit still as the train roared under the tunnel and up the island. Ella Fitzgerald was discovered at the Apollo; Cab Calloway played there, Duke, Count, Brother Ray, my own brother Aaron. The Apollo was the pinnacle. Got out at 125th Street, and when I saw this plain-looking theater in front of me, I stopped a brother and said, "Hey, man, can you tell me where the *real* Apollo is?" "You looking at it." I couldn't believe the Apollo looked like any ordinary movie house.

Nothing else about Harlem disappointed me — the great boulevards and the teeming population of black people, the clubs and the coffeeshops, the political posters, the street-corner preachers, the little hip bookstores piled high with black poetry, black biographies, black history. I imagined the figures of the Harlem Renaissance that I had read so much about — Langston Hughes, Zora Neale Hurston — roaming these very streets. I felt that I had a past to be proud of and a present to savor. Black music never sounded better. Record stores were blasting out the funk — Isaac Hayes and Curtis Mayfield, Shaft and Superfly, Aretha's "Spirit in the Dark," and a powerful new suite of supersophisticated soul Marvin Gaye was calling "What's Going On." I asked myself the same question. The pushers were up there, and the dope was dynamite. Staggerlee from back home was up there with me, and we ran together. I was a southern boy in the big city for the first time, and my head was reeling from the sights and sounds. I knew the excitement could do me in, and when Charles suggested the methadone program, I signed on.

Through the meth clinic, I got a job at the South Street Seaport Museum, where I helped restore old barges and tugboats. The job was fine, and the program also had me attending classes to advance my education. I took mathematics and spent lots of time in the Brooklyn library. These were the days of Richard Nixon, when the war was raging and the American empire, seen through the eyes of its minorities, looked evil. Despite whatever negativity still dwelled within me, the idea of finally facing my addiction was a positive step. Going on methadone gave me hope. Unfortunately, it was nothing but another dead end. Before long, I'd need a cure for methadone. Meth turned into a nastier monkey than smack. A few months later when I got back on heroin, I was actually relieved. Heroin was a drug I understood. Meth was a trick, a manipulation to fool your body into thinking you weren't a junkie when, in truth, meth was nothing more than a different kind of junk.

Charles

The New Orleans network kept me gigging. A homey called Cadillac had been Johnnie Taylor's road manager and got me on a couple of tours. Johnnie Taylor comes out of the Sam Cooke Soul Stirrers tradition of gospel/blues wailers. He had big hits with "Who's Making Love" and, later, "Disco Lady." Johnnie's problem wasn't singing — he could sing his ass off — but his inclination to strand his band. Johnnie would tell musicians to meet him someplace and simply not show. We'd be stuck with the hotel bill. That happened once in Detroit, and I had to call Sue to send me a ticket to get back to New York. I swore never again. But I was broke when Cadillac called to say Johnnie had a good gig in Knoxville. We played for two weekends and then, without warning, Johnnie left town, assuring us he'd be in touch when more dates were scheduled. I looked around Knoxville and decided to stay.

In the old days I'd go to the ghetto to score. But times they were a-changin'. Hippies had discovered smack, and hippies were all over the college campuses. At the University of Tennessee I discovered new blue morphine, a synthetic that did the job. That's also where I found a crash pad populated by Hell's Angels on the ground floor and hippies on the second floor. I hung with the hippies. It was a weed scene with wall-to-wall mattresses and albums by Blind Faith and Crosby, Stills and Nash singing "Suite: Judy Blue Eyes." One song called "Teach Your Children" had a country flavor, and during an acid trip, I imagined that, by playing the tune, the hippies were telling me, a black dude, I wasn't welcome. But that was paranoia from drugs. Drugs were everywhere. We were smoking mountains of hash and shooting this new morphine like it was going out of style.

Political tension was intense. President Nixon was coming to campus, with Billy Graham in tow. They were scheduled to speak in the football field, and the antiwar faction was getting ready. Coincidentally, the Grateful Dead were in town, with rumors flying that Owsley Stanley, the Dead's LSD chemist, was passing out pink pills of crystal mescaline. I was ready, and the day of the rally I was flying. There were more cops than protesters. We had to sit in a special roped-off section that faced a battery of cameras with long-ass lenses held by FBI agents. I moved out of that section — I didn't want my picture taken — and when the chopper landed on the field, Nixon and Graham got out along with Ethel Waters, who sang a religious song. The chief protester was a dude with long hair, a long robe, and sandals. He looked like Jesus. He started everyone shouting, *"Peace now! Peace now! Peace now!"* The cops made a move on him and, struggling to haul him out, turned him upside down. He was naked under his robe, his balls exposed to the world. All hell broke out. The next day the paper called it a riot, and the protester was charged with indecent exposure — fuck the fact that the cops caused the indecency. Other protesters who had been photographed were picked up in a dragnet. Some protesting professors were busted. Some undergraduates, scared by the incident, ran home.

I stayed, pulled in by the power of this synthetic morphine. One of the hippie girls in the crash pad could score the stuff with fake prescriptions. Me and two other cats accompanied her to a drugstore for just that purpose. We waited in the van while she went in to do her business. We figured it was taking her too long; we figured right because when she emerged, she had state troopers by her side. No time to react. Not only were we holding hash, we were high on hash. At the county jail the sheriff fingered the dope and asked, "What the hell is this?" The giggles rendered us inarticulate. "Look at this shit," said Mr. Sheriff, "three hippies and a nigger."

They locked us up. The DA took handwriting samples. The legal negotiations began. Turned out that the girl, who was the ringleader, was the daughter of a prominent doctor. Daddy got her off. The first guy, as grungy a hippie as the world was likely to see — stringy hair down to his butt, hadn't washed for days — was told if he cleaned up, he could walk. The second dude was the heir to a meatpacking fortune and, through his family's influence, was released. That left me. Since I had a record and had served time in the pen, they saw me as the ringleader. But when the handwriting analysis came back, it showed that the meatpacking heir was the one forging the scrips. They had no choice but to let me go. I dragged my ass back to New York.

Charles performing onstage with Chief Jolly (*All photos from private collection of the Neville Brothers unless noted otherwise*)

Aaron: "I can hear Jolly's voice right now."

Cyril in the late seventies, searching

From left: Aaron, Charles, Cyril, and Art — the newly formed Neville Brothers, the late seventies

The band, mid-eighties, from left: Charles, Willie Green, Art, Daryl Johnson, Aaron, Ivan Neville, Cyril, Brian Stoltz

Aaron and Linda Ronstadt, hit pop duo

Cyril and wife, Gaynielle

Art and wife, Lorraine

Aaron and wife, Joel

Charles and wife, Kristin, on their wedding day

Home turf: the Nevilles on Valence Street. From left: Charles, Aaron, Cyril, Art

We'll always miss him. From left: Cyril, Art, manager and friend Bill Graham, and Aaron

A night on the town. From left: Art, Charles, sister Athelgra, Aaron, Cyril

Our faithful entourage, late nineties, from left: Cyril Jr., Cyril, Shane Theriot, Saya Saito, Willie Green, Kenny Nestor, Earl Smith, Aaron, Art, Eric Kolb, Rocky Tornabene, Charles, Jeffrey Gex. Not shown: Nick Daniels (*NuNu*)

The Meters reunited, from left: Art, Leo, Zig, George (*NuNu*)

The Brothers today, from left: Aaron, Art, Charles, Cyril (*Michael Wilson*)

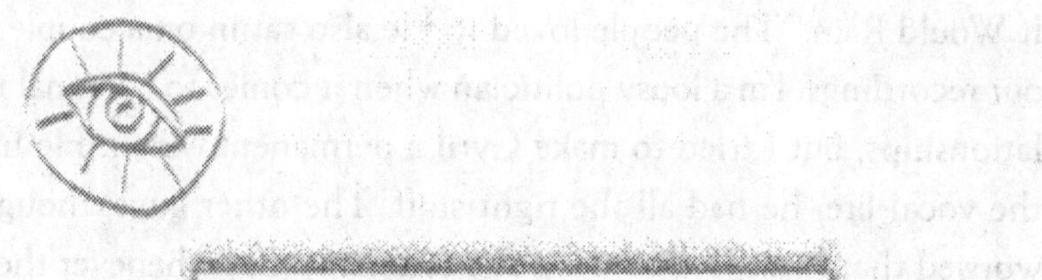

Graveyard Love/ Holy Love

CYRIL

One of the women from my life in New Orleans turned up in New York. It was a crazy situation that I didn't want to burden my brother with. Charles had a sweet scene going with Heather; they didn't need my graveyard love around them. So I took the lady back to New Orleans, where I still couldn't get it together. My domestic life had spun wildly out of control. I was like a leaf being blown by the wind in whatever direction. I missed my daddy, and I kept hearing his words of warning: "You'll wind up like a ball lost in the tall grass."

Art

When the Meters played the Ivanhoe, Cyril would sit in. He did an especially serious version of the Temptations' "I Wish

It Would Rain." The people loved it. He also sat in on a couple of our recordings. I'm a lousy politician when it comes to personal relationships, but I tried to make Cyril a permanent Meter. He had the vocal fire; he had all the right stuff. The other guys, though, worried that two Nevilles were one too many. But whenever there was a temporary vacancy, Cyril got the first call. That's how he happened to be playing in Philly with us. Can't remember the details, but Zig had gotten pissed and actually jumped out of the car on the way to some gig. He thought the group couldn't go on without him.

CYRIL

Aaron drove by where I was living, stuck his head out the window, and yelled, "Artie's looking for you. Wants you to gig with the Meters." I knew the Meters' material like the back of my hand. Playing and singing their shit was as natural as breathing. And besides, I was anxious to get out of Dodge. Threw a few things together and took off with Artie and them on the long-ass drive. They were talking about Zig, saying, "If he thinks by quitting he can stop the show, we'll show him." I'm thinking, *If they're saying this about a permanent member of their band, what are they going to say about me when I'm not here?*

Philadelphia was a revelation. At the Uptown Theater we were on the bill with the Last Poets, who were expressing a lot of the revolutionary rage churning through me. They shared a similar sensibility with Marvin Gaye, seeing protest, jazz, and funk as part of a single vision. We didn't know that these were the seeds of rap, the powerful poetry movement that exploded in the eighties. In the seventies, though, r&b was propelled by monster grooves that would be the basis of rap. The Meters were major groovemeisters, and so were Gamble and Huff, producers out of Philadelphia who had acts like Harold Melvin and the Blue Notes and the mighty O'Jays. It was at that same Philly gig that I heard the O'Jays live for the first time. Man, those cats could blow! Afterward they had us back to their hotel room, where they played some tracks they were working on. To hear the rhythm parts for "Back Stabbers," "Love Train," and "For the Love of Money" was to hear the future of funk.

Philly was in turmoil; racial tension was high. Mayor Frank Rizzo was cracking heads, and the Panthers were kicking ass. The Last Poets were saying shit the brothers and sisters needed to hear — just rapping over congas and bongos, testifying to the sorry state of the union. We did a couple of other gigs down in Greensboro, North Carolina, and then came home. Zig decided to go back on drums, and I was out. I was cool because deep down I never felt part of the group; I never expected to be asked to join permanently.

I was back to living between two women and two families, which meant living in the street and in the park. The one person who kept me from complete insanity was Jolly. Jolly had begun a transformation of character that would influence and change all of our lives. If my relationships with these two women could be called graveyard love, Jolly was showing me a holy love that took the form of poetry, music, and drama. Uncle Jolly became an Indian.

Art

The Mardi Gras Indian thing evolved slowly. Jolly saw it as a way to reclaim his birthright — he claimed American Indian blood — and reclaim his dignity as a man. That's why we respected him so much. Plus, he did it in a way that stayed true to the great tradition of New Orleans music, which is always about entertainment. His Indian rituals were sincere, but Jolly also knew how to put on a show.

Aaron

While we were lost, Uncle Jolly had found something to hold on to — something deep from the past that lived in his soul. We all watched it take shape because, starting from childhood, we watched everything our uncle did. We knew he was a king in the New Orleans underworld of nightclubs and cool music; now he was becoming more than a king. He was becoming Big Chief Jolly. There are other honored posts in the tribe — wild man, flag boy, spy boy, trail chief, and second chief. But big chief is the leader; he's the man.

CYRIL

The Mardi Gras Indian tradition has roots back in the nineteenth century. Some say it started during the Civil War when slaves were no longer allowed to drum and dance in Congo Square. There's evidence that some of the runaway slaves were taken in by Indian tribes. A deep bond between American Indians and African Americans became a sacred secret in parts of Louisiana. Both peoples were oppressed and slaughtered, both estranged from a system of belief — in Africa and America — that ran counter to the established culture. You hear in the Indian chants of New Orleans the soul of West Africa; you also hear the soul of Haiti and Trinidad, places with their own tradition of Mardi Gras Indians.

During Mardi Gras, a time when New Orleans celebrates and

shows off, blacks were cut out of the process; at best, a few blacks were given ceremonial roles, but only at the discretion of whites. The Mardi Gras black Indians said, *Fuck that. We don't need your fancy floats; we don't need no floats at all. We have our own stories, our own music, our own drama. We'll make our own costumes according to our own designs, and we'll design our own parades.*

The tribes were born out of the black neighborhoods, and in the old days there were reports of actual violence between them. The mythology of the tribes is based on territorial integrity — this is our plot of ground where we rule — and that sense of neighborhood pride prevailed as, over time, the violence dissipated into good-natured rivalry. The emphasis was on pageantry — extravagant costumes and haunting music. The emphasis was on self-assertion. As nephews, we were witnesses to Jolly's self-affirmation: *This is who I am; this is where I come from*. Rooted right in our Thirteenth Ward Uptown neighborhood, named after the street that ran perpendicular to Valence, where our mother still lived and where our lives would always be anchored, the Wild Tchoupitoulas tribe and the Wild Tchoupitoulas vibe would ultimately keep us from falling apart as individuals and as a family. When Jolly became big chief, he became a symbol of strength. It took us all a while to find that strength within ourselves, but Jolly showed us that it was there.

Art

If you break down the Mardi Gras Indian thing, you get what you always get in New Orleans — a big spicy gumbo. Some of those Indian chants sound French, some sound Spanish. Who knows where they came from? You'll hear call-and-response like you hear in a black Baptist church, and you'll hear rhythms that you swear come from some tiny island in the Caribbean. It's all over the map.

For decades blacks weren't allowed to mask, so Indian costumes were a way around that, a way to defy the white man but also to celebrate this wild-ass creativity that took on a life all its own.

Aaron

There were Downtown tribes like the Diamond Stars and White Eagles. But an Uptown tribe, the Wild Magnolias, was the first to combine the funk sound with the Indian chants. Willie Tee, who we knew from back in the projects, hooked that up. He went into the studio with his sax-playing brother Earl, Snooks Eaglin, the guitarist of life, and some other bad cats. The stars were Bo Dollis and Monk Boudreaux, who sang their Indian songs like "Handa Wanda" and "Smoke My Peace Pipe." Bo was big chief of the Wild Magnolias, and Monk led the Golden Eagles. The Wild Magnolias record was the first of its kind.

Art

You heard everything in that music — Sly Stone, James Brown, Parliament, Funkadelic, even the Meters. In turn, the Meters picked up a lot of that Indian feeling. You had to pick it up if you came from New Orleans.

CYRIL

It came from New Orleans, and it also came from a deeper place. It's a place of alienation, or if you think about it, double alienation — alienation for being black and alienation for being Indian.

To understand the phenomenon required study. Jolly was well versed in the history of Native Americans and pointed me to the texts I devoured — *Bury My Heart at Wounded Knee: An Indian History of the American West* by Dee Brown and *Custer Died for Your Sins: An Indian Manifesto* by Vine Deloria Jr. Jolly and his tribesmen gave me a new way of reading American history, through Indian eyes. Watching Jolly grow into his role, I saw its majesty. It came out of respect for the Native American to the point that within recent years official bodies of Native American tribes have recognized the legitimacy of Mardi Gras Indians.

For me, during one of the darkest times of my life, light came from Jolly's lead. I followed him in parades and picked up the rhythms; I became his percussionist. During long sessions when the tribe would sew those incredibly colorful costumes — millions of beads and feathers fashioned in ways that would make peacocks blush — I'd sit with my uncle and watch him work. I'd hear how he and his spirit brothers were connecting, not only to the ancient designs of their headdresses and headbands but to a feeling for the land that had been long lost. Many of the stories they told were privileged information and not to be repeated. I respected the mystery behind the mythology.

I was drawn to the lure of holy love. But graveyard love was still part of my sick mentality, and I'd spend days and weeks on the street, bouncing from one domestic crisis to another. I was also stealing. I pulled a little burglary in a school in a 'hood, taking a big box of meats and eggs and a portable record player. I sold the food but couldn't part with the record player. I was carrying it around one night when I noticed a car following me. I figured it was the police. Figured they were ready to bust me for some more vagrancy bullshit. "Cyril," said the driver, "it's Carl." Carl was guitarist for the Soul Machine. "We need you in Nashville," he explained. "They sent me down to drive you back up there."

I stood there, let a second or two tick by, and said, "Let's go."

"Don't you wanna go home and get your things?" asked Carl.

"No." I had everything I needed on me — my Aretha records, my Lou Rawls 45s of "Tobacco Road" and "Dead End Street." I'd been living on a dead end street.

On the way out of town, we stopped to buy half a gallon of wine, and I was fine. I called my mother. "Thank God you're leaving New Orleans," she said, worried that the police were unhappy as long as I was alive. When I got to Nashville, Aaron wasn't there. Aaron was having problems of his own.

Aaron

I was here, there, and nowhere. God had blessed me and Joel with our fourth child, Jason. I was grateful and glad, but emotionally I was also missing in action. Musically, the highlight of my life during those days was singing "Ave Maria" to the birds. That's when I felt most free. Toussaint and Sehorn opened a fancy new studio and signed me up to sing stuff like "Hercules," a story about surviving the streets. I dug the song, but there was no money coming in, no royalties, and I was getting madder by the day.

Started hanging with my old pal Treacherous Slim, who grew up with me on Valence. Things were looking down. I didn't have a car, and Joel, disgusted with my habits, threw me out. Sometimes I'd crash at the place Treacherous Slim kept with his lady; sometimes I stayed homeless and slept on benches. But I needed money real bad and knew one of the record rogues in town owed me a bunch. When I called, they kept saying he wasn't there. I knew they were lying, but by the time I went to the office to catch him, he was gone. The routine was getting old. He pushed me to the point of no return; I wanted my fuckin' money. One afternoon I went down there with Treacherous Slim. We both had pistols. But instead of busting in, I called him from a phone booth across the street from his office. After hearing it was me, the secretary said he wasn't in. "Fine," I said, "just tell him I'm on my way down." He figured I was calling from Uptown. Me and Slim walked across the street to his building. Just as I put my hand on the door to open it from one side, Mr. Record Rogue put his hand to open it from the other. When the motherfucker saw me standing there — and then saw Treacherous Slim by my side — he turned ghost white. No place to run, baby, no place to hide.

"Aaron," he said, "I was just about to call you."

"Well, I saved you the trouble."

"Should I shoot him in the balls?" asked Slim.

"He don't got none," I explained.

"Then I'll shoot him in the head."

Shooting people didn't mean anything to Slim, and this cat knew it. "If you need some advance on your royalties," he said, "I'll be happy to accommodate you."

He coughed up a little money, and I realized, given how the music business works in New Orleans, this was my only successful negotiation.

The Soul Machine had a spotty kind of success, back and forth between Louisiana and Tennessee. I moved in and out of Nashville for a week here or a month there, catching up with the band and brother Cyril. But when that gig started getting shaky, me and Cyril decided to bust a move. We made up our minds to make our fortune. We went to L.A.

King of Pimps

CYRIL

We had six bucks between us, and a bucket of Mommee's fried chicken. It's southern tradition for mothers to give their sons fried chicken when they go off on trips. I was excited about going out to L.A. but also bone tired. I slept for hours. When I woke up starving, I reached into the chicken bucket and came up empty. Aaron had given our food to a pretty lady sitting across the aisle who got off in El Paso and slipped into some dude's big fancy car with Marvin Gaye's "Let's Get It On" blasting on the radio. By the time we arrived in L.A., I was a wreck. Aaron had arranged it so that Larry Williams was going to pick us up — the same Larry Williams who had taken Artie and Aaron out on their first tours, *the* Larry Williams.

Aaron

We got off the bus in Hollywood, and Cyril, never having met the man, kept asking, "How will I know when Larry Williams gets here?"

"Don't worry, bro," I said. "You'll know."

A minute later, here comes my man driving a baby-blue Rolls convertible the size of a boat, wide-brimmed white fur fedora on his head, gold-plated shades hiding his eyes, glitter-gold suit brighter than the California sun. Cyril's mouth fell open.

CYRIL

I felt privileged to get next to Larry Williams, one of the pioneer rock 'n' rollers. He had a love and appreciation of all the Neville brothers, and beyond that, he had his own hard-boiled philosophy. For the most part, he was out of the music business; he'd become king of pimps. "I'm in a business," he proudly said, "where I don't have to pay Uncle Sam. I've decided to pimp rather than be pimped." He had a huge shag-carpeted, gold-chandeliered house in Baldwin Hills and no illusions about how the white world looked at him. "With all my money," he said — and the man had tons — "to the cops I'm just another nigger in a fancy car. The world judges you by the color of your skin because the world don't wanna know who the fuck you are. The world wants to keep the power where power has always been. And every day the powers that be get more powerful by stomping the powerless. So what the hell can *I* do? I can scam the system that's bringing us down, and scam it so I make more money than a motherfucker."

Aaron

In the ten years since I'd seen Larry, I hadn't lost my good feeling for him. He talked plenty shit, he was more gangster than ever, but he was still my man. He got me and Cyril a place not far from his house in Baldwin Hills and a gig waxing cars for Rocking Robin Car Wash way down La Brea. After we'd wax 'em up, rather than return them to the airport rental-car companies where they belonged, we'd ride 'em around town just for the hell of it.

I was hoping Larry might find us someplace to sing, but his connections were more criminal than musical. He gave us a bunch of counterfeit money to buy dope down on Crenshaw Boulevard. The dope dealer gave us the stuff and said we could try it right then and there. Then in the middle of our high, the man started inspecting the cash. When he popped one of the bills, the sucker tore in half. "Damn," he said, "this is some funny money. Y'all already shot up my shit, and all I got is this fuckin' funny money."

Cyril told him some bullshit about how we were with Fats Domino and managed to talk our way out of it. For a while we stayed with our cousins, who are beautiful people, Yolanda and Mildred. That seemed like a safe haven. Nice central city neighborhood, nice place to take a walk.

CYRIL

Same thing happened to me in L.A. that happened in New York and Nashville. My domestic situation caught up with me. One of my ladies came out to see me, making all sorts of demands. Rather than bug my brother Aaron with these problems, I rode off to northern California with the lady to try and make peace, but peace never came. I was back in New Orleans in no time, back at square one.

Art

We called it *Rejuvenation*. The Meters' second album for Warner described what the group was feeling — at least at that moment in time. There are critics and fans who say this is our finest funk. We were definitely back in the groove, bad vibes replaced by a group consciousness that went right to the heart of New Orleans merrymaking. Leo, Zig, George, and I had buried our differences in the cemetery of our city's musical ghosts. At the same time, we were hearing everything new and edgy coming over the radio — Herbie Hancock, Santana, Charles Wright and the Watts 103rd Street Rhythm Band, War. We had recently backed our friend Dr. John on his two big hits, "Right Place, Wrong Time" and "Such a Night." Ironically, Dr. John's career was taking off, partly because of his aggressive manager, Phil Walden, the same cat the Meters had rejected years earlier in Macon.

Rejuvenation contains some seminal Meters moments. The most memorable might be "Hey Pocky A-Way," by now a Big Easy anthem nearly as famous as "When the Saints Go Marching In." "Little bitty boy," I sang, "with a heart of steel, he can't boogie now, but his sister sure will / Feel good music, I've been told, good for the body and good for the soul / Hey hey hey, hey pocky a-way." This was an Indian chant born decades before me. No one knows how old it is. I worked up a piano part that gave some sense to the syncopation I felt growing up on Valence. I tried to make it original — and I think it was — but I also believe there is no originality; all we can do is put together old pieces in new ways. Over the years everyone and his mother have asked me what "Hey Pocky A-Way" means. My answer is simple — whatever you want it to mean.

Rejuvenation had a bunch of bad grooves. "People Say" was social commentary set to music, and "Africa" took us all the way back to the motherland, the original source. I can't tell you *Rejuvenation* was a huge hit, but its songs have survived the test of time. Among musicians, *Rejuvenation* was definitely heard. Our studio work got steadier. We cut "Sneakin' Sally Through the Alley" with Robert Palmer and went on the road with King Biscuit Boy. Rock superstars were courting us; we heard that the Rolling Stones were listening to our shit and thinking of having us open for them on a world tour. I'd believe it when I saw it.

Aaron

After leaving L.A., I stayed in the zone. The zone is the place where there is no place. The zone is where time stands still and you see the world through a fog. I was in the zone in New Orleans. The zone kept me from feeling the pain of being cut off from Joel and my children. I remember sneaking off to see my kids, meeting them in a park and having my son Ivan show me a snapshot of all of us when we were together. "We were a pretty family, Daddy, weren't we?" I couldn't answer him for the tears in my eyes and the lump in my throat. I couldn't answer him 'cause I was stuck in the zone. If the Soul Machine called for me to move back to Nashville, Nashville became the zone. If Cyril joined me up there, he slipped into the zone with me. Looking back, I see I tried to escape the zone by changing cities. But the zone was everywhere; I couldn't leave the zone because the zone was inside me.

Me and Cyril started talking about leaving Nashville for New York. I liked the idea. I'd been wanting to return to New York since I played the Apollo back when "Tell It Like It Is" was hot. Seemed like a million years ago. The city still called to me. I thought about all those cheap drugs. Besides, our big brother Charlie was living there, and by then Charlie knew all the ins and outs. Charlie was the horn man.

In the Zone

CYRIL

Me and Aaron were riding in on the Greyhound and hit the Port Authority bus terminal on Forty-second Street. It was bitter-cold dead of winter. We went down the subway and came up in Brooklyn, wind so strong that I felt freezing naked. Charles lived in Brooklyn, and Brooklyn was where I discovered new worlds of music. Trinidadians were all over Brooklyn; Jamaicans and Haitians and Puerto Ricans gave Brooklyn a taste that whetted my appetite for spicy rhythms and spicy food. For a while we stayed with Charles on Union Street, where I'd walk all the way to Fourth Avenue and buy a box of fish from the Muslims. Later I got a place of my own at 612 Putnam, where every floor had different flavors from different islands. I'd be frying up some tomatoes and onions when I'd hear a knock on the door. A dark-skinned brother would be standing there. "Hey, mahn, what you frying up?" I'd invite him in for a taste. "What island you from?" he'd ask. "The island of New Orleans." He'd laugh and invite me to his place to meet his mama. Mama would look at me and, in her Jamaican accent, swear I was a relative. It all felt like family. She'd give me jerk chicken, the spiciest bird I'd ever tasted, and I'd look around the apartment and recognize something from home — those burning candles, those flames of hope, those connections to the spirit world. I loved the spirit of Brooklyn and the fragrances coming from those big apartment buildings when everyone was cooking up beans and rice and savory dishes that had you dreaming of white beaches and swaying palm trees in the middle of concrete city. I know Manhattan is an island, but Brooklyn was really the island of my soul.

My soul was filled with the sound of reggae and ska, first heard in Jimmy Cliff's *The Harder They Come,* a beautiful and true movie that reminded me of every crooked record producer I'd ever known. Reggae became a permanent part of my worldview, pushing me on, pushing me out, opening my heart to its message of steadfast faith and liberation now.

Aaron

Memories of walking around New York City in the seventies with Cyril, singing on the street, harmonizing to "Morning Has Broken" or "Betcha by Golly, Wow" or "Tin Man." Some people turned around and smiled, some ignored us, some frowned. We were just trying to keep it together. We'd walk past Carnegie Hall, and I'd say to Cyril, "Sing something." He'd sing "Inner City Blues," and I'd say, "See, you just played Carnegie Hall." I was using my imagination not to go crazy because it was crazy that I was still contracted to Toussaint and Sehorn and not able to record or get a decent record deal.

Charlie hooked us all up in a group called Subway, a black band that let me sing some of my stuff. But mainly it was covers. For so many years, it was nothing but covers. We gigged around town for pocket change. I was there, but I wasn't there. I was in the zone.

CYRIL

I got chills when Subway played at the Audubon Ballroom in Harlem, the same ballroom where Malcolm X had been assassinated. I saw the bullet holes in the wall. I touched them with my fingers. All the shock and outrage returned. I didn't know how to process my thoughts until Charles finally said what we had all been feeling: "No one should have been able to find a black man anywhere who would kill Malcolm."

AARON

We were all getting in trouble in New York. I was hanging with a Puerto Rican brother named Angel who liked to call me Red and have me on the lookout while he yanked tape players out of cars. One night he asked me to help him, but I got a bad feeling. I wouldn't go. Cyril said he'd go instead. I never liked to play big brother, so I kept quiet. But the next morning the cops were knocking on the door saying Cyril's down in the precinct, booked for breaking into cars.

CYRIL

I was fascinated by Angel and never blamed him for the bust. My brothers were able to get me out in short order. I liked the New

York Puerto Rican lifestyle, the clubs, the music, the walk, the silky shirts, the pointy shoes, the sharp straw hats. Being with Angel, I imagined being in that Paul Simon song about Julio down in the school yard. We'd travel all over Brooklyn, ride over to Manhattan, and work those shops on Fourteenth Street on Union Square. Shoplifting in New York City was always exciting. Different ethnic groups had different hustles. Irish dudes showed me how to steal copper drainpipe from the top of an eight-story building and score quick cash. I noticed the tension between Italians and Puerto Ricans and stayed clear. The Puerto Ricans had incredible pastries, and the Italians incredible pizza. But the best pizza I've ever tasted in my life was street pizza slipped through a window and baked by a Puerto Rican.

Maybe because I had no car, or maybe just because the urban landscape was endlessly interesting, in Brooklyn I became a wanderer, walking from neighborhood to neighborhood, moving among Orthodox Jews, devout Muslims, Italians, Greeks, people of so many cultural complexions I could never be bored. To make the mix even more enticing, Charles hung with a group of musicians that included everyone from jazz cats from the Village Vanguard to violinists with the New York Philharmonic.

Aaron

Charlie hooked us up with David Forman, a songwriter who had a record out about returning from Vietnam. David was cool. He and I did some doo-wop things together, and I remember a high-class gig at the Long Island Yacht Club with everyone in tuxes and gowns. David harmonized while I sang "Tell It Like It Is." During the break one of the tuxes came up to me and said, "You sing that almost as good as the guy who did the record. What was his name?" I looked at him for a second and said, "Don't remember."

Charles

Aaron and Cyril and I were all strung out in New York. We were on and off methadone, on and off heroin, working out whatever hustles we could put together. I had recently been hustled by O. V. Wright, the soul singer who had hits with "Eight Men, Four Women" and "A Nickel and a Nail." I was a sideman on a short tour that featured O.V., Clarence Carter — remembered for "Looking for a Fox" and "Patches" — and starred Johnnie Taylor. When O.V. told us he was looking for songs, I showed him a tune Heather and I had written together. He said he loved it. In fact, he recorded it but somehow replaced our names as composers with his. Making matters worse, Johnnie pulled his old trick and stranded the band in Chicago. Heather was broke, so I had to ask Sue to send me a ticket.

When I arrived in New York, I was looking for Heather at the airport. When two women came up to me and said hello, I didn't recognize either one. Turned out to be Heather and Sue wearing wigs. At my suggestion, Heather had moved in with Sue, who had a baby and a nice place in Washington Heights. What I didn't know was that they'd begun a major scam together. In an odd twist of fate, Heather had taken my place as Sue's chief partner in crime. That's why they were wearing disguises.

They were working a pigeon con game. I'd seen a similar game in New Orleans: playing the part of a Jamaican immigrant fresh off the boat, the con artist would weave an elaborate story that would bilk a trusting white man out of several hundred dollars. In New York it was called the Drag, and the con also involved a long narrative. The difference, though, was that the Drag required two con women — the first older and more sophisticated (Sue), and the second an innocent secretary (Heather). After half an hour of brilliant storytelling about finding letters from Havana with cash enclosed, after running back and forth to nonexistent lawyers in nonexistent offices, after showing fake promissory notes and letters of accreditation, Sue and Heather convinced the lady pigeon to withdraw $2,500 from her bank account in order to receive $10,000. My job was to be in the bank and, once the money was turned over, ensure that Sue and Heather fled unhampered. There were so many Drags being foisted in the New York area that some of the banks actually had posted warnings. If I saw a detective approach while the ladies were waiting for their pigeon to withdraw, I'd give them a high sign and we'd scram. The amazing thing, though, was that several times the teller, aware of the Drag, would warn the pigeon. By then, though, the pigeon was so convinced of the truth of the tale, so certain she was going to get $10,000 in return for her $2,500, she'd become angry at the teller. "Don't tell me what to do," she'd say. "It's my money and I want it now!"

Heather was never a willing accomplice, but Sue convinced her that the Drag didn't have the moral consequences of a stickup. Heather didn't have to play the part of an innocent; she *was* an innocent. For a while it worked, but soon after, Sue, who had left her crooked cop husband, started dating a sax player and leading a more normal life. Heather and I went back to Brooklyn, which is when Cyril and Aaron arrived on the scene.

My criminal life had taken an alarmingly different turn. New Orleans crime — at least the kind I had pursued — lacked the raw violence of New York crime. New York crime was the kind that didn't give a fuck; didn't matter who you whacked or how you whacked them. New York crime was cold-blooded. For the first time in my life, I burglarized apartments. I hooked up with a crude cat named Indio who, learning no one was home, would kick in the fuckin' door and just grab shit. One time a tenant the floor below called the cops, who arrived in a flash. We were saved by being on the top floor of an eight-story walk-up. The fat cops were too lazy to climb the stairs, and we escaped, jumping from one roof to another.

Angel was a Puerto Rican I had introduced to Aaron and Cyril. For a while I went along with him on stickups. At first I closed off my mind and shut down my heart. We did what we had to do to get money to get dope. But then one night everything changed. I was with Angel and two of his boys when we stuck up an elderly white guy. I had him in a choke hold while the others took his money. Suddenly I saw Angel thrust his knife in the man's stomach. There was no provocation, no reason to harm him. The sound of the knife slipping into the man's skin — a slight sound, almost an imperceptible sound — roared like thunder in my brain. It's a sound I still hear. A million thoughts raced through my mind: *Why are we fucking over a man who's done nothing to harm us? All my life I've seen myself as a victim, yet here I am victimizing an innocent soul. I've always thought about getting even with the white man for what he's done to us, but this man hasn't done anything. I don't know this guy, yet I'm willing to terrorize him in a way that may mess him up for the rest of his life. What the hell is wrong with me? What have I become?*

After the assault, the others went to buy dope, but I didn't. I stayed behind and called an ambulance for our victim before seeking help for myself. Filled with self-disgust, I had had enough. I had to get off drugs. I was thirty-six and had been enslaved to this shit for half my life. Somewhere in the back of my mind, I clung to the myth, developed in my childhood, that a junkie could be normal. Now I had no choice but to admit that my drug use had brought on an insanity that slowly but surely was eating away at the moral fiber of my very being. I was desperate for help.

That same night of the assault I went to a public rehab center. The place was closed, but I banged on the door till someone came.

"You gotta let me in now," I said.

"Come back in the morning."

"If I kill myself," I told the cat, "it'll be on your head."

He let me in. I stayed for a day or two; I got with the program. Staggerlee from back home went into the program with me. We both struggled and we both slipped. I kept my vow to swear off personal violence of any kind, but I still could not find the strength to give up shit. Years of agony, years of alternating hope and despair, were still ahead.

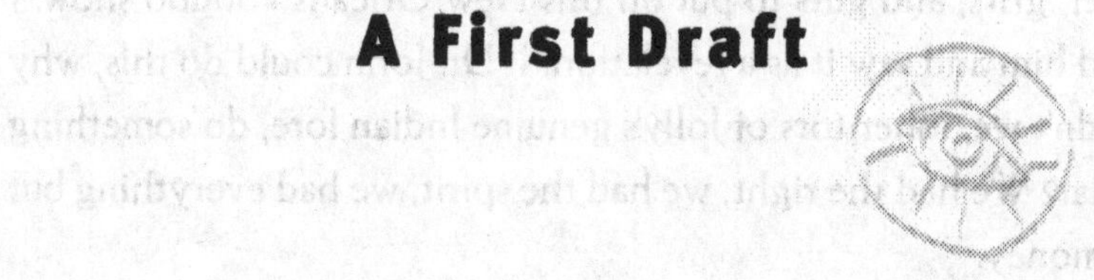

A First Draft

Aaron

Out of all that craziness in New York, one good thing happened. When the gigs dried up, Charlie, Cyril, and I looked at each other and said, "Why do we need to look around for a band? We *are* a band." That's when the first musical unit called the Wild Tchoupitoulas was born. It was ragtag, and we sure as hell were flying by the seat of our pants, but it was the start of something — or the continuation of something — that's still happening: the Nevilles playing together. It warmed my heart then, just as it warms my heart now, to be up there making music with my brothers.

CYRIL

Musically, many things were going through my mind. The Wild Magnolias had a record out, and it was screaming.

Meanwhile, the Meters were throwing everything into their funk bag — Indian chants, Caribbean beats, second-line grooves. Then one night Dr. John invited us up to his concert at Carnegie Hall. Dr. John has always been a friend of ours. He was doing his witch-doctor-gris-gris-gumbo-ya-ya-Night-Tripper thing. The stage was strewn with feathers, beads, and burning candles. Dr. John had the glitter, grits, and guts to put on this New Orleans voodoo show. I loved him and saw it as a revelation. If Dr. John could do this, why couldn't we, inheritors of Jolly's genuine Indian lore, do something similar? We had the right, we had the spirit, we had everything but the money.

The full-tilt Wild Tchoupitoulas band was still ahead of us, but while Aaron, Charles, and I were living in New York, we put together what I'd call a first draft of that group. Wasn't polished, wasn't all that thought-out. Fact is, it was pretty fuckin' crude. But the seed of the idea, planted by our uncle, was there. So we borrowed the name of his tribe and went to work.

Aaron

We dressed in old jeans jackets with sequins sewed all over them. We tied bandannas around our heads and wore long-ass feather earrings. We'd cover songs by Marvin Gaye and Curtis Mayfield, Bobby Womack, and Bill Withers. We'd sing whatever was on the radio and throw in our own stuff for good measure. We found work at one little joint where the owner told the crowd, "When these guys showed up, we thought we were being robbed — that's how rough they looked. Once they started playing, though, we knew we were safe." I played piano — if there was a piano in the club — Cyril handled percussion, and Charlie was the horn man. All three of us sang.

Charles

We were a motley crew, but we were mighty soulful. This was the first time I'd performed with my baby brother, and I was knocked out by the power of Cyril's voice. Naturally Aaron was a proven master, but Cyril was proving himself as someone with a strong message to deliver. His drumming chops were remarkably sophisticated, yet he knew how to put it in the pocket. He also had a notebook filled with sparkling original tunes.

CYRIL

That little Wild Tchoupitoulas trio worked some strange gigs in some strange clubs. No one knew what to make of us, especially when we started in with Uncle Jolly's jams. I remember performing at Catch a Rising Star, where we opened for Richard Belzer, the comic. He floored me. There were times when we floored the audience and other times when it seemed that we were playing to the walls. Musically, we were in an incubation period, and not everyone heard what we were doing.

Charles

When the trio wasn't working, we'd wander off on our own and stumble onto different scenes. Once, I was called up to the Palms Café on 125th Street to play with a band called Sleepy King and the Sandations. I arrived early. The place was empty except for this old bald man sitting on top of his amp, playing this little bitty guitar.

"Who you?" he asked.

"The sax player," I said. "I'm subbing."

"Me, too." And with that, he started warming up, running through the most incredible bebop riffs I'd ever heard on guitar. His ideas were scintillating, his fingers lightning fast.

"Excuse me," I said, "but what's your name?"

"Tiny Grimes."

"*The* Tiny Grimes? The Tiny Grimes who cut all those sides with Bird?"

"The same."

That night Tiny was deep into his gin, but that didn't stop the flow of feeling coming out of his guitar. I never complained about subbing as a sideman, especially when it put me on the same bandstand with brilliant beboppers like Tiny Grimes.

Art

I didn't expect it. It happened in 1974, when my brothers were living up in New York. The rumors had proved true. The Rolling Stones were planning a big tour for the following summer and wanted the Meters to open. First person I thought of was Cyril. If we were going to play in giant stadiums before fifty thousand screaming rock 'n' roll fans, we sure as hell needed something more than four instrumentalists. We needed a lead vocalist, a front man, who could turn it out. We needed Cyril. If the others were opposed, tough shit. They could go face those screaming fans without me.

CYRIL

Back when Aaron and I were living in L.A., Larry Williams had given me some righteous advice. Cat said, "Look here, baby bro, if you got some hurt feelings about shit happening between you and Artie, express yourself. Tell him what you're thinking. Work it out." I knew Larry was right, but I never quite got to it. Kept a lot of that hurt bottled up. When Mommee called me in New York and said Artie was looking for me to go with the Meters, I was excited to be invited back. Artie was the one brother hardest for me to relate to, but Artie was also someone I admired with all my heart. Emotionally, it was confusing. What I didn't know — and what I wouldn't know until years later — was that Artie had given the other Meters an ultimatum: if they didn't accept me, they'd lose him. That attitude, though not openly discussed, was always under the surface. Weird vibes were always there. Me and Artie might have had a heart-to-heart discussion to clear the air. But it wasn't his style, and it wasn't mine. I became a Meter, but I felt like a Meter who had to sit in the back of the bus.

Like a Rolling Stone

Art

Cyril was all over the Meters' *Fire on the Bayou* record. It's the first album where he was a full-fledged member of the band. He'd remain with us for the duration. Along with "Hey Pocky A-Way," "Fire on the Bayou" was a classic Meters moment. It's an expression we sang at basketball games when we were kids. I'd call it an ambiguous phrase. Some say it's got to do with smoking weed — and that's a legitimate interpretation. But it's also about a deeper kind of fire, the kind of heat that Cyril brought to the group. It's about the fire of creativity that we found down on the bayou, the downhome creativity that you hear on "Talkin' 'Bout New Orleans," the fun of that Big Easy crawfish and Creole gumbo we talk about on "They All Asked for You."

CYRIL

A lot of those Meters songs were nothing more than jams we put together in the car or right there in the studio. For the first time my name appears as a cowriter along with Artie, Zig, Leo, and George on *Fire on the Bayou*. And for the first time I felt that I had made the transition from a guy who could sing to a real-life singer. All that was great. But as far as business decisions were concerned, I was never consulted or invited to meetings. I didn't say anything. I lived with tension. With the Meters, tension was the glue that held their music together. The thicker the tension, the funkier the beats.

Touring with the Stones was like running off to join the circus. The shit was surreal. There were more drugs than you'd find at your local drugstore. For three straight months, I was high with no danger of running out of stash. I remember the mirrored dressing room in Glasgow where one of the Stones gave me a little bitty brown rock before the show. I snorted it up and started flying. Started tripping. I'm thinking, *Here I am, a kid from the Thirteenth Ward, on tour with the fuckin' Rolling Stones*. I flashed on the cops in New Orleans who gave me and Jake such grief — *Kiss my ass now, you motherfuckers; try to bust me over here in Scotland, you assholes*. And just when my mind was working overtime, I heard the strands of "Fire on the Bayou." That meant the other Meters were already walking down the aisle of the amphitheater, clanging those cowbells on the way to the stage, making their entrance through the crowd of God knows how many thousands of fans. I needed to join them, but as I looked around the dressing room, which was wall-to-wall mirrors, I couldn't find the door. I was confused by the images of myself, lost in the reflections, too high to orient myself. I started to laugh, then I started to panic. I kept hearing "Fire on the bayou! Fire on the bayou!" and I couldn't get out. It was crazy, it was stupid, but it wasn't funny anymore. How could I break down the door if I couldn't find it? Suddenly the door opened and Keith Richards was standing there. I like Keith — Keith has that raggedy nasty attitude on guitar, Keith has the best collection of blues 45s in the world — and Keith was smiling, Keith was saying, "How's it going, mate?"

"Cool, man," I said, "just lead me to the stage."

I absorbed so much from what the Stones did onstage. Talk about showmen! They knew how to rock a crowd. It wasn't just their riffs, it was their stage movements, their fierce energy, their commitment to give it up and turn it loose. After the shows I mainly stayed to myself. In London I discovered Ronnie Scott's, the jazz club, where I hung every night, listening to Elvin Jones, Coltrane's incredible drummer. Along with Tony Williams, whose every sound on Miles's *Seven Steps to Heaven* is imbedded in my brain, I consider Elvin Jones a master. In Yugoslavia I understood how America had mastered the world of hip fashion. Some fan offered me $300 for my studded bell-bottom jeans. I'd been wearing them for more than a month and offered to wash them first. "No," said the fan, "three hundred just the way they are." I disrobed, took the money, and paid my hotel bill.

It was a heady time. The Meters might not have been selling millions of records, but the rock superstars looked on us like royalty. The Rolling Stones had us on another tour. And when Paul and Linda McCartney gave a party in 1975 on the *Queen Mary* docked in Long Beach, California, they could have hired anyone in the world to entertain. They hired the Meters. I remember that night not only because the Hollywood stars were out in force but because Michael Jackson, when he still looked like Michael Jackson, was tearing up the dance floor while we were sending out the "Cissy Strut" and the "Rockin' Pneumonia and the Boogie-Woogie Flu."

Art

If you look at the CD they put out from that McCartney party — *Uptown Rulers! The Meters Live on the Queen Mary* — it's listed as a Marshall Sehorn and Allen Toussaint production. That never made us happy, since we were our own producers. And we were even unhappier when they put out a Meters album called *Trick Bag* while we were in Europe, hoping to capitalize on our Rolling Stones association. The trick was that we never approved that album. They threw together some scattered tracks, dumped on some scratch vocals, and made it seem like an authorized Meters record. They mixed it without us. We were incensed. "Trick Bag" was an old Earl King tune where we had Earl come in and cut it with us. "Trick Bag" was part of New Orleans r&b lore. An album called *Trick Bag* carried the name of some serious history; it should have been worthy of the legacy we represented. Instead, it was some slapped-together bullshit. Still pisses me off to think about it.

CYRIL

Anger was everywhere. Not just anger because records were being issued without approval but anger at management. Rupert Surcoff was Artie's man, the manager Artie had picked. But the other Meters didn't have the same closeness to Rupert, and the skirmishes never stopped. The mood was this passive-aggressive mix that had everyone uptight.

During my stint with the Meters, my own aggressiveness had hardly diminished. I still saw the police as my enemy, and they could still smell my anger a mile away. When two plainclothes cops saw me and two friends pull into a gas station, for instance, they had no reason to hassle us except for our color. I was holding a small bag of heroin that I slipped under my tongue. One of the cops told me to open my mouth, I tried to swallow the shit, but he grabbed me by the throat, and the stuff popped out and landed in his hand. I spent the night in jail but beat the charge because they never had probable cause to stop us.

Art

Everyone was volatile; everyone had his own pumped-up ego, his own agenda, his own problems. But suddenly the Meters' problems seemed petty. Everything seemed petty.

When it happened, none of us could quite believe it. As a family, the Nevilles had never faced anything so painful.

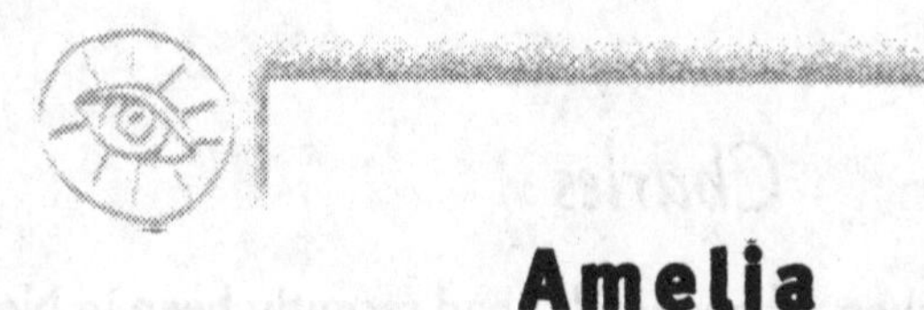

Amelia

Aaron

I wrote a song called "Amelia." This was years after it happened, but I wanted to sing her name in my song, I wanted that feeling my mother gave us. I wanted to remember everything about her.

I remember the morning it happened: I was living on Valence, and she woke me up so I could get to the gig on time. I was working on the river. I was still separated from Joel and my kids, trying to keep my head and heart together. Mommee was the one who kept saying it would be all right. She turned me on to Saint Jude, patron saint of hopeless causes. Mommee was the one who took me to the church, where I walked up the steps on my knees. Mommee took me to the shrine and said, "This is the saint of miracles. This is the saint who will turn your life around." Mommee had a way of talking that wasn't preaching or scolding. She spoke softly and sweetly, and nothing but love for her children came out of her heart. She never stopped believing in her children, even when we seemed lost to the world.

She always said, "You have talent. Once you let God lead you, you'll get where you need to go." That morning I went to work feeling blessed that God had given me a mother like Amelia Landry Neville.

Charles

I was in New York when it happened. I had recently been in New Orleans, where I helped her draw diagrams for her RN courses. She was working as a nurse's assistant at the hospital and was energized with positive determination. She was a natural nurse. She always had talent — as a dancer, a hairdresser — but now she wanted to help people heal. She loved the technical side of medical care and had a particular genius for the emotional side. The woman was all about love.

CYRIL

At the time it happened, Mommee was living with Athelgra downtown, but she was up on Valence Street almost every day to see about us. We'd been getting closer and closer. She saw how I was hurting. I'd gotten back from being with Artie and the Rolling Stones all around the world, and I felt no better about myself. She was an example of how to feel good about yourself. She had passed her nurse's test but was refused her license because of her age, sixty-five. The news put a knot in my stomach; I got enraged. I saw it as hidden racism. But Mommee accepted it as part of a larger plan. She showed me how there is no serenity without acceptance. She looked at me and saw what I was doing. I couldn't lie to her, couldn't hide my drug addiction. She asked whether there was anything she could do to help. I didn't know what to say. She said, "Look, Cyril, I know you're hurting, but I also know you've wasted enough time." Her words stayed with me.

A week later I'm driving around the city. The radio's playing and suddenly the radio is talking about how Mrs. Amelia Neville had been in a serious accident and was in need of blood. It was a call for help. With my heart beating like crazy, I raced to the hospital.

Art

When I got to the hospital, Mommee was still alive. They told me what had happened. Going to work, she got off the bus and began crossing the street. As she walked in front of the bus, a truck came charging out from behind the bus and ran over her with both the front and rear tires. You can't imagine her pain. The tires went over her midsection and crushed her pelvis. She was bleeding internally.

Aaron

When I got to the hospital and saw her there, I could hardly look. She was so helpless, yet she never lost any of her dignity or patience. To be patient with pain — especially your own pain — is something to see. I started thinking of the guy who did this to her. I went looking for him. I'm glad I never found him.

CYRIL

This was a period when we identified with Sitting Bull and the warrior spirit of Native Americans. We felt we were within our spiritual rights to avenge. If they caught the driver and he went to jail, I planned to get busted and be sent to the same jail so I could kill him.

Aaron

Looking in her eyes, I could hear her thinking. If she lived, she knew she'd be an invalid. That would be torture for my mother, who never wanted to burden anyone. She was an independent woman. She couldn't deal with the idea of not getting along on her own.

CYRIL

Jolly was there with her. Jolly loved her as much as anyone. Jolly comforted her with the assurance that he would look after her boys.

I saw in her eyes the peace she had made with her creator. She had made her amends and was ready for her transition. Her eyes said it all; she wasn't afraid. The pain was unimaginable, but she didn't complain. I believe she left with peace in her heart. As life drained out of her, my legs turned to water and I slid down the wall of her hospital room.

Art

I was the last to see her alive there in the hospital. She was smiling. Her teeth, recently fixed, had been smashed during the accident; what a shame, she said, to waste all that money on new teeth. Her beautiful smile told me she had not lost her humor. We passed many moments in silence. I sat beside her and held her hand. Finally she said, "This is it." Her last words to me were "Keep them boys together." "Keep them boys together" was a phrase that would live inside me. I couldn't forget those words. My mother gave very few direct orders in her life — she wasn't that kind of woman — but there could be no doubt about what she was asking me to do. "Keep them boys together" meant that, one way or another, me and my brothers needed to join forces.

CYRIL

The force of God is powerful. The man who drove the truck was found by the police — not by us — and convicted. I heard him speak about the accident and knew he was genuinely remorseful. As a result of what he had done, I also knew he would never be the same. It didn't matter that negligence charges weren't brought. I know he suffered. God took care of him.

Charles

Our mother's funeral at Saint Stephen's Catholic Church was overflowing with family and friends. Amelia was much loved. In the community where she had lived her entire life, she was respected as a woman who lived according to the simple principles of goodwill. Our mother didn't have a mean bone in her body. As we laid her to rest, I thought about the days in our house on Valence when she and her brother, Jolly, danced the dance of life. That was the dance that told us that the rhythm of music was the rhythm of joy. Mommee was about joy. The tragedy of her death could not destroy that lesson. Nothing could.

"Keep Them Boys Together"

Charles

The death of our mother changed the emotional equation of our lives. Our father's death eight years earlier was no less tragic, but when Mommee was killed so unexpectedly, we were without parents. The void was enormous. The only person who could possibly fill it was Uncle Jolly.

I had seen Jolly mask during Mardi Gras in the sixties. Before I went to Angola, I'd spot him running down Valence in a costume or hanging with his cronies in the bar where he led them in Indian chants. In addition to being my uncle, Jolly was also my running partner. We had a history of hustling and shooting up together. After I got out of the pen, though, when me and Aaron were still fucking around with heroin, Jolly got clean. Just like that. We couldn't help but be impressed. That's why I hated to see him start using again. It happened during one of my trips home when he came around looking for stuff. Aaron and I might have been hooked, but we weren't about to watch Jolly get rehooked. We said we wouldn't come around him with any shit — and we didn't. Jolly didn't get angry. He went off and took care of business. Without any announcement or fanfare, he got clean and stayed clean. His sobriety gave him the clarity to forge a musical project that, when you think about it, had been hatching our entire lives. His sobriety also enabled him to grow into a spiritual force. It was that force that called me back to New Orleans to help him and my brothers put together *The Wild Tchoupitoulas,* the first album in more than two decades of professional recording on which all four Nevilles play together. It took our uncle to do that.

Art

When Jolly told me he wanted to do his own version of the kind of funk the Wild Magnolias had done, I was down with the program. It was his idea for all the brothers to join in. I heard Mommee's words — "Keep them boys together" — and knew this was part of the plan. The Meters were still together, and the Meters — me, Cyril, Zig, George, and Leo — were a vital part of the project. The Meters' "Hey Pocky A-Way," reinterpreted by Jolly, was one of the key songs on *The Wild Tchoupitoulas*. Jolly's concept was simple: he wanted music that would express the heart and soul of his Uptown tribe. We were still under contract to Toussaint and Sehorn, so I had them set up the deal with Island Records. The musicians were the real producers.

Aaron

When Jolly called us together, it was like a call from God. God was reuniting me and my brothers. Here we were — I was thirty-six, Charles thirty-nine, Artie forty, and Cyril thirty — and we'd never been together in the studio as a family, not once. After years of separation, I was also getting back with Joel and the kids. Healing was coming from all sides. You can hear that healing in the Indian music.

CYRIL

When the call came from Jolly, I was deep in the streets, but the call had me zooming to the studio like a rocket. The years I spent shadowing Jolly — hanging out at his Indian sewing sessions, drumming in his parades, and listening to the secrets of the Native American–Negro connection — were finally culminating into something more magical than I could have ever imagined. I was beyond enthusiastic. I was in heaven. But if it was heaven for us, it was also heaven for Jolly to be playing with his boys. I wrote a song of my own — "Brother John" — and another with Jolly — "Hey Hey (Indians Coming)" — showing some of the excitement coursing through my body. "Brother John" is about John "Scarface" Williams, the vocalist for Huey Smith's Clowns who was stabbed to death on Rampart Street. There have been many songs about John. I hoped mine expressed that weird mixture of violence and beauty that was part of our r&b street life.

Art

The Wild Tchoupitoulas came to life in the studio. That's how great records rise to levels higher than great. Nothing was written out; the arrangements were loose; Charles and I did some on-the-spot charts; Aaron played piano; all the brothers sang; Willie

Harper helped out on vocals; the Meters funked it up. And of course the stars weren't us but the Wild Tchoupitoulas, Jolly's tribe of Uptown Indians. Jolly was a helluva singer. His big gruff voice gave the record its flavor. The other Indians played percussion and sang background.

Aaron

We were happy to be in the background and let our uncle shine. Most of the songs were his, old songs he redid his own way — "Meet the Boys on the Battlefront," "Here Dey Come," "Indian Red," "Big Chief Got a Golden Crown." Jolly was wearing that golden crown — he'd earned it — and was singing with the pride of a man who'd found redemption. The record came out with a picture of Big Chief Jolly, Second Chief Norman Bell, Spy Boy Amos Landry, Flag Boy Carl Christmas, and Trail Chief Booker Washington. The Wild Tchoupitoulas trio that me, Charles, and Cyril had put together in New York was only a warm-up. These guys were the real thing.

CYRIL

If you listen to the record, you know it's about courage. Big Chief Jolly isn't scared of lightning or thunder; he'll walk through the graveyard at midnight kicking over tombstones. He's so powerful that when his enemies see him, their blood runs cold. Jolly's power comes through his singing voice, his piano playing, the majesty of the colors of his costumes — the sun-golden plumages, the dark purples and the pale blues, the scarlet reds and the snow-white shades of his headdresses. It was royalty, funky royalty. The grooves were dance grooves, parade grooves, party grooves. It was a music of motion, a music that moved us to change our lives.

Art

After *The Wild Tchoupitoulas* I had to go through one more change with the Meters. We were obligated to make another album. We decided to do it in California. We set up shop in Tiburon, outside San Francisco. A big budget was set. David Rubinson was hired as producer. And then the shit hit the fan.

CYRIL

I was still a ghost Meter, so none of this bugged me like it bugged Artie. After all, he was the Meters' mother and father. But his children were rebelling, and the egos were going crazy; everyone wanted to sing lead. At one point the bickering got so bad that Rubinson got up and left, saying, "When you decide who you want to sing what, call me." No one could agree on nothing.

Art

After being in California for weeks, after finally cutting the damn album, the Meters were scheduled to appear on *Saturday Night Live*. That was supposedly our big break. By now, of course, I'd been hearing about a "big break" for ten years. Now I couldn't take the bullshit anymore. I refused to appear on television with the Meters. Far as I was concerned, I'd go off and play with my brothers.

CYRIL

After Artie made it clear he was out, the Meters were certain I'd go to New York with them anyway and do *Saturday Night Live*. They were waiting for me in the cab to go to the airport. I was back in the studio thinking it over, remembering all those times I'd been kicked to the curb. *Fuck it: if my brother wasn't going, there was no way I was going*. The cab pulled away without me.

Art

The last Meters album wasn't terrible. Nothing the Meters played was ever terrible. Like James Brown and Sly Stone, the Meters came up with some serious grooves that are stolen and sampled every day of the week. I'm proud of the Meters' music.

We called the last album *New Directions* because the music took something of a rock turn. Meanwhile, though, I had moved in a different direction altogether, one that brought me back to the bosom of my family.

Charles

By 1977 it was clear my uncle and brothers wanted me to work with them. After *The Wild Tchoupitoulas* was released, there was talk of nightclub appearances and even a national tour. I figured it was time to go home. I loved New York and, despite its mean streets, had survived there for ten years, six of them with Heather. My hope was that Heather, her son, and our daughter, Rowena, would all live in New Orleans with me. I'd been telling her about the beauty of the city, hoping to sell her on the idea. She agreed to drive down there with me to look around. Everything went well until we were stopped by a cop for no reason at all. He looked at us, a mixed couple, and asked Heather point-blank, "What the fuck you doing with this nigger?"

That was enough to turn Heather against the Crescent City. She stayed back East and eventually settled in Rhode Island. When I finally made the move back home, it was all the way back to Valence Street. In the years ahead, all the brothers moved back into those shotgun bungalows from the deepest part of our childhood. In order to move forward, we had to move back.

Art

Moving forward meant capitalizing on the Wild Tchoupitoulas thing. The initial record did well. Critics were calling it a masterpiece of American music. There should have been a follow-up. Jolly was in favor of a follow-up. But then the money got funny from the first album. Jolly felt he never got his due and said, "Screw 'em. I ain't recording for those guys again. Let's just take it on the road." We had one tour that took us to California and included Professor Longhair. That was a beautiful thing to see, my uncle and Fess working side by side. They'd been forever friends, and here they were, two masters finally getting the credit they deserved. My brothers and I weren't official members of Jolly's tribe, but the tribe allowed us to wear their costumes onstage.

Aaron

I've heard critics say we were commercializing the Mardi Gras Indians. Fuck the critics. We were spreading the word about the Indians in a way that glorified their tradition. We were playing the music the way it should be played. And best of all, the crowds were loving it. Word was out; we were putting on a helluva show. I was thrilled to be onstage with Jolly and my brothers, and just as thrilled to see my son Ivan join us. Ivan had turned into a superbad keyboardist, singer, and writer. He helped put together a band called the Uptown Allstars that had everyone rocking out. The Uptown Allstars, like the Wild Tchoupitoulas, like the brothers themselves, had that second-line funk boiling in their blood. I loved how the spirit had been passed on to my son, just as my uncle had passed it on to me.

Charles

While I was living in New York, I reestablished contact with my daughter Charmaine, who, like Ivan, became a third-generation member of our Wild Tchoupitoulas show. Charmaine had grown into a lovely woman with a superb voice. In addition to the work we did with my uncle and brothers, Charmaine and I put together a little jump band that played around New Orleans. We'd play Louis Jordan tunes, and Charmaine sang Billie Holiday stuff. Being with my daughter onstage, being part of her life, was a great comfort to me. During my dark New York years, I had lost track of my children, just as I had lost track of myself. Back in the sixties, after I blew my cool about their mistreatment, they were sent to a foster home in Texas. I had no address or way of reaching them. The only time I heard anything was when my sister Cookie, then a young teenager, went to camp and met these girls whose last name also happened to be Neville. They turned out to be her nieces, my daughters Charlene and Charmaine. From then on, at least I knew where they were. But it wasn't until the late seventies that Charmaine became part of the musical family that, in miraculous fashion, was taking form and gaining fans.

CYRIL

We did some tours, made a little money, and kept the thing alive. We were all still getting off on the novelty of playing together, our uncle, our kids, our brothers, everyone shoulder to shoulder. There were no big record contracts and no number one hits. It was a way to stay together as a family and survive economically. But for all the modest success, the good write-ups, and a steadily growing base of fans, our other problems didn't go away. Not by a long shot.

Black Male

Art

You gotta remember what was happening in music in the late seventies to understand what was happening with us.

Disco was still happening. Disco was everywhere. Disco had washed over the shores and swept the business like a fuckin' tidal wave. Everything was disco, from Donna Summer to "Disco Duck." Back in '76 even the Meters, the least disco group you can imagine, cut "Disco Is the Thing Today," hoping that the mere mention of the word might mean sales. It didn't. The music the Meters made was essentially the same music I'd been making since the days of the Hawketts. It was New Orleans rhythm and blues, a music that's simple and, at the same time, not simple at all. But whatever it is, it sure as hell ain't disco. As me and my brothers started out on our own, we had the definite disadvantage of going up against disco. We could sing ballads, we could sing blues, we could take you to the islands with a heavy dose of reggae, we could play straight-up soul all night long, we could kill you with our uncle's Indian funk, but disco? I don't think so. That's one of the reasons it took us so long — at least on a national level — to get over. We were swimming against the tide.

After Cyril and I were out of the Meters and *The Wild Tchoupitoulas* had been released, we needed a backup band for our tour. With the Meters gone, where would the funk come from? It came to me one night in a New Orleans club and hit me right in the gut. The band was called Black Male. These cats were badder than the Meters; I mean, they were playing Meters shit funkier than we'd played it. I couldn't believe it. Young dudes, too — Newton Mossip on drums, the Poche brothers, Renard on guitar and Roger on bass — and their leader, the one we dubbed Professor Shorthair, Gerald Tillman.

CYRIL

Gerald was a genius. He earned the title of professor at probably the youngest age of anyone in the history of New Orleans. He was younger than me, but where I was still searching for it, Professor Shorthair had found it. Tillman was our teacher. He taught me more about songwriting than anyone. I called his approach more arranged than deranged; there was a method to his madness. He was a brilliant keyboardist in the great Professor Longhair/James Booker/Art Neville tradition. And he was more: one time I was jamming with Black Male and heard this cool alto blowing behind me. Turned around and saw Gerald blowing sax like it was his main ax.

Art

It all came together in Dallas. Our good friend and promoter Angus Wynne booked us at the Bijou Theater for a couple of months. Angus really helped us out. Me and my brothers took an apartment. This was the first time we had lived together under one roof since we were kids. The vibes were good. We were still wearing Indian costumes onstage but realized we needed our own identity beyond our uncle's tribe. With Black Male supporting me in the rhythm section, we saw we had the right stuff for a great band. That long, hot Texas summer is when the Neville Brothers were born. It wouldn't be easy. No instant hits. No national notoriety. The grind would be long and, you'll soon see, filled with new frustrations. At times the shit nearly came apart at the seams. But the uncontestable fact is that, despite brotherly disputes bordering on brotherly warfare, the Neville Brothers have stuck together since that gig, some twenty-three years ago, in Dallas.

CYRIL

The Bijou gig was 1977, the year *Star Wars* came out. I remember because Artie is such a sci-fi freak he couldn't stop talking about the movie. About the same time, we got an insurance settlement from our mother's death — something like $6,000 each — which we used to start Neville Productions. That company, still strong today, wouldn't exist if my mother hadn't shed her blood. That's why I say that Amelia Landry Neville will always be our chief executive officer.

Companies inevitably have conflicts, and ours, despite the good family feeling, began early. It had to do with recording. I've always taken the position that we're our own best producers. I'd studied the best producers and reached a point where I understood the skill. It was Allen Toussaint, an accomplished producer himself, who said, referring to me, "You can't produce a producer." I saw my brothers in the same situation; each one was a wonderful producer.

Then there's the issue of the giant record companies. To me, they're plantation owners who see us as sharecroppers. Personally, I'm not interested in sharecropping for anyone. But my brothers take a more practical approach. They're more willing to be produced by outside producers, more willing to let the label determine the kind of material and styles of songs.

Charles

At the time of the Neville Brothers' first record deal, I'd been around the business for three decades. I knew how it worked. The label evaluates the artist, evaluates the market, and tries to take the artist to market with a product that has the best chance of selling. I respect the label's expertise. I also know that without their promotional push, nothing happens. That doesn't mean the Brothers would fuck with the integrity of our own sound. During disco we never chased fashion; we stayed true to our roots. But if an a&r man had a suggestion about how to mix or modernize our sound without corrupting it, I was all for it. We all wanted a wider audience. At the time we got our first deal — this was 1978 on Capitol — we had high hopes.

Art

Our debut album was called simply *The Neville Brothers,* and I loved it. Jack Nietzsche was an outside producer, but he understood how to keep us in the pocket. We had one jam, "Dancin' Jones," that should have hit big. Problem was the label. The executive in charge of us was a man we didn't like. He didn't know whether to sell us to a black audience or a white one, and wound up selling us to neither. He flushed the album down the fuckin' toilet.

Aaron

I remember two ballads I sang on our first album that filled my heart with pleasure. They made me feel that I was back on track. One was "If It Takes All Night," written by our friend David Forman, the guy we gigged with in New York. The other was "Arianne," a gentle melody that moves real slow and lets me take my time getting lost in the lyrics about a woman "made of feelings so I milk her of her kisses and swallow up her breathing and taste her where she loves me." I loved the story. My own story was that some of my frustration was ending. I was getting to record again. And with "Arianne," recording with lush strings soaring over me was a gift from God. Singing was the important thing, just singing about the beauty and loneliness of pure love. I was happy to be out of those old contracts and free to record with family. Didn't matter who the producer was. Singing was the thing.

Charles

If I'm not mistaken, one of the items in the budget for that first album was $10,000 designated for drugs. And no one was complaining. Cyril wrote "Vieux Carré Rouge," a musical postcard from the French Quarter, a fantasy about a dancer who intoxicates with bodily movements liquid as love. Art wrote "Speed of Light," a slow burner expressing deep feelings about captivity. I was still captive to drugs, and the drawings I was doing — where the needle held me chained to the crucible of addiction — said the same thing. Cyril also wrote "Break Away," which had a similar motif, only this time the captive was the victim of a twisted romance. Brother Cyril sang that song like his life was on the line.

CYRIL

"Break Away" hit me hard because I realized that's just what I needed to do. But to break away from my sick associations of the past took more than an act of will. It took an act of God. It was God, I'm convinced, who brought me to Gaynielle. And whatever the great spirits put together, no one — not even my silly ass — can put asunder.

When I met Gaynielle, I was still sick, still a druggie, under the influence, living in my car, running around in a rage, fueled by discontent and disillusionment. Gaynielle was much younger than me, and much wiser, too. She was the first woman to say I had to forgive myself before I could forgive anyone else. Just to hear a woman speak about forgiveness was so new and refreshing, I found myself filled with hope. For so long, I had seen my relationships with women as struggles; the metaphors in my mind were battles, wars, endless antagonism. Gaynielle changed that thinking. She showed me that relationships are based on tenderness, compassion, understanding. She brought me a new sense of my own worth. Gaynielle brought me love.

Gaynielle also introduced me to the music of Bob Marley, whose *Kaya* album rocked my world. "Is This Love" became our song, providing the soundtrack for our romance. If John Coltrane was a divine instrument of universal love, Bob Marley embodied that same divinity. Marley's "No Woman, No Cry" and "Natty Dread" took off the top of my head. His "Rebel Music (Three O'Clock Roadblock)" taught me that, although the island spirit was free, the islands themselves were no freer for a black man than anyplace else. I loved early reggae because every song was political. Everything about me was political.

Gaynielle's dad, Mr. George, was slow to accept me. He was a master carpenter who, when I was out of work, took me on his gigs. I'd try to hang sheetrock, and he'd tell me, "Good thing you're a musician 'cause you ain't shit on this job." He was brutally honest but underneath a cool dude who had raised a strong family. It was Gaynielle's strength of character — the strength of a black woman rich with self-esteem — that put me on a healing path. She accepted my children, *all* my children, as though they were her own. She loved me not for who I was onstage but for myself. When I was a little boy, Percy Mayfield's "Please Send Me Someone to Love" touched me in a special place. I heard it as a prayer. When I found Gaynielle, when we grew to know each other, when I asked her to marry me and be my queen, that prayer was answered.

From that day on, renewed by the devotion of a righteous woman, I became a different man. Challenges were still ahead. I'd fuck up a few more times. But something in me was changed forever. A light had been switched on. I guess it's the same light my mother had been telling me about ever since I was a kid — the light of love.

Big Chief Got a Golden Crown

Aaron

Uncle Jolly had been in and out of the hospital for a couple of years, but when I admitted him in the summer of 1980, I knew it was serious. He had held many jobs — from merchant marine to doorman at the Roosevelt Hotel — but the one that did him in, I believe, was the asbestos plant where he'd worked for years. That shit got in his lungs and gave him cancer. In the beginning, with *The Wild Tchoupitoulas* and the touring, he could handle it. His voice was still strong. But then the coughing got worse, his voice cracked, and we knew something was real wrong. By May of that year, I could see he was dying.

Until he went into the hospital, Jolly had been living next door to me, Joel, and our kids on Valence. I was especially close to him — but so were all my brothers. Which is why I got pissed at them for not visiting him more often in the hospital, especially when the end was so near.

Art

There are certain things you don't want to face. Certain things you don't want to admit, even to yourself. Maybe I was denying how seriously sick he was; maybe I didn't want to see a man whom I loved since I was a little baby wilt away like that. We spoke, he knew how much I cared, but unlike Aaron, I couldn't hang at the hospital night and day.

Charles

When I moved back home, I found myself in love with a long series of white women. I was still trying to make up for those dark days when interracial sex was punishable by death. The lure of forbidden fruit was irresistible. But beyond the symbolism, these were women I deeply loved. Nancy, for instance, was a prim and proper lady who moved comfortably in high society. Our affair was wildly passionate; she moved out on her husband and, because of our liaison, lost her friends and job. Complicating matters more, these relationships were not monogamous on my part. My addictive/compulsive behavior was not limited to drugs. While with Nancy, I also fell madly for Carol, a well-bred southern girl whom I found absolutely intriguing. In addition, there were Lotus and Deborah, beautiful hippie chicks who today are beautiful women and remain two of my closest friends.

Deborah was in nursing school with Ruth, who also became a casual lover. As nursing students, both Deborah and Ruth tried to help me get off methadone. I'd get scrips from doctors for drugs to counteract the effects of meth. But nothing helped. It was crazy; the cycle of taking one drug to get off another was unending. The more my determination, the more disillusioning my slips. At one point Deborah put me in touch with Sister Phyllis, a nun in New York who ran a rehab with an astoundingly high recovery record. I went up for the cure. Dr. John and I shared a tiny apartment in SoHo, where I waited around for days. At the last minute I learned that there was no room in Sister Phyllis's program. In disgust, I spent all my money on drugs except for twenty dollars, hardly enough to get me home. Dr. John said not to worry. "We gonna do some voodoo," he promised, and with that he took my twenty, wrapped it around a candle, stuck it in a dish of water, tied some root around the thing, mumbled some prayers, and assured me more money was on the way. Well, after a couple of minutes, my twenty caught fire and burned to a crisp. "Fuck this voodoo," I said. "Don't worry," said the good doctor. "That means our prayers have been accepted." I suffered for two days, but on the third a royalty check from BMI arrived for $300. I was able to score some shit, plus a ticket home.

Back in New Orleans I met and fell in love with Roberta,* who would be with me for many years. Roberta was a photographer and painter, a Jewish woman, soft-spoken, sweet, and gentle. It was Roberta who later helped care for my aunt Cat and aunt Espy during their last days. It was also Roberta who, more than anyone, was disgusted with my dependency on dope.

Lucky had moved back to New Orleans — the same Lucky who'd been my hustling buddy in New York — and had access to some cold-blooded cocaine. I got hooked up to my eyebrows. When it was time to pay our rent, I confessed to Roberta that the money had gone for coke. "How in hell could you choose dope over rent money?" she asked. "I'll show you how," I said. "Try some of this shit, and you'll see." For the next month Roberta did coke with me. When the rent was due and we were out of dope, I asked her to choose. "Buy the coke," she said.

*Fictitious name

I couldn't jump off the treadmill, and when Jolly was desperately sick, I was too preoccupied with my addictions — drugs and women — to do him much good. Jolly had been a father, an uncle, and a friend. He was also the musical catalyst who drew me back to my brothers. I owed him everything, but a junkie has only one real allegiance, and that's to the sacred proposition of scoring more junk.

Aaron

I can hear Jolly's voice right now. I'd go to the hospital and pull up a chair next to his bed. He'd take my hand and say, "Baby, let's pray." Jolly called all his nephews and nieces "baby." The sound of that "baby" had more love in it than any word I'd ever heard. He was suffering something awful. The lung cancer was eating him away; the decay was steady and terrible to see. But he had made his peace with God. He had gone through his changes and come out a man. I saw his manhood in how he treated the nurses and everyone around him. He never lost his manners, never had anything but a kind word for everyone. There were French Gypsies who came to visit him, friends he had made who treated him like he was their father.

CYRIL

When my uncle first befriended the Gypsies, I was skeptical. The Gypsy father was a painter who had come to New Orleans with his wife and two children to soak up the artistic vibe. He and Jolly became tighter than tight. Jolly seemed as close to them as he was to us. He embraced them like long-lost family. Maybe I was jealous. After all, they were white. Then Jolly started telling me about what the Gypsies had gone through in Europe — how, like the Jews and homosexuals, they had been tortured and murdered in World War II. "This is how some people," said Jolly, referring to the Nazis, "treat other white people. It just ain't about whites hating blacks. It's about hatred — *period*." Jolly was always telling me to get past skin color. "Don't let the racists turn you into them," he warned. Slowly I warmed up to the Gypsy family.

Aaron

I had a cot in the hospital and sometimes slept there. I watched Jolly go through his suffering, but I never let him see me cry. When I had to cry, I'd walk down the hallway and hide in the men's room. I might weep for five minutes, wipe my eyes, and go back and hold his hand like nothing had happened. Joel was there, too. Once, she and I had to authorize a test the doctors wanted to do. They stuck in a long, long needle to draw fluid from Jolly's lungs; I watched the blood come streaming out of his mouth and thought of the power of his voice — to chant and sing and shout out his Indian songs — now reduced to nothing. I watched him go from a big strapping man to a helpless child. I tried to visit him before and after every gig. One night, before I went to the hospital, I called the doctor just to check Jolly's condition. "He's gone," the doctor said. It was August 9, 1980. He was sixty-three.

Art

The funeral of George Landry was a noted event in the history of New Orleans. The newspapers ran page-long articles and dozens of pictures; history books on the Mardi Gras Indians devoted whole chapters to the day his body was laid to rest and his life celebrated. Only four months before, he had led his Wild Tchoupitoulas tribe on the Mardi Gras parade. Now there was another kind of parade, a funeral parade, honoring Jolly with the glory of the tradition he had helped keep alive.

First came a Catholic mass. The casket sitting up there was draped with the headdress of Big Chief Jolly. Afterward, outside the church, a brass band played a haunting funeral blues that followed the casket down Constance Street. The other tribes participated in full regalia — Chief Pete of the Black Eagles, Bo Dollis of the Wild Magnolias. Everyone was singing "My Big Chief Got a Golden Crown." The song was slow, the song was sad. People had drums and tambourines; it was one of the biggest second lines the city had ever seen. Kids who knew him and kids who didn't know him, old folks weeping, Indians chanting, their costumes — green and yellow and blue and red — lighting up the world, everyone going from sad to glad and breaking into "Hey Pocky A-Way," the song that said so much about the love we had for the man whose name described the way he viewed the world. The tributes for Jolly went on and on: when the parade reached Valence Street, one Wild Tchoupitoulas all in yellow did an intense dance before dropping to his knees and kissing the sidewalk, all out of respect to his fallen leader. Long into the afternoon, long into the night, you could hear the sound of singing, "Brother Jolly's gone . . . Brother Jolly's gone . . ."

Aaron

It all started at my house, where Jolly was laid out in an open casket in his Indian costume. I don't remember everything because, to tell the truth, I wasn't in good shape. Hundreds of people were converging on my house. There was so much commotion and sadness inside me, I just wanted to escape the crazy scene. I went next door and shot up dope. I meant no disrespect to my uncle. I wish I could tell you that his death sobered me up, where I wouldn't get high no more. But the devil wasn't through with me yet. I was still dealing with heroin, and if anything could make the pain go away, if anything could numb the loss of a man I loved with all my heart, it was that fuckin' white powder.

Charles

I never made it to Jolly's funeral; I was too busy looking to score. Looking back, I see it as one of the saddest days of my life. I was seriously strung out, trying to get off methadone, hunting down some smack to get me through a few hours. I was running from pillar to post, but no one had anything. For whatever reason, my dope supplies had dried up. I was scrambling like a wild man, desperately looking to connect, not able to think about anything else — not even my uncle's last hurrah. Of all people, Jolly would have understood. I was sick, but my sickness didn't take away the shame I felt. I wasted the whole day searching for smack.

Art

One lousy aftertaste left over from Jolly's funeral concerned his costumes. Some of his friends wanted to borrow them for the parade. I said sure, certain that's how Jolly would have wanted it. But the so-called friends never returned the magnificent costumes, which were priceless. Now ain't that a bitch?

CYRIL

After Jolly was gone, the Wild Tchoupitoulas part of our show slowly but surely faded away. We would put banners carrying his big-chief image across the stage — we still do that — and he remains strong in our consciousness. But the Neville Brothers, along with Black Male and the Uptown Allstars, were entering a new period.

Art

One reason we dropped the Wild Tchoupitoulas were those damn Indian costumes. They were beautiful, but hell to carry on planes. They couldn't really be dry-cleaned, and because we performed in them under hot lights, they got sweaty and smelly. I think we were all glad to see them go.

Charles

We were going through something of a tough time. Our first record on Capitol didn't really sell, and the industry hardly saw us as moneymakers. Our main audience was white college kids in New Orleans, especially students at Tulane. We often played on campus — not that far from Valence Street — and developed a devoted fan base. The kids would go home to Mississippi or Missouri or Illinois, tell their friends about us, their friends might tell their local clubs, and we'd be booked. You'd hear our shit on college radio stations interested in real-deal black music. But because we weren't following any disco or postdisco fashions — we sure as hell didn't sound like Michael Jackson or Luther Vandross — black stations ignored us.

Aaron

After the Capitol album came out, we didn't have a deal for a couple of years. A big-time producer in New York, a man who became a close friend, Joel Dorn, shopped us to all the labels. Everyone passed. But one night Bette Midler was in New Orleans and heard us at Tipitina's, an Uptown club not far from Valence Street that got hot among the college kids. Named after the Professor Longhair song, Tipitina's became our second home, the place where we built our reputation.

Maybe it was the death of Jolly, maybe it was the dope, but I was feeling increasingly discouraged. I wasn't singing much more than "Tell It Like It Is" and "Arianne." Artie and Cyril were handling most of the vocals while I hid behind dark glasses. I wasn't really there. So when Bette Midler started singing our praises, it was a wake-up call. She convinced Jerry Moss, who along with Herb Alpert owned A&M Records, to let Joel Dorn produce our next album. It was a great opportunity. I prayed to Saint Jude to be there in spirit when we started to record. I prayed to find the strength to overcome my addiction. I realized I had to take the initiative to find a way out of hell. And this time I was determined to do it.

Lovely Lady Dressed in Blue

CYRIL

It should have been a big moment in the history of the Brothers. We were about to cut the album for A&M, a great opportunity to record with Black Male and the Uptown Allstars, which included Nick Daniels on bass and Mean Willie Green on drums. I didn't like how some members of our management tried to sabotage the career of Black Male. Now this new album might make up for that. Management viewed Black Male as our competition; I viewed them as our children — and Professor Shorthair was no less than our guru. Musically, we were all cut from the same cloth; we were made to record together.

But Dorn had different ideas. He had New York session players he wanted to use. They were cool, but they sure didn't know us like Black Male. No one did. Charles didn't even play the tenor solos; Fathead Newman did.

Charles

My attitude was that I was glad to get the A&M deal. Fathead is a wonderful player, and if they wanted to use him, fine. I was still busy chasing down drugs and glad to leave the production to the producer. I was also distracted by problems with management. Money wasn't reaching us in the right proportions. I had warned one particular manager that we wanted to be paid, but he really didn't pay too much attention until I snuck into his backyard, waited for him to arrive, and put a shotgun to his head. Must have been the reality check he needed; shortly thereafter, the money started flowing to us.

Art

The A&M record was called *Fiyo on the Bayou,* a modification of the title and tune I had done with the Meters. The studio cats gave it a different feeling, and I liked the results. The whole album kicked ass. Dorn got Cissy Houston and her young daughter Whitney to do background on "Sitting in Limbo," with me singing lead. "Limbo," composed by Jimmy Cliff, is one of the most serious reggae jams ever written.

CYRIL

I was against putting "Brother John" on the record. We'd already done it on *The Wild Tchoupitoulas* and never been paid the writer's money due me and Uncle Jolly. Until that shit was straightened out, I saw no reason for other people to make money off my efforts. I sang it anyway, but I wasn't happy.

Aaron

I was happy with *Fiyo on the Bayou* because Joel Dorn understood our music. Keith Richards told *Rolling Stone* magazine it was the best album of the year. What makes it special for me were a couple of precious ballads. Joel Dorn had me testifying to "The Ten Commandments of Love," a song that dips all the way back to the Moonglows in the fifties. I also sang "Mona Lisa" with a slew of strings all around me. That was a special thrill because "Mona Lisa" was my mother and father's favorite song. There are many vocalists I have loved: Sam Cooke was a master; Clyde McPhatter was a genius; in my own hometown, Johnny Adams, called the Tan Canary, could sing any song in any style — Johnny was superbad. But I don't think any vocalist was as loved as when Nat "King" Cole sang "Mona Lisa." The older generation in my household looked at Nat Cole as the beginning and end of romantic music, and when I recorded "Mona Lisa," I pictured my parents standing there next to me.

Fiyo on the Bayou was a heavy time. I had promised myself that once the record was cut, I would check into rehab. I had never gone that route. My old method was to take a bus to New York, curl up in the backseat, and go cold turkey. That method worked but never lasted long. Here it was, the eighties, I was forty, and like Marvin Gaye wrote in "Flyin' High in the Friendly Sky," I was "still hooked to the boy who makes slaves out of men." "Boy" was heroin; heroin was my undoing. But devotion to Jesus and Saint Jude gave me the courage to finally sign up for the rehab program at DePaul Hospital in New Orleans. I'd be locked down for the first week. After that, I had no idea what would happen.

I was afraid. I was also confused — happy I'd made the commitment, scared I couldn't keep it. Part of me felt lucky that rehab places even existed; another part of me wanted nothing to do with them. The week before, I was in New York — this was when *Fiyo on the Bayou* was nearly complete — staying at a friend's apartment. I sat at his piano, thinking about my future and singing about the past, singing all the old stuff, the Soul Stirrers' "Any Day Now," "Touch the Hem of His Garment," "Be with Me, Jesus," "Jesus, Wash Away My Troubles." I played those old songs over and over. I knew I needed to make my transformation, needed to get back to the place where I was a little boy who believed in the goodness of God and the power of prayer. I remembered the Catholic Church of my childhood. Now I needed to remember how to pray. My fingers ran over the keys on the piano as these words poured out:

Lovely lady dressed in blue
Teach me how to pray
If God was just your little boy
Then you know the way
Did you lift him up sometimes
Taking him on your knee?
Did you tell him stories of the world
Like Mother did to me?
And when he fell did you lift him up
And make everything all right?
Did you tell him his prayers at night?
Lovely lady dressed in blue
Oh, God was just your little boy
And you know the truth
Did you whisper in his ears sweet lullabies?
I want to know — did he cry?
Lovely lady dressed in blue
Oh, won't you please teach me to pray
'Cause God was just your little boy
I want to know, please teach me how to pray

When I was through, my eyes were filled with tears and my heart was happy. If the Blessed Mother could mother God, she could mother me. I felt the love of my own mother and, at that moment, knew I could go into the hospital and do what needed to be done.

I was in there for a week without any drugs of any kind before I went to group therapy. I was shy and didn't speak much. An older lady said to me, "When you first came in here, I was afraid of you. Your eyes frightened me. But now I see there's a light in your eyes. I believe the Lord is working with you. I want to give you this book and pray it helps you as surely as it helped me." The book was called *The Greatest Miracle in the World* by Og Mandino. The kind-hearted woman was right; the book filled me with inspiration. It said the same thing Saint Jude had been saying, that miracles were possible. It said I could reclaim my sense of myself, my own worth and my ability to stay clean. I stayed two more weeks in the rehab unit because I didn't feel ready to deal with the outside. I stayed in prayer, and I felt a calmness come over me I had never felt before. When I left, I left clean. I vowed to stay off drugs. With God's help, I've kept that vow.

When I got out, I changed friends. I separated myself from the users and abusers. If anyone came to me or my brothers with dope, I'd get in their face and scare them so bad, they'd never come back again. I became a watchdog. But a lifetime of drug taking taught me no one stops till they're ready. I tried to keep the scene clean, but I sure as hell wasn't going to start preaching. Naturally I knew when one of the brothers was high. The tempo would be too fast or too slow; I could hear it in their voice or see it in their eyes. Brothers know brothers. I knew when my brothers were hurting.

Charles

The hurt was deep — deeper than a sense of loss or disappointment. For me, it had reached a level of self-loathing. I had struggled with my fuckin' addiction for decades and gotten nowhere. I had sworn to stop, I had availed myself of half a dozen programs, I had gone off and on methadone more times than I care to recall. Now I was feeling hopeless. Hopeless lives next door to despair, and despair can be as much an addiction as any narcotic. My depression was profound, my thinking unrelentingly negative.

I started thinking how I was letting down my brothers. Here we had finally come together as a family, we were finally making a decent living as musicians, and I was endangering the whole setup; one drug bust could bring it all down. With my connections to the underworld, with the dealers coming around me, I could ruin Neville Productions. At the same time, I was incapable of functioning without substituting methadone for heroin — and vice versa. There was no way out.

My mind was closing in on me. The world was closing in on me. The only way to protect my brothers from myself was to eliminate myself. The thought startled me. Was I capable of the ultimate self-punishment? Had my self-disgust reached the point of no return? I saw myself as intelligent; I knew I had talent; I had survived the back alleys of New Orleans, the world of Angola, and the cold-blooded streets of New York City. Surely I had something going for me. Maybe I did, but in the meantime I was going crazy. I saw my addiction as an intolerable, inexcusable weakness, and I no longer wanted to live.

Roberta and I were living on Valence with Auntie Cat and Aunt Espy. God bless Roberta. She nursed Auntie Cat through her last days. And when that remarkable lady — Mrs. Virginia Harris — passed away, Roberta devoted herself to Aunt Espy, a blind invalid who required round-the-clock care. In her self-sacrificing love for me and my aunts, Roberta was something of a saint. Her goodness only made me hate myself that much more.

The full weight of these dark thoughts was heavy on my head. I felt like my head was in a vise smashing against my temples. I wanted the pain to stop, the hideous cycle to end. I knew of only one way out. I took my shotgun from the closet, loaded it, walked out to the back porch, and stuck the fuckin' thing in my mouth. Roberta saw what was happening and called our neighbor. Donnie is a masseur, a warm and wise man with a strong gift for language. "I respect you, Charles," he said, "but are you sure you know what you're doing?" Quietly, deliberately he engaged me in a dialogue of reason. "Reasonable men," he said, "find solutions. You *will* find a solution. It's only a matter of time. This is a chemical and an emotional malaise. It's a sickness. To call it personal failure is a way to punish yourself. You don't have to do that." As Donnie's arguments sunk in, I remembered something my mother had once said. Before, I had dismissed it as a cliché, but now the words resonated with truth: *A quitter never wins and a winner never quits*. I took the gun out of my mouth.

A few more years would pass before I found a program that let me see the light of clarity. I'd keep stumbling, but never again would I toy with self-destruction. I recommitted myself to the struggle, no matter how long it took. And in the meantime, at certain moments on certain days, I had flashes of insight. Once, for instance, when I was trying to kick methadone, the withdrawal was horrendous. I suffered seizures and uncontrollable vomiting. I fell and couldn't raise myself off the floor — that's how weak I was. Suddenly I had a vision: I was outside in Rosenwald Park near the Calliope projects where we lived as kids. A person was standing over me, not a human being of flesh and blood but a figure made of light. The figure was neither male nor female, just pure light, the same light that settled on my forehead and filled me with strength. I felt the light flow through me. Then a voice spoke these words: *"Remember the children."* I could see children in the park playing on swings. I could hear their laughter and see their smiles. It was an epiphany that comforted and calmed my soul. I might not have completely understood the vision, but its essence was positive; its message was that the light had not been extinguished. There was hope ahead.

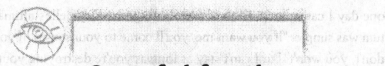

Grateful for the Deadheads

Aaron

Once I got clean, I was able to do some things that were important to me. I began the Uptown Youth Center for needy kids and took a personal interest in its programs. We took over a playground and an old firehouse in the Thirteenth Ward; it was a grassroots effort that really took hold; grown people today tell me they'd be lost if that place hadn't been there.

With Allen Toussaint, I also started NOAH, New Orleans Artists Against Hunger and Homelessness, an organization that did a world of good and is still going strong. I sang in dozens of benefits for officers who died in the line of duty. Whenever I could lend my voice to raise money for good causes, I did so. Being off dope was a godsend.

CYRIL

It wasn't so much God who sent me a message, but my wife, Gaynielle. By then our beautiful daughter, Lirica, was born, and one day I came home to find them both gone. Gaynielle's ultimatum was simple: "If you want me, you'll come to your senses. If you don't, you won't. But I can't stay as long as you're destroying yourself with those hard drugs."

I went to a friend's house and hid in the back bedroom. I went cold turkey. I wore out Bob Marley's *Natty Dread*, the sound of "No Woman, No Cry" playing over and over again, a holy mantra on my mind. I went to Bonnebal Hospital and stayed five weeks. The program worked well until I got the bill — $12,000 — which made me wanna get high all over again. I didn't. I attended a bunch of AA meetings around town. I liked the idea of one drunk helping another, one junkie gaining courage from the story of another junkie. I thought of using again, but the question kept coming back — *Do my balls belong to me or the dope man?* I wanted my balls back, my self-respect, my wife, and little girl. For a while I would trade off — I'd drink beer and not coke up, or coke up and not drink. But that was dumb. I knew I had to stop everything — heroin, cocaine, speedballing, and booze. I did. Stopped everything but pot. I saw no harm in pot, and besides, I viewed myself as suffering from the posttrauma of being a black man in America. I was the member of one subculture being controlled by another. Pot helped me deal with that. Besides, I'd never heard of anyone high on pot going on a murder spree or driving a car a hundred miles an hour. Pot was benevolent. Pot was the Rasta herb. Pot helped numb me from the world that was shattered when my father, my little sister, and my mother all died. Pot was cool. It would take me another fifteen years to realize that even pot, and the rationalizations surrounding it, might not be a cure-all. Meanwhile, the hard stuff was behind me, even if hard times were still here.

Art

After *Fiyo on the Biyou,* we had a hard time getting a deal. Fact is, from 1981 till 1987 we had no deal. For all its good reviews, *Fiyo* didn't sell and no one was willing to take a chance on us. These were the years when we were slammin' at places like Tipitina's. These were also the years when although our fan base was mixed, I'd say it was mostly white. I love my own people with all my heart, but if the Nevilles had to depend on them for our musical livelihood, we'd go broke. In terms of real audience breakthrough, it was white bands like the Rolling Stones and the Grateful Dead who brought us to their fans. It began when we played some gigs with the Dead and I saw Jerry Garcia digging on our shit. "Jerry," I said, "why don't you bring us along on a tour?" "Cool," he replied. And that was it.

Charles

When we opened for the Stones in the eighties, that was a way to widen our exposure. Unlike the record companies, the Stones didn't give a shit whether we had any radio hits. They felt the same way as our hardcore fans; they wanted their funk full strength. The Stones helped us a lot. The big turning point, though, was the Dead. We did a New Year's show with them that rocked the planet. After that, we started noticing Deadheads at our concerts, whether we were actually playing with the Grateful

Dead or not. The tie-dyed crowd had fallen in love with us, and as someone who always has and always will identify with the hippies, I loved them as well.

Art

We appreciate fans of any kind, and for those years that the Deadheads adopted us as their own, business was good. You had to watch the water you were drinking, though, 'cause the 'Heads were always happy to drop in a little high-powered acid as a token of appreciation. I had already gone through my purple haze days and wasn't interested in tripping. Unfortunately, I was interested in some shit that I should have never touched.

Some years back I had met a young woman named Jenny. Eventually we married. Together we had a son, Ian, who's now a bright young man in college. Jenny brought out the wild in me, or I brought out the wild in her. I guess it worked both ways. The wild part is that while I had always been someone who avoided drugs while my brothers were getting blasted, they were now getting clean while I fell down the dark hole of addiction. I can't tell you why I waited so late in my life to fall. Freebase cocaine was sweeping the country in the seventies and eighties, and it sure as hell swept me. My thinking got twisted. I was so messed-up I didn't see freebase as a drug; I thought it was just stuff for the good people. I kept hearing the echo of the question my relatives used to ask my brothers, "Why can't you be like Artie?" Artie was always clean, straight, the one who got away without a scratch. But now Artie got caught up in some shit that brought out his devil. These were some demonic times. Jenny didn't survive. She died at a tragically young age. I barely survived myself. Finally I was able to put it away. Those years are gone, like pages ripped out of a book. I don't want to think about them; I don't want to remember. All I can do is thank God that Ian, who was born in the middle of the craziness, turned out so healthy and strong. A lot of credit goes to Lorraine, the woman who is my wife today.

CYRIL

The eighties were marked by the death of men who molded our musical universe: In 1980, only months before Uncle Jolly, Professor Longhair passed. In 1983 James Booker expired in a waiting room at Charity Hospital. He was a troubled man, but the city of New Orleans, birthplace of a slew of piano players who changed the world of sound, has never produced anyone better than James Booker. A few years later my soul brother and eternal inspiration, Gerald Tillman, our beloved Professor Shorthair, died a young man. Gerald had been sick, and I believe that, like Booker, he died of a broken heart. The world never gave these geniuses their due.

Black Male hadn't played with the Neville Brothers in some time. I had taken over the Uptown Allstars when my nephew Ivan, who'd proved himself a stupendous writer-singer-keyboardist, went to California to start his solo career. Ivan — like me, like everyone Gerald ever encountered — was devastated by Gerald's death. Gerald had been sick for more than a year, and in testimony to their love and esteem, the members of Black Male refused to play without him. The night of his death we were at Benny's, the Uptown club around the corner from Valence Street where I loved to jam with the Uptown Allstars. We were working on what I call the first second-line reggae groove. When we heard the news about Gerald, we stopped playing. We could hardly breathe. We walked outside and someone said, "Look at the moon." The moon was encircled by a triple rainbow; suddenly a shooting star streaked across the sky. Even now, so many years later, when the funk starts to sizzle onstage and the groove's good and greasy, we say, "That's Tillman." In introducing the Nevilles, I tell audiences all over the world, "We are brought to you by the spirit of our founder and mentor, Gerald Professor Shorthair Tillman." Believe me, the brother lives on.

Charles

We lived through some brutal deaths. When the brother of our drummer, Newton Mossip, was killed in cold blood, Newton was understandably enraged. His brother's funeral was held at a church a block from Valence. We all attended — and so did the two dudes allegedly responsible, almost as a dare. A few days later there were murderous repercussions. One dude was dead; another had a big chunk of his neck blown away. Newton was arrested but later released because they never found a weapon or a single witness. Some claimed me and my brothers were involved. But the truth is that we did not kill anyone. And I'm glad to report that Newton, an intelligent and talented man who has been to hell and back, is an active drummer again.

Art

During the eighties, even when we weren't selling records, we were burning up the clubs. We were developing a coterie of die-hard fans all over the country, especially in northern California. If you caught us at Wolfgang's in San Francisco or the Catalyst in Santa Cruz, you were certain that you were hearing the hottest band ever.

Our music was tight, but our business thing wasn't. We had some good managers who did their best to get us through — Rupert Surcoff, Bill Johnston, Harry Duncan, Steve Egerton, Pamela Gibbons. Shannon Chabaud, who helped us get organized, is still running Neville Productions. We didn't know what was missing, though, until we found it. The missing link was Bill Graham.

Bill was a Jewish guy born in Germany. He and his sister escaped the Nazis. He came to California and during the height of the hippies promoted acts like Jefferson Airplane and the Dead. He opened the Fillmore West and turned it into the music palace of the flower children. Bill was a strong character, tough talking and right to the fuckin' point. We bonded one night standing in the wings while Booker T. and the MGs were onstage. When I saw Bill digging on Booker as much as I was, I knew he was cool. This was in the eighties, when Bill was running Bill Graham Presents, one of the most powerful management/concert concerns in the country. To some he seemed gruff, but to me he was just straight-up sincere. I believe he loved the Neville Brothers, and we loved him.

Aaron

Graham once said to me, "I come to your shows whenever I'm down 'cause I know you'll lift me up. Someone should make a Neville pill for depression. If you squeeze all that Neville spirit into a pill, no one would ever be unhappy again."

We were happy to hook up with Bill, who assigned Morty Wiggins to the Neville Brothers. Morty put in a helluva lot of time with us. He was devoted. We got a deal on Rounder/EMI, which meant, for the first time in five years, we were back in the studio.

Charles

Bill Graham Presents is supersavvy big-time management. That's why they still represent us and why Arnie Pustilnik, who took over after Morty, is still our man. But it took a while to put us in the right recording environment. The album on Rounder/EMI, the one called *Uptown,* was pretty fuckin' flat. It came out in 1987 and, with drum machines and synthesizers, tried to catch a techno-dance feeling that, by the time of the record release, was already out of fashion. The producer was gung-ho on getting us radio play. But in doing so, he gave us a tinny sound that had nothing to do with our souls. The thing flopped.

CYRIL

Uptown was ridiculous. We had basically worked out the entire album over at Artie's shotgun on Valence. We had a little equipment over there, no air-conditioning, and sweated our way through the material. When we took it to the studio, though, we saw we had no control. The record company representative had an engineer spend six hours recording a thunderstorm. I didn't know what the fuck was happening. Everything got diluted; our spirit was sucked dry. Finally, the record had nothing to do with us except for a couple of tunes. Ivan, our bass player Daryl Johnson, and I wrote "You're the One"; Ivan, our guitarist Brian Stoltz, and I wrote "I Never Needed No One" — which could be the story of my life — but both songs got drowned in a sea of bad production. I can't think of any other album of ours that sounds so dated.

Charles

One cool thing about the record was the guests who played on it, guys who pitched in to give us support — Keith Richards, Jerry Garcia, Branford Marsalis, Carlos Santana, and Richie Zito. I was touched and, at the very same time, had something weightier on my mind. I was moved to make good a promise long overdue. Cyril was off smack, Aaron was clean, but I was still fucking around. I finally realized that the only way was to simply drop out of the rat race and devote all my energy to recovery. When I made that decision, everything changed.

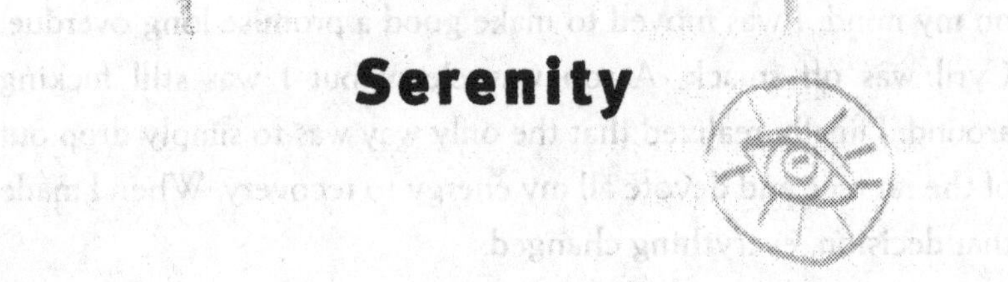

Serenity

Charles

Earlier in the eighties, we had played on the campus of the University of Oregon in Eugene. The moment I stepped off the bus and planted my feet on the grass, I felt at home. There was peace and calm in the air, hippies reading beneath shady trees and sending loving, welcoming vibes my way. A couple of years later, studying various rehab facilities and their recovery records, I noticed a place called Serenity Lane located in Eugene. I read that their success rate was highest among all treatment centers. Their main methodology was a twelve-step program modeled on Alcoholics Anonymous. I decided to go.

It was a major decision, especially in light of the fact that the Neville Brothers were booked on the Amnesty tour with Miles Davis. I hated to miss that, but there was no way around it. I was forty-eight, and for twenty-nine years I'd been hooked, periodically vowing to stop while staying in an environment that crushed my vows into dust. Serenity Lane had no more than a hundred patients, broken into groups of ten. Before Serenity I had been to a few AA meetings, but in those days the program drew a sharp division between alcoholics and drug addicts; the alcoholics thought they were better. Serenity ignored such distinctions. Substance abuse was substance abuse. There were ongoing meetings night and day, and it didn't take long to understand the single ingredient I had been missing in trying to kick drugs. I had been counting on my mind. My reasoning went like this: *If I understood what was wrong, if I knew why I got high, if I clearly saw the reasons behind my self-destructive behavior, surely I could stop*. But the people at Serenity — all of whom, including the cat who swept the floor, were recovering addicts themselves — took another approach. Their program was based on spiritual maintenance. The first of the twelve steps asked that I admit that I'm powerless over my disease. The power to recover comes not from my willpower but from my willingness to trust a power higher than myself. The source of healing is not the logic of the mind but the mystery of the heart. Some call that higher power God, others simply call it love. I remembered a metaphor I read in Oriental mythology in which the mind is seen as a monkey who can't stop fucking up. That was me.

Working these steps represented a gentler, more compassionate approach. In the past I had excoriated myself for being weak. Now I admitted I needed help beyond my own power to reason; I came to believe that something bigger than me — a spiritual force — could provide that help; I decided to let that force guide my journey; I made a decision to do God's will, not mine. No one dictated any definition of God. I wasn't pressured to accept any specific theology or moral code. It was the God of my own understanding.

At first clichés like "Let go and let God" sounded corny. But the more I lived with such ideas, the more I allowed the wisdom of the program to wash over me, the more relief I felt. A weight had been lifted from my shoulders because, at long last, I saw I didn't have to do it alone. I chose sponsors, mentors to help me through the ups and downs of recovery. One of my counselors was a Native American of deep understanding and patience. I worked those steps and listened intensely when someone quoted the AA Big Book: "Half measures availed us nothing." I saw that I had tapped a higher power within, which gave me calmness and clarity. It wasn't just drugs that had imprisoned me all those years, it was also my ego. My ego, my mind, my stinking thinking had me convinced that I alone could figure it out. Now I saw none of that was necessary. At Serenity I learned to simply surrender.

The recovery worked. When the program was over, I decided to stay in Eugene, where I experienced an emotional equilibrium I had known nowhere else. Roberta moved up there. Lara Lavi, a good singer and friend, formed a jazz band with me. When I felt strong enough, I joined my brothers out on the road, using Eugene as my base. Guided by the time-honored mantra of "one day at a time," I've been sober ever since.

Aaron

Some good things started happening to all the brothers. For me, a key moment was meeting Linda Ronstadt. That was back in 1984 when the Brothers were playing the World's Fair. After her gig, she came to ours with Nelson Riddle, Sinatra's famous arranger who had done Linda's *Lush Life* album. That night Linda sang duets with me onstage, old-time stuff like "Earth Angel." Linda knows as much about American music as anyone. She has great taste in songs. Afterward I asked her for an autograph. She said singing with me made her feel like Cinderella at the ball. "Aaron," she said, "I'll sing with you anywhere." A year later I was doing a NOAH charity concert in New Orleans and asked her to join in. Singing "Ave Maria," we had the whole place crying. "Listen, Aaron," she said, "these live performances are wonderful, but you and I need to record together." I told her I was ready whenever she was. Four years later she made good on her word.

Her album was called *Cry Like a Rainstorm, Howl Like the Wind*. We did four duets, and she put my name on the cover in big letters, "Featuring Aaron Neville." Most artists wouldn't share billing so generously, but Linda isn't most artists. She also shared the artists' royalties with me fifty-fifty. One of those songs, "Don't Know Much," blew up into a huge pop hit, going all the way to number two. It was the first time my voice had been heard on the radio with such frequency since "Tell It Like It Is." That was twenty-three years earlier. It was a thrill to have another hit — a dream I never gave up on — but even more of a thrill to have it with Linda, whose voice is as sweet and pure and strong as any vocalist out there.

After we cut "Don't Know Much," I turned to Linda and said, "See you at the Grammys." Sure enough, she and I were sitting at the Grammys when they announced the winner for Best Pop Vocal Performance by a Duo or Group. "Linda Ronstadt and Aaron Neville." That was a celebration I'll never forget. I got to be in a room with Curtis Mayfield for an hour, just talking and feeling his beautiful spirit. In spite of the accident that cost him his mobility, Curtis's soul remained strong and inspiring. I had my picture taken with Jerry Butler, Ben E. King, and the Shirelles. Best of all, though, that same night my brothers and I had a breakthrough of our own. We won our first Grammy. "Healing Chant" won the Best Pop Instrumental Performance. I wouldn't exactly call it pop, but I've never understood those categories too well. Besides, who gives a shit? A Grammy is a Grammy, and that night I got two.

"Healing Chant" came off a Neville Brothers album called *Yellow*

Moon. After being together for twelve years, me and my brothers finally had a record the world recognized. I was proud that "Yellow Moon" was a song that I wrote. Joel had gone off on a cruise with her sister, and I was feeling lonely. It came from a poem, and all my poems come from my heart.

CYRIL

I've always said that the brothers are our own best producers. But when we signed with A&M in 1989 and they hooked us up with Daniel Lanois, the chemistry was right. Lanois was the baddest outside producer the Nevilles have ever known. He came to New Orleans and turned a house on St. Charles into a studio. Artie brought in a stuffed bobcat, some big ol' rubber snakes, and thickets of moss to hang from the ceiling. Lanois had the voodoo vibe going strong; he had psychics dropping by; he let us hang loose; he encouraged using all sorts of sounds — crickets, the whistling wind, you name it — to catch our family flavor. Lanois knew how to kick back and stay out of the way while bringing out the essential Nevilleness of me, Artie, Aaron, and Charles.

A big turning point came when Daniel came to Benny's, where the Uptown Allstars were playing originals I'd been working on — "Wake Up," "Sister Rosa," and "My Blood" — that expressed my politics. "That's my blood down there," I sang, thinking about the Indian nations, Nicaragua, El Salvador, Belfast, South Africa, Haiti, and the ghettos of America. "Jah, please come to the crossroads, you can save the children I know / Jah, please come to the crossroads, tell them to let my people go."

Daniel asked why these songs hadn't been presented to him. The truth is that management was worried they were too political. But Daniel felt the strength in message material, and it was message material that helped redefine the Neville Brothers and give us a distinct musical character.

Of the twelve tunes on *Yellow Moon,* we wrote seven. And the other five, things like Dylan's "With God on Our Side" and Sam Cooke's "A Change Is Gonna Come," were right up our alley. I was happy that "Sister Rosa," our tribute to civil rights pioneer Rosa Parks, became an anthem while "Wild Injuns" kept Uncle Jolly right there next to us as, commercially speaking, we reached a new level. When I learned that they knew "My Blood" down in South Africa, I was heartened that our worldwide message had gotten through.

Charles

Lanois got more of our spirit and emotional content on record than anyone before or since. He had the smarts not to dominate — as many producers do — but elicit the magic burning at the bottom of our souls. It helped that he's a fine musician himself and played on the tracks. What helped even more was Bill Graham Presents. Bill and his people had it all mapped out. The year leading up to *Yellow Moon,* we did TV shows and high-visibility appearances everywhere from Europe to Japan. When the record hit the streets, we were in every magazine from *Playboy* to GQ. Finally, after a lifetime of false starts and frustrating failures, we had a bona fide runaway success on our hands. *Yellow Moon* went gold. The motherfucker is still selling today.

Art

I liked A&M. Over the next eight years, we put out five CDs on the label, and every one was solid. Nothing took off like *Yellow*

Moon, but they were all true to our musical selves. If you look at the overall package — the artwork, the song selection, the production values — you'll see a certain class that no other label had ever afforded us. I appreciated their respect. We also made real money with A&M. After thirty years of being fucked by jackleg label owners and two-bit hucksters, it was a pleasure to do business with reputable people like Jerry Moss, Herb Alpert, and Al Cafaro.

CYRIL

I still felt like odd man out. Even with the success, I was the brother who spoke up too much and mouthed off too often. Maybe that's because I still felt like a junior member of the fraternity. I also saw control — musical and managerial control — slipping away into the hands of others, while I've always been convinced that control should rest with the brothers. Maybe it's a generation gap; my brothers may be more willing to go along with authority. If I don't think it's in our best interest, I challenge that shit.

Charles

It was clear that, just because we had a bestselling album, the conflicts wouldn't end. Aaron now had hits on his own. He had proved what we all knew. "Tell It Like It Is" was no fluke, and he'd once again become a pop star. His love for us and concern for our welfare never weakened — he never left us and never will — but he suddenly had another career on another track. That could create potential conflicts. Cyril had a temperament and a political agenda that did not always coincide with everyone else. Artie was fighting demons of his own. I still faced problems with addiction — not drugs, but women. I was still going through changes. The nineties — just like the eighties and seventies — weren't easy, but different in at least one respect: our audience expanded beyond New Orleans and the United States to the world. That meant more to us than making money, although earning a good living is nothing to sneeze at. Even before the term was used, I always felt we were playing world music, sounds that resonated in different hearts in different cultures. Now I saw for myself — in France and Haiti, in Israel and Italy, no matter where we traveled — the universality of our family groove.

Warm Your Heart

Aaron

In the mid-eighties Joel Dorn produced six songs on me, doo-wop classics like "Pledging My Love" and "For Your Precious Love." Joel's a great producer; the record was sweet but never found a major label. But now in the nineties, with "Don't Know Much" under my belt, big labels were expressing interest in me.

When the Brothers signed with A&M, the label wanted me as a solo artist as well. That definitely warmed my heart. "Warm Your Heart" was a song sung by Clyde McPhatter and the Drifters back in the distant fifties. Turned out so well, we decided to use it as the title of my debut A&M CD. Linda Ronstadt and her friend George Massenburg, an engineering genius, produced the record. Because Linda is such a fine singer herself, she understands what a singer needs in the studio, the material and the production to make me comfortable. I've never been more comfortable than when we made *Warm Your Heart*. At that point, Linda and I knew we were a great musical team. A second song from Linda's *Howl Like a Rainstorm, Cry Like the Wind* — "All My Life" — not only was another smash hit but got us the Grammy for Best Pop Vocal Performance by a Duo or Group for the second year in a row. If any producer could kick off my solo career with sensitivity and care, it was Linda.

I covered "Everybody Plays the Fool," the Main Ingredient song I used to sing with the Soul Machine, and it hit. Linda sang behind me on "Ave Maria" and brought in the Grace Episcopal Choir from San Francisco. Linda pulled out all the stops to make *Warm My Heart* a milestone in my career. After the record went platinum — as almost all my solo records did — I was off and running, and had Linda to thank.

Art

One of the reasons our brotherhood has survived is that we're independent, even when we're together. While Aaron was singing solo, Cyril was off with his Uptown Allstars, Charles formed a jazz band, and I put together a new edition of a famous funk band. I called it the Funky Meters. George Porter, the original Meters bass man, joined me, along with Brian Stoltz on guitar and Russell Batiste on drums. I found that the hip-hoppers, rappers, scratchers, and deejays had placed the original Meters high up in funk heaven. Our original jams were known to two or three younger generations, and there was an audience out there hungry for our old beats. Keeping the Meters spirit alive, even as the Neville Brothers maintained their identity, has proved a blessing. When I get pissed at my brothers — or when they get pissed at me — we each have a musical place to go that's all our own.

CYRIL

Some of the cats in the Neville Brothers band — especially Willie Green and Nick Daniels — also became a mainstay of the Uptown Allstars. I loved the Allstars, not only because of my devotion to second-line reggae but because it was the one area where I was autonomous. I started Endangered Species Records and recorded whatever I wanted. I called my first CD *The Fire This Time,* riffing off James Baldwin. I was able to show my respect for New Orleans roots music and also protest injustice to my heart's content. Songs like "Genocide" put my politics on the line. I called my second CD *Soulo* and wrote deep songs with Gaynielle, my best friend and business partner: "The Road to Unity (Don't Kill Your Brother)" and "No Justice, No Peace." I also sang "Be My Lady," a Zig song I used to do with the Meters. When I sang it now, the love was directed at Gaynielle. We had a second child together, our talented son, Omari, and my home life had never been more satisfying. Gaynielle treated all my children with great love. She's also a great writer and singer who formed the Diamonds, the vocal group that backed up the Uptown Allstars and did a CD of their own on Endangered Species Records.

Charles

It was 1990 and I was living back in New Orleans. Roberta stayed in Eugene, and despite the love between us, we were going separate ways. I had returned to old habits when it came to women — the more the merrier.

One night at Tipitina's I couldn't take my eyes off a beautiful young woman in the crowd. I was up there playing with my brothers, but my mind wasn't on the music. I approached her afterward and learned that her name was Kristin. She was there because she wanted to hear Aaron sing. Aaron was attracting fans who normally would not have come. I asked if I could call her, and she gave me her number. She was a VISTA volunteer and worked at the food bank. We dated and fell in love. There was something about her — a gentleness, a serenity — I found irresistible. Her ex-boyfriend told me, "If we all had built-in bullshit barometers, Kristin's would register zero." She spoke with her heart, and her heart was filled with poetry. I knew she was everything I wanted in a woman. But I wasn't through with some old patterns. You could call it compulsive behavior or plain cheating; it all boiled down to the fact that, after a lifetime of slipping and sliding, I found myself doing it again.

Kristin had gone home to Massachusetts to visit her folks. While she was away, I'd been loving on a woman who worked at the health-food store. My rationalization was that Kristin had been talking to her ex-boyfriend. It was a pitiful excuse, but I'd use any excuse I could find. When Kristin returned, she knew I wasn't right. Women know those things. She confronted me, and I confessed. She reminded me that when we started living together, we pledged to be true. *Everyone says that shit,* I thought to myself, *but no one honors it.* "If you don't honor it," Kristin warned me, "I can't stay." I remembered the spirit of guru Kirpal Singh on such matters: *If I am your lover, I am your partner; and if I am your partner, I must believe your every word, I must trust everything you do.* My old rationalizations — I'm a black man making up for all the romantic love the white world denied me — was nothing but played-out jive. Different women I had been with had different qualities I loved. But in Kristin, I had finally found a woman who contained all those qualities. Here was a stable relationship in which I could be fully honest or continue to double-deal and ruin everything.

It helped that she insisted we see a counselor. At first I refused, arguing that a stranger couldn't possibly know more about us than we know about ourselves. Besides, I said, I'd been through counseling. But Kristin wouldn't yield, and I'm glad she didn't. She dragged me to the counselor, who turned out to be a woman of unusual perception. She helped me open that last door that led me out of the chamber of self-imprisonment. To be hooked on promiscuity isn't all that different from being hooked on drugs. It all goes back to ego. The counselor had the objectivity — the emotional distance — to let me see how I was running from my feelings and escaping intimacy by compulsively bouncing from woman to woman. It was a great revelation; I saw another addiction blocking my serenity. Kristin and I spent seven months going to the counselor. When the sessions were over, I pledged monogamy — and this time meant it. We married in 1995 and had a baby boy, Khalif. At age fifty-eight, I was a new daddy and a new man.

Art

I'm no different from most men; I've had my struggles with women. On a Neville Brothers CD cut in 1992, though, *Family Groove,* I sang a song called "On the Other Side of Paradise." Brother Cyril, Eric Kolb — one of my main musical partners of these past years, a beautiful man who recently passed away — and I wrote it together. It had an island lilt. "I get away from city life," it said, "leave behind trouble and strife . . . sweet Lorraine, she's my best friend, she's my wife." Lorraine changed my life.

I'm not an easy man. I can isolate and irritate. This road my brothers and I have been on, touring the world year after year, is no walk in the park. But through it all, Lorraine has given me something no other woman has — a sense of security and the flow of a love I know is real. She's raised my son Ian as though he were her own — and done a fantastic job. Together we had a baby daughter, born on my mother's birthday and bearing my mother's name, Amelia. When I look at Amelia, when I look at Lorraine, I realize there's nothing more precious than a woman's love. Lorraine has made all the difference.

Charles

I wanted to play a different music in addition to what I play with my brothers. I needed the kind of expression that spoke to my earliest excitement — bebop. As a kid playing behind bluesmen, as an Angola inmate honing my skills, I've quietly kept at my craft. My models remain the same, Bird, Monk, Gene Ammons and James Moody, Stitt and 'Trane and Rollins, the giants who, for me, define modern jazz. I've appeared on avant-garde records like Kip Hanrahan's *All Roads Are Made of Flesh* and enjoyed the artistic stimulation, but my true soul is on the records I've made under my own name — *Charles Neville and Diversity* in 1990, and *Safe in Buddha's Palm,* from 1997, where I revisited straight-ahead standards like "Stella by Starlight" and " 'Round Midnight." My devotion to what you might call mainstream modernism is absolute. It's taken me a lifetime to master the grammar and vocabulary of a music that, to my ears, never grows old.

I've grown physically since staying off junk. I've long been interested in martial arts, starting with study of tai chi at the Brooklyn Academy of Music in the seventies. I became proficient at judo. For years now, I've practiced chi kung, which involves a standing or sitting meditation I practice for half an hour twice daily. Chi kung focuses my awareness and lets me feel my mind resonating through my body. I've learned to control my body and allow the even flow of energy to reach the spaces between my muscles. It's all about proper alignment, centering, and maintaining open channels. It all ties in with my music, which I also practice daily, whether on the road or at home. As Kirpal Singh first pointed out in his study of comparative religions, the creative impulse is an energy that manifests itself in a vibration. I want to connect with the highest of those vibrations, the lightest and purest tones. To do so, I myself must be light and pure. Cigarettes, booze, drugs, meat, excess sex kept me from that state. To move from a gross vibration to a light vibration is to open up a third eye that sees spiritual reality. To stay connected to that reality requires a discipline, a spiritual practice that depends not only on sobriety but on a physical posture rooted in a balanced, even-minded strength.

With my mind clear, I, along with Cyril, got involved in the Peoples of the Land/Prophesies for Peace, an amalgamation of aboriginal tribes of North America whose goal is sovereignty and self-sufficiency. In the aftermath of the Wild Tchoupitoulas, the Neville Brothers have maintained a deep and warm rapport with Native Americans, whose struggles and wisdom have become part of our own path to political and spiritual enlightenment.

Brother Blood

CYRIL

I still feel the losses. On *Brother's Keeper,* our second album for A&M, we wrote "Brother Jake" for my friend Alfred Rudolph, sometimes called Jake the Snake and also known as Kumbuka. He was my man, a fellow soldier in a war waged on the mean streets of New Orleans when the cops were out for black blood.

Aaron

Jake had to leave town on a rail. When he came back, he got into a fight and hit his head on a curb. The cops came, took their time in taking him to the hospital, and left him there to die. That's what the song is talking about. When Cyril and I sang it, we were thinking about how, after his death, those same policemen taunted us by saying, "We sure were happy to hear about what happened to

Rudolph." "I bet you were," Cyril snapped back, "I bet you came, you motherfucker." The song tells Jake's story in a way we hope will keep him alive. He was a good cat. And as we sang on the record, "Brother Jake is finally home."

Bill Graham was another loss that hit us hard. Flying from one of his gigs, he died in a helicopter crash in 1991. He was our brother. When the Nevilles toured Israel, Bill came along and gave us a private tour of the country.

CYRIL

Bill got sick over in Israel, but he still stuck with us on that tour. He was definitely a die-hard business guy, but his soul was incredible. We became friends during that trip to the Holy Land, and I've never had deeper discussions on the subject of Jewish-black relationships with anyone. His knowledge about the Middle East and the history of his people impressed me. I'll also always be grateful to Bill for involving us in meaningful causes like Amnesty International. Last time I saw him, we walked up a mountainside together. "That ski lift is for sissies," he said. During that hike I felt his enormous energy, I felt that he saw into my heart. Bill saw me for who I really am.

Charles

The Israeli trip was just after the Gulf War. Jack Bruce and Ginger Baker were opening for us, and Bill was as enthusiastic as a little boy. He took us on all these side trips. He hooked us up with the Black Israelites who, in addition to designing and making clothes, made music. I could feel the satisfaction Bill derived from reuniting us with our long-lost brothers. We jammed with them and discovered our grooves and riffs matched up beautifully. Bill was digging it; his face lit up in a big smile as he danced to our self-styled freedom song.

Aaron

Brother Bill loved to dance. That's how I see him — out there on the floor doing the mambo. Bill could dance up a storm. God bless him and the good things he did for us.

Art

Good things were happening all around us. On *Brother's Keeper* we sang a movie theme called "Bird on a Wire" written by Leonard Cohen. Suddenly we were shooting long-form videos with stars like Dennis Quaid, Bonnie Raitt, and Jimmy Buffett. Things were getting a little Hollywood.

Aaron

I don't mind Hollywood, but I hate it when someone acts like my friend, gets close to me, then takes lines from my poetry, and turns them into a song without giving credit. When my brothers and I were having big disagreements, I wrote a poem reminding them that brotherly love is nothing you ever want to lose. Turned out the poem turned into someone else's song. Never asked me, never thanked me, never credited me, never paid me. That ain't right.

As far as me and my brothers went, I always said that until all of us have made it, none of us have made it. No matter how big my solo career was getting, I never played with notions of leaving them. I never could. It comforts me to travel and sing with them night after night. I'll go off and do concerts on my own, but the family connection is the one I cherish most. At the same time, new fans wanted me to sing songs different from the traditional Neville Brothers. On my second solo CD, the title tune, "The Grand Tour," was country, and because it was a hit, country fans started coming to our concerts. I sang a duet with Trisha Yearwood, "I Fall to Pieces," that got a Grammy, and a duet with the great Tammy Wynette, "All I Am to You." I was asked to sing on the tribute to Jimmie Rodgers, one of the old cowboys, and did "Why Should I Be Lonely?" Now the Neville Brothers had a whole new audience that didn't look anything like the Deadheads.

Art

We can bicker. Aaron will be wanting to sing ballads, Cyril will be wanting to preach, I'll be wanting to play funk. Sometimes I'll be thinking we've gotten too far away from the original funk, and I'll go back to the source. Recently, for example, I was invited to play on a CD, *Organ-ized*. Different organists — Jimmy Smith, Jimmy McDuff — were asked to contribute tunes. I wrote something borrowed from Uncle Jolly that went all the way back to my childhood. Called it "Mickey Fick," an expression invented by Jolly. "Mickey Fick" was a subtle way of saying "motherfucker." "Mickey Fick" is where I want my music to stay — the same place I stay — right there on Valence Street.

After our A&M contract expired in 1998, we switched over to

Columbia and did an album called *Valence Street*. Me and my brothers had some arguments, but we also had some musical successes. I sang a song I wrote called "The Dealer," another throwback to our early years and the good sense of Auntie Cat. She used to talk about playing the hand you're dealt. The dealer is the Lord, and the Lord's not giving you anything you can't handle. That's the philosophy I'm trying to live.

Aaron

Some of the work I love most didn't sell that well. I'm thinking of gospel songs I recorded on Johnny Adams's last CD, cut just before he died. We sang in the style of Sam Cooke and the Soul Stirrers, the righteous way to praise the Lord I learned as a little boy. I also collaborated with Father M. Jeffery Bayhi on *Doing It Their Own Way: A Contemporary Meditation on the Way of the Cross*. The good father tells the story of the crucifixion while I sing about the sorrow and glory of salvation. Artie, Eric Kolb, and I played the keyboards. All proceeds went to charity.

Charles

Sometimes the cord that ties us together feels like steel, other times it's threadbare. I've worried that the Brothers might break up — conflicting temperaments, conflicting agendas, jealousy, bickering. But just when it looks like the bough will break, the bough bends. Maybe it's because each of us knows we can quit whenever we want — and the other brothers will go on without us. But more likely it's because once we're onstage, harmony heals the hurt. Seeing our children and grandchildren jamming up there with us is also a great source of satisfaction; the Neville vibe passes on from generation to generation without losing a drop of passion.

I'm a blessed man. I know so many jazzmen, talented souls with exquisite gifts, who died sordid deaths. I remember when we were touring Europe and leaving our hotel in Denmark. An old musician was part of our tour. He had deep wrinkles in his face, hardly any flesh on his bones. He looked like a bum. When he got on the bus, Cyril and Daryl Johnson were playing a tape of one of our concerts on a boom box. The old musician started screaming how the music sounded like shit. He grew abusive. Daryl, a big cat, came roaring down the aisle and was about to kick his ass. I stopped Daryl and said, "Leave him alone. He's Chet Baker." A few months later the great jazz trumpeter was dead. He jumped — or was pushed — from his hotel window in Amsterdam. There but for the grace of God . . .

Aaron

I believe it's God's grace that answered my prayers. With the help of Saint Jude, my dreams came true. All those years when I couldn't give up dope, couldn't get out from under those slavery-styled contracts, couldn't get a deal to sing, found myself hauling shit from the dark hole of a ship — they were trials I had to endure. "Once I was a deceiver," I wrote in a song, "but now I'm a believer . . . it took me who I was and where I've been to make me who I am."

Who I am is a man grateful for the gift of song. I get chills when people write me and say that my voice was the only thing that could calm an autistic child. A mother told me her wild children wouldn't sleep until she played my records. In England there's a club called BANANAS — British Awfully Nifty Aaron Neville Appreciation Society — that has cases of people whose suicides were avoided by listening to something I've sung. I was moved to tears when they named a bridge after me in the poorest part of India. Rehab doctors have said my voice has chilled out addicts in detox.

I think of all the great producers who brought beauty to my records — Linda Ronstadt, George Massenburg, Steve Lindsey, David Anderle, Mark Mazzetti; I think of the talented musicians in the Neville Brothers band — Eddie Freche, Saya Saito, Shane Theriot, Earl Smith, Daryl Johnson, Michael Goods, Eric Kolb, Willie Green, Nick Daniels, Ivan Neville, Charmaine Neville. So many good people helped us along the way. Looking back on the long journey, I see that it was all part of God's plan. Without those dark, dark days, I couldn't appreciate the light that now leads my way.

Art

Miracles happen. Recently during Jazz Fest in New Orleans, my wife, Lorraine, suggested I invite three guests to my home. I wasn't sure they'd come, but they all did: George Porter, Leo Nocentelli, and Joseph "Zigaboo" Modeliste — the original Meters all under one roof. I never thought that would be possible. We ate, joked, and laughed till we cried. We saw that despite the bitter and long-lasting differences, there was love underneath it all.

CYRIL

I guess I've come the closest of anyone to packing it all in. Sometimes it seems that me and my brothers will never see eye-to-eye.

I'm still striving for autonomy, for absolute ownership of everything we do. I'm tired of being exploited, tired of the manipulation by management to divide and conquer — and the ease with which they've accomplished that goal. I feel more isolated than ever, but I also feel stronger and more in control of my personal life — thank God.

My head knows there are personal differences that go deep, soul wounds from the past that haven't healed. My brothers and I are from different generations and view the world differently. The chasm between us is wide. Yet my heart is filled with sentiment and love for family. But just when that sentiment swells up and makes me think everything will work out, reality will step in. My brothers and I can't agree on issues surrounding management, production, and record labels. All those things make me think I just want to concentrate on the Uptown Allstars and the Diamonds and the New Orleans Music and Culture Preservatory, where I'm taping and honoring New Orleans's forgotten pioneers.

For all my sense of separating and being autonomous, something still happens when I hear my brothers play and sing. I think back to when I was a boy and I worshipped the ground they walked on. I think of their guts to go out in the world alone; I think of their talent to create a music that expresses the language of the heart; and I know I'm lucky to be a Neville. Those are the moments I must admit that, in spite of the differences, which remain profound and sincere, my brothers are still my heroes. Those are the same moments when I turn to them and see in their faces the faces of my mother, my father, my sisters, my aunts, my nephews and nieces, my children, and my grandchildren. I also see in their faces the relatives I never saw, the families of my parents' families going back in time through the history of hope and pain that has defined my people. When the moon is full and the stars shine bright, I see it all in a waking dream, a vision in which all the world is composed of Nevilles, black Nevilles and white Nevilles, yellow and brown Nevilles, generations upon generations of Nevilles, all making music, all living in peace, all understanding that there is only one race on the planet — the human race.

Art

I built a studio above where I grew up and still live on Valence Street. I go up there and, like a little kid, play with my toys — my computers and jet-pilot video games, my sci-fi books, and my keyboards. In wintertime the trees outside my window are bare, but when the spring arrives and the leaves bloom on the branches, one particular tree blossoms into a remarkable form; the tree takes the shape of Uncle Jolly wearing his golden crown and full regalia. I know that's Jolly saying hello, reminding me that just as the world revolves on its unending axis, his essence is continually born again. His is the spirit of the muse, the spirit words can't define, the same spirit that, no matter the obstacle, will keep Cyril, Aaron, Charles, and Art together . . . forever.

Discographies

BY JOHN BRENES*

Current Discography

The following records are currently available on compact disc:

The Wild Tchoupitoulas	Island Records ILPS 9360
Fiyo on the Bayou	A&M Records SP 4866
Treacherous — A History of the Neville Brothers, 1955–1985	Rhino RNFP 71494
Yellow ÏMoon	A&M Records SP 5240
Brother's Keeper	A&M Records 5312
Treacherous Too! A History of the Neville Brothers, Volume Two, 1955–1987	Rhino R 270776
Family Groove	A&M Records 5384
Live on Planet Earth	A&M Records 0225

*A leading Neville Brothers scholar, John Brenes is also proprietor of the Music Coop, a retail store where many of these discs are available: 9 Petaluma Boulevard North, Petaluma, California 94952, (707) 762-4257.

Mitakuye Oyasin Oyasin/ All My Relations	A&M Records 0521
The Very Best of the Neville Brothers	Rhino Records R2 72626
The Neville Brothers Live at Tipitina's (1982)	Rhino Records R2 75330
Valence Street	Columbia CK 68906
Uptown Rulin' — The Best of the Neville Brothers	A&M Records 490403
Orchid in the Storm	Rhino 70956
The Classic Aaron Neville: My Greatest Gift	Rounder 2102
Warm Your Heart	A&M Records 5354
The Grand Tour	A&M Records 086
Aaron Neville's Soulful Christmas	A&M Records 0127
The Tattooed Heart	A&M Records 0349
To Make Me Who I Am	A&M Records 0784
The Very Best of Aaron Neville	A&M Records 490482
Art Neville: His Specialty Recordings 1956–58	Specialty SPCD 7023
Safe in Buddha's Palm	Small Circle Records SCR 9701
Cyril Neville and the Uptown Allstars/The Fire This Time	Endangered Species Records ES 1702
Cyril Neville Soulo	Endangered Species Records ES 1706

Neville Brothers Complete Discography

The Wild Tchoupitoulas (First time the brothers recorded together) Producers: Allen Toussaint/ Marshall Sehorn	Island Records ILPS 9360	1976
The Neville Brothers Producer: Jack Nietzsche	Capitol Records ST 11865	1978

Fiyo on the Bayou Producer: Joel Dorn	A&M Records SP 4866	1981
Live Nevillization (Recorded at Tipitina's 9/24/82) Producers: Hammond Scott, Art Neville, W. Barry Wilson	Black Top/ Spindletop BT 1031	1984
Treacherous — A History of the Neville Brothers, 1955–1985	Rhino (2 lps) RNFP 71494	1986
Uptown Producers: Jim Gaines, Richie Zito, Clive Langer, and Alan Winstanley	EMI America ST 17249	1987
Nevillization 2 (Recorded at Tipitina's 9/25/82) Producers: David Torkanowsky and the Neville Brothers	Spindletop Records SPT 115	1987
Yellow Moon Producer: Daniel Lanois	A&M Records SP 5240	1989
Brother's Keeper Producers: Malcolm Burn and the Neville Brothers	A&M Records 5312	1990
Treacherous Too! A History of the Neville Brothers, Volume Two 1955–1987	Rhino R 270776 (CD only)	1991
Family Groove Producers: the Neville Brothers, Hawk Wolinsky, and David Leonard	A&M Records 5384 (CD only)	1992
Live on Planet Earth Producers: the Neville Brothers	A&M Records 0225 (CD only)	1994
Mitakuye Oyasin Oyasin/ All My Relations Producers: James Stroud and the Neville Brothers	A&M Records 0521 (CD only)	1996
The Very Best of the Neville Brothers	Rhino Records R2 72626 (CD only)	1997

The Neville Brothers Live at Tipitina's (1982)	Rhino Records (2 discs) R2 75330 (CD only)	1998
Valence Street Producers: the Neville Brothers	Columbia CK 68906 (CD only)	1999
Uptown Rulin' — The Best of the Neville Brothers	A&M Records 490403 (CD only)	1999

Aaron Neville Discography

Tell It Like It Is	Par-Lo No. 1	1967
Like It Is	Minit/Liberty LP 40007	1967
Orchid in the Storm Producer: Joel Dorn	Passport PB3605 CD, Rhino 70956	1985
Humdinger (English collection, Minit material)	Stateside Records SLL 6011	1986
Make Me Strong (English collection of 1968 to mid-'70s singles and unreleased material)	Charly CRB 1111 CD 64	1986
Show Me the Way (English collection of Minit/ Instant singles and unreleased material)	Charly CRB 1127 CD 8203	1989
The Classic Aaron Neville: My Greatest Gift (Collection of 1968 to mid-'70s singles and unreleased material)	Rounder 2102	1990
Tell It Like It Is (Reissue of Par-Lo No. 1)	Collectibles 5132	
Aaron Neville Greatest Hits (Collection of Minit and Par-Lo material)	Curb D2 77303 (CD only)	

Warm Your Heart Producers: Linda Ronstadt and George Massenburg	A&M Records 5354 (CD only)	1991
The Grand Tour Producer: Steve Lindsey	A&M Records 086 (CD only)	1993
Aaron Neville's Soulful Christmas Producer: Steve Lindsey	A&M Records 0127 (CD only)	1993
The Tattooed Heart Producer: Steve Lindsey	A&M Records 0349 (CD only)	1995
To Make Me Who I Am Producers: Keith Andes, Marc Nelson, Darrell Spencer, Robbie Nelson, Bradley, Tony Rich, Aaron Neville, Khris Kellow, Linda Ronstadt, George Massenburg, Mark Mazzetti	A&M Records 0784 (CD only)	1997
The Very Best of Aaron Neville	A&M Records 490482 (CD only)	2000

Art Neville Discography

That Old Time Rock 'n' Roll (Specialty singles and unreleased material)	Specialty SP 2165	1987
Mardi Gras Rock 'n' Roll (English, Specialty singles and unreleased material)	Ace CHD 188	1986
Rock 'n' Soul Hootenanny (English, Instant singles and unreleased material)	Charly CRB 1177	1988
Art Neville: His Specialty Recordings 1956–58	Specialty SPCD 7023	1992

Charles Neville Discography

Charles Neville and Diversity	Laserlight 15 331	1990
Safe in Buddha's Palm	Small Circle Records SCR 9701	1997

Cyril Neville Discography

Cyril Neville and the Uptown Allstars / The Fire This Time	Endangered Species Records ES 1702 (Reissued as Iguana Records 070, 1995)	1993
Cyril Neville Soulo Producers: Cyril and Gaynielle Neville	Endangered Species Records ES 1706	1998

Reference Discography

Johnny Ace

Memorial	MCA 31183

Mose Allison

Allison Wonderland (2-CD anthology)	Rhino 71689

Gene Ammons

Boss Tenor	Prestige 7180
Boss Tenors	Verve 837440
Funky	Original Jazz Classics 244

Louis Armstrong

Best of the Decca Years, Vol. 1	
Satchmo the Great	Legacy 53580
16 Most Requested Songs	Legacy 57900

Count Basie

Best of the Roulette Years	Bluenote 97969
April in Paris	Verve 521402
Count Basie and the Kansas City 7	Impulse 202

James Booker

Junko Partner	Hannibal 1359

Resurrection of the Bayou Maharajah: Live at the Maple Leaf Bar	Rounder 612118
Spiders on the Keys: Live at the Maple Leaf Bar	Rounder 612119
Booker T. and the MGs	
The Very Best of	Rhino 71738
Charles Brown	
Driftin' Blues: The Best of	Collectibles 5631
James Brown	
20 All Time Greatest Hits!	Polydor 511326
Live at the Apollo, 1962	Polydor 843479
The Clovers	
Down in the Alley	Rhino 82312
Nat "King" Cole	
Hit That Jive, Jack (Nat "King" Cole Trio)	Decca/GRP 662
Greatest Hits	Capitol 29687
Sam Cooke	
Greatest Hits	RCA 67605
Sam Cooke with the Soul Stirrers	Specialty 7009
Cousin Joe	
Bad Luck Blues	Evidence 26046
Miles Davis	
Birth of the Cool	Capitol 92862
Cookin' with the Miles Davis Quintet	Prestige 7094
Kind of Blue	Columbia 64935
Seven Steps to Heaven	Columbia 48827
Bill Doggett and His Combo	
All His Hits	King 5009
Fats Domino	
The Fats Man: 25 Classic Performances	EMI 52326
Dr. John	
Goin' Back to New Orleans	Warner Brothers 26940
Dr. John's Gumbo	ATCO 7006
Mos' Scocious (2-CD anthology)	Rhino 71450
The Drifters	
Very Best of	Rhino 71211
Let the Boogie Woogie Roll, 1953–1958 (2 CDs)	Atlantic 81927

Billy Eckstine	
Mister B. and the Band	Savoy 0264
Everything I Have Is Yours (2-CD anthology of the MGM years)	Verve 819442
Ella Fitzgerald	
Ella and Friends	Decca/GRP 663
Something to Live For (2-CD retrospective of Decca and Verve recordings)	Verve 547800
The Flamingos	
Best of	Rhino 70967
Marvin Gaye	
The Best of	Motown 530529
What's Going On	Motown 530883
Guitar Slim	
Sufferin' Mind	Specialty 7007
Lionel Hampton	
Greatest Hits	RCA 68496
Midnight Sun	Decca/GRP 625
John Lee Hooker	
His Best Chess Sides	Chess 9383
The Ultimate Collection: 1948–1990	Rhino 70572
Elvin Jones	
Elvin	Original Jazz Classics 259
Dear John C.	Impulse 126
Louis Jordan	
Let the Good Times Roll (2-CD anthology, 1938–1953)	MCA/Decca 11907
B. B. King	
Singin' the Blues/The Blues	Flair 86296
Greatest Hits	MCA 11746
Live at the Regal	MCA 11464
Smiley Lewis	
I Hear You Knocking — The Best of	Collectibles 5630
Little Willie John	
Fever — The Best of	Rhino 71511
Bob Marley	
Legend: The Best of	Polydor/Tuff Gong 846210
Natty Dread	Polydor/Tuff Gong 846204

Clyde McPhatter	
The Forgotten Angel	32 Records 32089
The Meters	
Very Best of	Rhino 72642
Funkify Your Life (2-CD anthology)	Rhino 71869
Amos Milburn	
Down the Road Apiece, Best of	EMI 27229
Thelonious Monk	
Solo Monk	Columbia 47854
Thelonious Monk with John Coltrane	Original Jazz Classics 039
Wes Montgomery	
Bumpin'	Verve 539062
Full House	Original Jazz Classics 106
The Incredible Jazz Guitar of Wes Montgomery	Original Jazz Classics 036
James Moody	
Moody's Mood for Love	GRP 823
Hi-fi Party	Original Jazz Classics 1780
The Moonglows	
Their Great Hits	Chess 9379
Jelly Roll Morton	
Greatest Hits	RCA 68500
Birth of the Hot: The Classic Chicago Red Hot Peppers	RCA Bluebird 66641
The Orioles	
Greatest Hits	Collectibles 5408
Charlie Parker	
Genius of Charlie Parker	Savoy 0104
Yardbird Suite: Ultimate Charlie Parker Collection	Rhino 72260
The Platters	
The Best of	Rhino 75326
Lloyd Price	
Greatest Hits	MCA 11184
Lawdy	Specialty 7010
Louis Prima	
Louis Prima	Capitol 94072
Say It with a Slap	Buddha 99614

Professor Longhair	
New Orleans Piano	Atlantic 7225
Fess (2-CD anthology)	Rhino 71502
Arthur Prysock	
Morning, Noon and Night: The Collection	Verve 557484
Sly and the Family Stone	
Dance to the Music	Legacy 66427
Stand!	Epic 26456
The Spaniels	
40th Anniversary	Collectibles 5584
Joe Tex	
Very Best of	Rhino 72565
Tuts Washington	
New Orleans Piano Professor	Rounder 11501
Johnny "Guitar" Watson	
The Very Best of Johnny	Rhino 75702
The Wild Magnolias	
They Call Us Wild	Polydor 519419
Larry Williams	
Bad Boy	Specialty 7002
Lester Young	
The Kansas City Sessions	Commodore/GRP 402
Lester Swings	Verve 547772

Collections

New Orleans Party Classics	Rhino 70587
More New Orleans Party Classics	Rhino 75506
Best of Doo-Wop — Ballads	Rhino 75763
Best of Doo-Wop — Uptempo	Rhino 75764

Authors' Acknowledgments

Art Neville thanks first of all, our Lord Savior Jesus Christ, without whom none of this would be at all possible; my parents, Arthur and Amelia Neville Sr.; Miss Virginia Harris; Mr. George Landry; Rowena "Cookie" Neville; Athelgra Neville; Gabriel, our number one fan

My immediate family: my beautiful and loving wife, Lorraine Ponce Neville; my children: Michael, Arthel, Ian, and sweet Amelia Jane; Mr. and Mrs. Vincent Ponce

The Neville organization: Shannon and Arnold Chabaud, Jan Bateman, Steven and Rushell Chabaud, Aaron Neville Jr., Craig Hayes

Bill Graham Management: Bill himself, Arnie Pustilnik, Cynthia Parsons, Michael Jones, Laura Farenza, Morty Wiggins, Kenny Nestor

The William Morris Agency; Mike Kappus at Rosebud

From the beginning: John and Charlotte Brenes, Steve Eggerton, Lynne Batson, Pamela Gibbins, Chuck Randall, my friends Malcolm Baker and Issacher Gordon

My band members: George Porter Jr., Zigaboo Modeliste, Leo Nocentelli, Brian Stoltz, Russell Batiste Jr., Ivan Neville, Willie Green, Gerald Tillman, Newton Mossip, Renard Poche, Roger Poche, Daryl Johnson, James "Hutch" Hutchinson, Tony Hall, Nick Daniels, Eric Struthers, Shane Theriot, Earl Smith, Michael Goods, Saya Saito

To All of Our Past and Present Crews: Kenny Nestor, Rocky, Mick, Jeff, Chopper, and Kelsey. And friends Anita Keys and David Hearst.

And a special thanks to my buddies Eddie Freche and Eric Kolb, who are truly missed.

And to David Ritz. We never could have found anyone hipper to write our story. Thank you.

Aaron Neville thanks God, Saint Jude, the Blessed Mother; my mother and father, Mr. and Mrs. Arthur L. Neville Sr.; Uncle George "Big Chief Jolly" Landry; Slaughter and Sly Neville; Auntie Cat; Espy; Lealuh; Odile; and Lena. Joel, my wife of forty-one years; my children, Ivan, Aaron Jr., Ernestine, and Jason. My mother-in-law, Beatrice Roux Taylor; Vincent, John, and Bettina Roux. Artie for inspiring me to sing, Charles for being my mentor and soul brother, Cyril for being my friend, travel buddy, and one of my favorite singers, also to a wonderful sister, Athelgra, with whom growing up was a pleasure. I have more precious memories with her than anyone else. She helped mold me. I also want to thank Father Roger Temme, Father Ray Jean, Father Jeff Bayhi, Father Franco; Sister Damien and all the nuns who taught me. My growing-up friends, Melvin Wright, Marvin and Johnny Metoyer, Staggerlee, Idris Muhammad, Junie Boy, Hartzell Craig, Bobby Knight, Carleatis Kennedy, Roonie, Jake, Vernon Bellings, Poochie Boo, Bobby Smith, Skin Booty, T. June. The Braud family, Gerald Tillman, Roger and Renard Poche, Newton Mossip; Solomon Spencer, for giving me my first gig; Sam and the Soul Machine; our first business managers, Bernard Sontag and Pamela Gibbons; Pam Sontag; all of our past band members, especially Eddie Freche, Lynne Batson for having faith in my poetry, Maureen Weil, Linda Ronstadt, George Massenburg, Janet Stark. John and Charlotte Brenes for their hospitality while I was recording *Warm Your Heart,* Steve Lindsey and Gabe, Dianne Warren, Doreen and Real Songs, all the musicians and background singers on my solo albums, Steve Tyrel, Mark Mazzetti for being a great a&r guy and making such a great recording with *To Make Me Who I Am,* Robbi Nevil, Bradley Spalter, Emanuel Officer, Neville Productions crew, Shannon, Jan and Stephen, Bill Graham Productions, Larry Williams, Larry McKinley, Morty Wiggins, Arnie Pustilnik, Bernie Cyrus, Johnny Miller, Junior Prout, Elliot Boisdore, Steven Segal, Bret "the Hitman" Hart, Dutch Morial, Mayor Marc Morial, Chief Richard Pennington, Barbara and Rosa Hawkins, Alvin "Shine" Robinson, James Booker, Johnny Adams, Plas Johnson, Herbert Hardesty, Issacher "Izzy

Koo" Gordon for having faith in me; Clyde McPhatter, Sam Cooke, Pookie Hudson, the Clovers, the Flamingos, Chief Rudy, Chief Bordelon, Warden Robert, Attorney General Richard Iyoub, Mona George for the rosaries, Burl Cain, Mickey and Sidney Barthelemy, Phillip and Terry Manuel, Judges Marullo and Quinlan, Officer Debbie Prejean; my personal trainer, Tazzie Colomb, throat doctor Richard Spector, Ronald Swartz, Craig and Pamela Hayes, Rita Coolidge, Ed Bradley, Sister Jane Remson, Sister Blaise, Aaron Fuchs, Vincent Fumar, Leo Sacks, Tex Stevens, Joel Dorn, Bobby Cure and the Summertime Blues, all my nieces, nephews, and my six grandchildren. If I missed anyone, I thank you also.

Charles Neville thanks Sant Kirpal Singh Ji, who helped me make the journey from the dark to the light — and the many friends at Serenity Lane in Eugene, Oregon, who also played a part of that journey — and to those who put love in my life — and all representatives of the Great Spirit, who moves through all things.

David Ritz thanks the Neville brothers for their candor and trust. I love each of you. Thanks to sister Athelgra Neville, and to the wives — Joel, Lorraine, Gaynielle, and Kristin. I deeply appreciate the help of Leo Sacks, Aaron Priest, Lisa Vance, John Brenes, Michael Pietsch, Chip Rossetti, Arnie Pustilnik, Cynthia Parsons, Craig Hayes, Angus Wynne, Shannon Chabaud, Steven Chabaud, Alan Eisenstock, Harry Weinger, Joel Dorn, and Linda Ronstadt. And to my loving wife, Roberta, and my wonderful daughters, Alison and Jessica, I love you with all my heart.

Index

CPSIA information can be obtained
at www.ICGtesting.com
Printed in the USA
BVHW071953160822
644753BV00002B/16